Values and Evaluations

American University Studies

Series V
Philosophy

Vol. 183

PETER LANG
New York • Washington, D.C./Baltimore • Boston
Bern • Frankfurt am Main • Berlin • Vienna • Paris

Julius Kovesi

Values
and Evaluations

Essays on Ethics
and Ideology

Edited by
Alan Tapper

PETER LANG
New York • Washington, D.C./Baltimore • Boston
Bern • Frankfurt am Main • Berlin • Vienna • Paris

BD
232
.K68
1998

Library of Congress Cataloging-in-Publication Data

Kovesi, Julius.
Values and evaluations: essays on ethics
and ideology / Julius Kovesi; edited by Alan Tapper.
p. cm. — (American university studies V: philosophy; vol. 183)
Includes bibliographical references and index.
1. Values. 2. Ethics. 3. Theology. 4. History—Philosophy. I. Tapper, Alan.
II. Title. III. Series: American university studies.
Series V, Philosophy; vol. 183.
BD232.K68   190—dc21   97-20823
ISBN 0-8204-3808-1
ISSN 0739-6392

Die Deutsche Bibliothek-CIP-Einheitsaufnahme

Kovesi, Julius:
Values and evaluations: essays on ethics and ideology / Julius Kovesi. Ed. by
Alan Tapper. –New York; Washington, D.C./Baltimore; Boston; Bern; Frankfurt
am Main; Berlin; Vienna; Paris: Lang.
(American university studies: Ser. 5, Philosophy; 183)
ISBN 0-8204-3808-1

The paper in this book meets the guidelines for permanence and durability
of the Committee on Production Guidelines for Book Longevity
of the Council of Library Resources.

Printed in the United States of America.

Contents

Acknowledgements

I wish to thank the editors of the following journals for permission to reprint six papers in this collection: *Jowett Papers* for 'Valuing and Evaluating' (1968-69); *Proceedings of the Aristotelian Society* for 'Descriptions and Reasons' (1979-80); *Philosophy* for '*Principia Ethica* Re-examined: The Ethics of a Proto-Logical Atomism' (1984); *The Journal of the History of Ideas* for 'Marxist Ecclesiology and Biblical Criticism' (1976); *Midwest Studies in Philosophy* for 'Against the Ritual of 'Is' and 'Ought'' (1978); and *Proceedings of the New Norcia Humanities Symposium* for 'Nature and Convention' (1987).

Some minor grammatical and stylistic amendments have been made to the previously published papers. The unpublished papers have been clarified in places where the expression was unclear.

This collection has been a team effort. I have had the benefit of good advice from Ted Watt, Bob Ewin, Selwyn Grave and Chris Ulyatt. Many others made valuable suggestions, particularly about the introduction. Lee Carter typed the early drafts. Olga de Moeller proofread the script. Chris Ulyatt has handled the page layout and final text.

Janet Kovesi Watt contributed to the book in many ways, large and small. Julius Kovesi used to argue that books can't be burned. In the sense in which (as conceptual creations) they can't, this book is his. In the sense in which (as words on paper) they can, it is largely Janet's.

Alan Tapper

Julius Kovesi

Alan Tapper and Janet Kovesi Watt

Julius Kovesi, who died in 1989, published only one book, *Moral Notions*, which appeared in 1967. This present book brings together most of his published and unpublished papers. It is a substantial collection, covering a variety of topics, and it will help to assuage the regrets of many of his friends that he did not produce the books that we felt he was uniquely equipped to write. That feeling arose in part from the impact that *Moral Notions* had on those who read it carefully, but even more from the impact that Julius Kovesi had on those around him. He seemed to have so much to say that was quite unlike anything being said by others. We expected that he would eventually say it in books—a successor to *Moral Notions*, a book on modern theology, an analysis of Marxism, something on Plato—but at his untimely death the books were unwritten. What he did write is here.

Philosophers who are 'known' are, of course, known by their surnames: Russell, Austin, Quine etc. Julius Kovesi was not in that sense a 'known' philosopher. To all who knew him, from first-year students to eminent professors, he was known simply as Julius. That is how he wanted to be known. For some years his office wall carried a child's story book picture of a genial gorilla emerging from the jungle and announcing 'My name is Julius'. The convention is that in a book such as this he should be known as Kovesi, but to those who knew him this will feel wrong; those who did not know him might want to know that about him.

Hume exhorted philosophers to 'Be a philosopher; but amidst all your philosophy, be still a man'. Two hundred years later, when philosophy has become more than ever a professional occupation, and some even make professional philosophy their life, this is good advice, but it perhaps assumes that philosophers are somehow philosophers first, and men or women second. In Julius's case it was clearly the other way around: he was a philosopher because he was someone who had lived the life he had lived. Julius the person preceded Kovesi the thinker; he became the thinker he was in order to remain the person he had always been. Not to think as penetratingly as he could about the world he lived in—a world of conflict, ideology and moral confusion—would have been a self-betrayal, a deliberate forgetfulness about his everyday experience. All those who knew him felt the force of his honesty, simplicity, humour, integrity and unconventional wisdom. This introduction will attempt to introduce the thinker and the man, and preferably both at once, for his philosophy and his life were all of one piece.

A brief biography is called for here, to give an outline of the experiences that helped to shape his thinking. He was born in Budapest in 1930, and grew up in a country town in western Hungary, Tata, a lakeside resort favoured by previous occupying powers, including the Romans and the Turks. His brother described their idyllic life in pre-war Hungary as 'like growing up in the nineteenth century'. The mid-twentieth century brought war, invasion and occupation, first by German troops and then, after prolonged fighting in the countryside near their home, by the Soviets.

At the time when communist government was established in Hungary Julius and his brother were students at Budapest University, where Julius attended the philosophy lectures given by Lukacs. As communist rule became increasingly oppressive, and barbed wire began to encircle the country, they decided to escape while it was still possible, only to be caught at the Austrian border. Julius, even then ideologically quick on his feet, told the guards that he and his brother were not rejecting communism, they were only foolish young bourgeois students who wanted to see Paris before the final collapse of capitalism. Whether or not this was a convincing defence they were released, after a beating, but only on condition that they reported on fellow-students who might also be planning to escape. Within days they again headed for the border, and this time succeeded in crossing it.

Eventually they made their way to Innsbruck and studied there for a year before deciding, with their parents who had now joined them, to take the opportunity of migrating to Australia.[1] Understandably it was not an easy decision, but their apprehensions about committing themselves to a new life and language in a remote and unknown country were soon dispelled by the realities of life in Perth.

Six years after arriving in Western Australia Julius had mastered English, completed a first class honours degree in philosophy, and had been awarded a scholarship for postgraduate study at Balliol College, Oxford. No sooner had he arrived in Oxford however, in late 1956, than the Hungarian revolution broke out, and he was given leave to go to Austria to work as an interpreter for refugees, thereby helping others in the same predicament that he had himself been in a few years before. From them he learned at first hand what it was like to try to resist a communist government that was now backed up with Soviet tanks and artillery as well as guards and barbed wire at the border.

Back at Oxford, besides studying for the degree of B. Phil. and writing his thesis (on 'How good is "The Good"?'), Julius collaborated with Anthony Kenny in producing a journal of philosophical parody called *Why?* which is still widely remembered.[2] The first editorial (there were three issues) set the tone by declaring: 'The value of philosophy is to protect us from other philosophers. But who will protect us from ourselves if we take ourselves too seriously?' Julius was never in danger of that, but he meant the first sentence to be taken seriously, and often had occasion to quote it later on. He knew only too well the power of apparently impressive arguments to bemuse and oppress, and for the rest of his life devoted his energies to helping others to see through them and resist them. While the jokes and parodies in *Why?* were overwhelmingly light-hearted and good-humoured, on later occasions, notably in the writing of *Trialogue*, a privately-circulated journal lampooning the 'modern' theology of 1970, the jokes had a sharper edge. This more aggressive approach was foreshadowed in the second *Why?* editorial: 'There is only one sort of philosophy we intend to attack: that is, any philosophy, anywhere, which cannot afford to laugh at itself.'

The philosopher who had the greatest influence on Julius's thought during his time at Oxford and for some years afterwards was his supervisor, J.L. Austin, whose penetrating, precise and witty analysis of ordinary language was the embodiment of the Oxford linguistic philosophy which flourished in the 1950s. His style of philosophising was affectionately parodied in *Why?* in a spoof book review of *The Philosophy of Cookery*, which described

Professor A*st*n's completely original approach to the problem. Instead of simply considering 'to cook,' he investigates 'cook with,' 'cook for,' 'cook at' and 'cook up'. One must mention his well-known lecture on the distinction between 'boiling' and 'broiling'. We do say we embroil but we do not say we emboil…. He prefers the language of a plain cook who says 'take two eggs'. But how do you separate two eggs? Do you separate two eggs as you separate two eggs when they are stuck together or as you separate two separate eggs? Do you do the same when you separate two potatoes as when you separate two eggs? You can separate *an* egg. Now separate *a* potato. Why cannot you separate a potato? Usually we say that we *cut* a potato.

Julius's gifts, both intellectual and social, blossomed at Oxford. He was particularly delighted by the many Oxford societies, from the seriously intellectual Socratic Club,[3] to the rather less serious or even exuberantly frivolous societies based on Balliol. During his final year at Oxford Julius himself founded a society, modelled on the Socratic Club, for the discussion of philosophical and religious topics from a specifically Catholic viewpoint, and attracted a remarkably distinguished group of Catholic philosophers to its meetings. Later in his academic life he was to gather around himself other more informal groups, modelled on the Leonardo Society at Balliol, for the reading and discussion of papers on a wide variety of philosophical, historical and literary topics. It was an aspect of his life that gave him enormous pleasure, and he cherished the friendships that grew out of such gatherings.

After leaving Oxford Julius spent a year at Edinburgh University, and three years at the University of New England in New South Wales, before returning to the University of Western Australia in 1962. He remained on the staff there for the rest of his life, and there he taught until a week before his death. Though he died before the full collapse of communism in Eastern Europe, he did live to see the opening of the Hungarian border, and the symbolic presentation to President George Bush of a piece of barbed wire.[4]

Just before his final exams at Oxford, Austin gave Julius a note reading: 'Be relevant. Read and answer the question.' It was a note he framed and kept on his desk for the rest of his career. Readers who have glanced at the Table of Contents will have noted the diversity of subject matter, and perhaps have wondered what, if anything, might hold it together. Marx, Moses Hess, G.E. Moore, biblical criticism, myth, convention, fact and value—these look like diverse interests.

Not only do they seem somewhat unrelated to each other, they seem even less obviously related to the problems of the mid-to-late twentieth century. Yet Julius's philosophy was *about* this world, even when it involved thinking about the past, and the philosophers of the past. And, in his own view at least, his interests had a unity which he was always trying to articulate, and which made his conversation always likely to jump unexpectedly from the present back to Socrates or to *The Epic of Gilgamesh* or anything else between then and now.

Julius's interest in history was not of the sort which looks simply for parallels or precursors of the present. It was far more original than that. Comparisons were his stock in trade, but the kind of comparisons he sought can best be expressed by the phrases 'the same, yet different' or 'different, but the same'. The capacity to discern differences in sameness and sameness in differences was the skill which he most sought to cultivate and inculcate. It is a theme in *Moral Notions* and it is a theme running through his writing on ideological issues. Thinking responsibly about important matters, in his view, just is the process of teasing out similarity and dissimilarity. And thinking philosophically just is thinking carefully and formally about how we recognise samenesses and distinguish differences. (In everyday life this deeply rooted habit of mind showed itself in a tendency to make puns, often rather bad puns, which depended on a mispronunciation of English, and he was always pained when others did not immediately see the point.) In his view, it is our lack of skill in handling comparisons and examples that makes our moral life so difficult. His own constant, vivid and memorable use of examples is characteristic. He used to say that he collected examples, even if he did not yet know what they would turn out to be examples of. One notable philosophical example which he was able to display in actuality, and of which he was very proud, was a blown-glass fly-bottle such as he, like Wittgenstein, had been familiar with in childhood. He delighted in asking admirers of Wittgenstein what they thought it was. They never knew.

Moral Notions was notable for the inventiveness and liveliness of the examples and newly-coined concepts ('misticket,' 'saving-deceit') which were discussed. A central theme of the book was that our moral concepts, like all other concepts, embody shared rational standards. It was a deft and many-sided attack on the distinction between matters of fact and matters of value which had dominated English-speaking philosophy since the eighteenth century. Julius, as a newcomer to the

English language and to the established traditions of philosophy in that language, was able to survey those traditions with a fresh and quizzical eye. His central thesis was that 'Moral notions do not evaluate the world of description but describe the world of evaluation'. In his Critical Notice of the book in *Mind*, Bernard Mayo described it as 'a lightning campaign of a mere 40,000 words which, I think, decisively and permanently alters the balance of power' in the debate about fact and value. The effect, Mayo observes, is both 'strongly original' and 'somewhat intoxicating'. 'Time and again a startling paradox brings us to a halt, and we want a recapitulation of the steps in the argument that got us there. Nearly always we are driven back to realise that a favourite preconception has been subtly charmed away.' Its philosophical framework, as Mayo says, is 'a general theory of concept-formation, meaning, and rules of usage' which is used 'to solve or dissolve an impressive list of standard problems in moral philosophy'.[5]

The argumentative strategy of *Moral Notions* is to show that *both* 'descriptive' concepts ('table,' 'horse,' 'yellow,' etc.) and 'evaluative' concepts ('murder,' 'lying', etc.) can function as concepts only if they serve our rational purposes and needs. Without our moral concepts and the standards they embody there could be no moral argument or disagreement. If we want to know what is moral then we must investigate the relations between these various moral concepts. The concepts and the distinctions between them *constitute* our moral knowledge. If we make the effort we will find in them a schematic rightness that we commonly overlook. And about this we have no choice, because we can only think by means of concepts. (Similarly, if we want to know about sport, or transport, or cookery, we need to investigate and master the relevant concepts. Only so can we work out whether, say, professional tennis is sport or business.)

In another way, however, as Julius argued, it is the conceptual structure which can distort everything, and it may do so in ways which lie far deeper than ordinary mistakes of reasoning. Ideologies are ways of thinking in which a twist in the conceptual structure so governs our mental responses that we become unwitting victims of a systematic distortion. This is particularly likely to occur when one system of ideas is replaced by another. This is memorably illustrated by the *Peanuts* cartoon referred to elsewhere in this book, in which Lucy, having at first mistaken a potato chip on the ground for a butterfly from Brazil, then asks indignantly how a potato chip could have flown all the way

from Brazil. Jean-François Revel made the same point when he remarked that 'our tendency to maintain habits of thought after we have
abandoned the premisses on which they were based, guides much of
our thought today'.[6]

Ideologies not only mask hidden interests from those with whom we
argue; they hide from *ourselves* knowledge of what it is we are really doing. They do this by eliminating from consideration those with whom we
should be arguing. It is this that makes ideologies dangerous and permits
us quite literally to eliminate our opponents. It is in this way that belief
systems can be used as instruments of oppression. A society which institu-
tionalised belief in peripatetic potato chips, and which treated those who
called them 'butterflies' as mad or bad, would be an ideological society.

How are 'ideologically distorted' and 'undistorted' conceptual structures to be distinguished? More generally, if moral notions are collective
achievements in which the interests of all parties are respected and through
which social life is made possible, how can whole social worlds be governed and dominated by radically unjust and intellectually absurd schemes
of belief?

Julius wanted to draw a distinction between 'closed' and 'open' conceptual systems. As he outlines the distinction, an 'open' system is open
to reasoning and evidence, and open to modification, even to refutation,
in the light of that reasoning or evidence. Awkward facts, inconvenient
arguments and evidence *have* to be listened to, and answered. A 'closed'
system, by contrast, does not answer inconvenient reasoning and evidence; it *explains* them, usually as attacks on itself. The 'closed system'
purports to explain *why* the outsiders are attacking it, and why it would
be out of place to listen to them seriously or to reason with them. So no
fact, no event, no evidence, no argument can do any damage to a 'closed
system'; on the contrary, they all confirm and elaborate the truth of it.

Julius had a keen eye for illustrations of the 'closed system' cast of
mind. He thought he detected it in the dictum of Lukacs that the truth of
Marxism would be unaffected even if every one of Marx's assertions were
shown to be false. He remarked on the combination of what he described
as 'the greatest possible "humility" with the greatest possible megalomania' displayed in Teilhard de Chardin's assessment of his own work:

In me, by the chance of temperament, education and environment,
the proportion of the one and of the other are favourable, and the
fusion has spontaneously come about—too feebly as yet for an ex-

plosive propagation—but still in sufficient strength to show that the reaction is possible and that, some day or other, the two will join up. A fresh proof that the truth has only to appear once, and nothing can ever again prevent it from invading everything and setting it aflame.[7]

That a system of concepts is closed is made apparent by situating it in a larger conceptual framework. But this will not fully explain why it is so difficult to break out of a closed system. The answer to that lies in the way in which the kind of closed system that interested Julius provided a 'place' for the believers or adherents of the scheme and a very different sort of place for those outside it. And since the schemes that he has in mind usually embody philosophies of history, this 'place' is (he believed) to be thought of as a role in a kind of drama.

As a moralist Julius expected that the scheme of concepts which constitutes our moral life would assign me a place in my social order (e.g., parent, son, colleague, teacher, citizen). 'Places' of this kind are not intrinsically objectionable. We could have no social life without them, or something like them. Dramatic placement is quite different; it provides its proponents with a privileged place which owes nothing to reason or morality. It is characteristic of ideological thought that in it the drama comes first, and the background concepts—upon which reason depends—are distorted to fit the requirements of the plot.

Julius always kept distinct the issues that he regarded as ideological from those he saw as simply social or rational in the normal senses of those words. Some of the arguments for and against socialism (to do with economic efficiency, the power of the state and the bureaucracy, the value of personal liberties, etc.) were in his view quite unrelated to the arguments for and against Marxism, so that a recognition of Marxism as ideology in no way constitutes an argument against socialism in any of its aspects.

Some will be inclined to dismiss these essays as 'conservative,' just as Julius himself was often so dismissed. His opposition to communism, of which he had first-hand experience, and from which he had with difficulty escaped, was often brushed aside as 'mere prejudice'. This kind of dismissal nicely illustrates all that he was concerned to argue against, and it can be used to show in simple form his moral theory working in harness with his critique of ideology. 'Conservative' used in this way as a term of dismissal is itself ideologically loaded, for it permits, indeed requires, the rejection of arguments on wholly extrinsic and irrelevant grounds. To 'conserve' is to do something which is morally neutral, but it is here being treated as a complete moral concept, comparable to 'stealing' or 'cheating'. That it is not a complete moral concept is easily shown by the fact that even those who use it in that dismissive way will themselves sometimes want to conserve things—historically significant buildings, for instance. The real issue is whether those things Julius wanted to conserve were things that ought to be conserved.[8]

Julius's thought was more a matter of questions than of answers. It is hard to recall any philosophical theories, other than his theory of concepts, which he can be said to have believed in. His lack of philosophical theories went deep. He once said that he thought that of all the great philosophical systems Spinoza's was perhaps the most consistent. Had he not said so no-one would have guessed this to be his opinion. He was, it can be said, very little interested in the truth, in the sense of having a problem so well defined that we can start to talk about having 'the truth of the matter'. He found from experience that it is far more important to get to grips with the kind of error that prevents us from even starting to think relevantly about what might be true. He thought most political discussion to be a form of moral exhibitionism. He never moralised. When a real moral issue arose—an issue about what to do here and now—he dealt with it mostly in silence, looking for the unexpected angle which might be the crucial one.

This lack of positive assertion came from the fact that he did not have answers to the many questions he thought we should be interested in. In place of answers there could only be puzzlement. He had a remarkable capacity for puzzlement, for not even knowing what the question was when others were half-way towards working out their answers. A set of boxes he kept on his office shelf illustrates his attitude—a large one was labelled 'major premises,' a smaller one was labelled 'minor premises,' and a still smaller one contained 'conclusions.' All were empty. This kind of philosophical joke (there were two more boxes, labelled 'facts' and 'values,' linked by a plastic bridge from a model railway layout) was one aspect of his teaching style which intrigued some students while baffling others. One group, having noticed that he would illustrate the patterns of argument in most of his tutorial topics, however varied, with similar sets of circles drawn on the blackboard, delighted him one day by drawing some plausible-looking circles in advance *before* a tutorial. Not all were so attuned. One student described the experience of endeavouring to follow his lectures as being like running past a garden and trying to see what flowers were in it through the cracks in the fence.

If comparison was his characteristic strategy, puzzlement was his characteristic mode. On the surface this was playful, underneath it was not. The madness he sought most to combat was a madness which supplied answers without questions, and in this respect, as well as in his gleeful skill at drawing out unwelcome and unexpected conclusions to the arguments and assumptions of others, it is not unduly far-fetched to compare him to Socrates.

Most of Julius's philosophy was an attempt to think about the conceptual tangles which bedevil our shared life. This made him very much a public person, though one who held few public positions. Throughout the turmoil of the late 1960s and 70s his door was shut only when he had a class or was talking with a student. He seemed to be perpetually in conversation, and, like Socrates, he practised his philosophy on his feet. This collection shows that he wrote more than we had realised. It represents him as a thinker, and indicates some of his qualities as a person.

Moral Philosophy Papers:
Introduction

R.E. Ewin

Julius Kovesi's main contribution to work in the field of moral philosophy was a book, *Moral Notions*, not papers. In the period leading up to his death, he was working on a second book; discussions with John Colman had interested him in Locke's idea of 'mixed modes,' and Julius was using that idea to further his views on moral philosophy. Between the first book and the projected second book there appeared a number of papers on moral philosophy, directed mainly at clarifying his views in the face of widespread misunderstanding, and those papers are reprinted here.

The other papers that Julius wrote in the field were usually done as the basis for discussion in honours classes, never polished, and not prepared with a view to publication. It would be unfair to him were they to be published here. Little points come up in them that are typical of Julius and his concern with everyday arguments in morality, as also about the everyday operation of concepts. As well as the 'potato chip fallacy,' mentioned elsewhere in this collection, he recognised, and introduced to his students, the fallacy of One Good, One Bad, which he described as a real case of the naturalistic fallacy: 'There might be all sorts of things wrong with Mr Paisley's views and policies, but one would like to point out that fascists are quite different. In pointing this out one's intention is not to defend him, and not to defend fascists. One would like to make an important distinction while continuing to disapprove of both.'[1]

Julius was not one to run away from paradox, or, at least, apparent paradox: 'Surprising as it may sound, the fact/value distinction of moral philosophy is not about the distinction between facts and values'.[2] Such identification of fallacies and embracing of paradox meant that his discussion was always lively and colourfully expressed. He was always teaching. At first year level, the students could readily be divided into those who were fascinated by what he said and were won to the puzzles of philosophy, and those who understood not a word of it. From second year on, Julius aroused great enthusiasm, interest, and industry in his students. His effect on colleagues was almost exactly the same as that on his students.

To be won to an interest in philosophy by Julius was just that: to be won to an interest in *philosophy*. He always put his problems in historical and philosophical context: he was interested in a wide range of philosophers, but especially in Plato, and later in Locke. He was original in his interpretation of these thinkers, and to that extent he probably underplayed the originality of his own thought. What might otherwise have been treated as moral philosophy was, therefore, often presented as a contribution to the history of philosophy or the history of ideas.

The appearance of *Moral Notions* in 1967 caused quite a splash, as is evidenced by Bernard Mayo's review of the book in *Mind.* Then, however, the book dropped from view. This, I think, was partly a matter of its subtlety being misunderstood and partly simply a change in philosophical fashions: concern about the foundations of ethics was replaced by a desire to deal with problems in moral philosophy mathematically, and, at the same time, there grew up a desire to apply philosophy directly to problems of immediate public import (the Vietnam War, abortion, and so on) in a way that took those problems away from their place in the tradition that is the history of philosophy, the context in which Julius always worked. In recent years we have seen from philosophers such as Alasdair MacIntyre and Bernard Williams a move back towards dealing with the problems in that context. The publication of Julius's papers should, therefore, be welcome, and might encourage a return to consideration of *Moral Notions.*

Valuing and Evaluating

In a lecture-seminar at Oxford a few months ago I heard the following turn of argument. After some discussion of the similarities and differences between the good or virtuous man and the good carpenter or good musician, it was suggested that perhaps similar comparisons could be made to elucidate our social virtues. For these similarities and admitted differences we were asked to turn to the world of bees. It was felt that a musician can exhibit excellences that concern only his own abilities and potentialities, and so this can illustrate only those virtues that concern our individual development into excellent persons. Morality, however, concerns our dealings with other people. So we had to turn to the bees. Of course we could have turned to a concert pianist instead, but even this would not have made me happy. I would have been happy only if we had abandoned the whole pattern of argument by saying that the concert is over, the pianist has pocketed the whole takings of the charity performance and gone on holiday on the proceeds, and now let us talk about moral problems. But then we would have been at a loss because we would not have known what our pianist is good at or bad at; we could not have said that he is bad as a this or a that. So we turned to the bees because there we were able to say that the bee which goes off with the honey to Majorca on his own, instead of bringing it back to the hive, is bad as a bee. He is not functioning properly. Actually, the example was not even this, but, as far as I remember, a bee which is not interested in honey.

After a lecture-seminar it is not easy to question in a few words the whole procedure of the enterprise, so I tried to make only one small distinction. I tried to distinguish between a bad bee, who is bad as a bee, and a bad little bee. For this I was greeted with perhaps well-deserved laughter. The distinction I was trying to make is that between a bee which is indeed insensitive to honey and is just buzzing around aimlessly and a bee which performs his beeish functions properly, but cleverly puts aside a bit of honey in a corner, wakes up at night and eats it up secretly by himself. He is not bad as a bee, he is a bad little bee.

Incidentally, I am not sure whether we would really say of the first one that it is a bad bee. We are very egocentric in our use of 'good' and 'bad'. We do not say that the weather is good when it—whatever 'it' is—functions properly as 'weather,' but we say that the weather is good when we can go for a picnic. (Of course this is why we talk about 'weather' at all, not because there is such a thing but because we want to have picnics and get in the harvest.) We say that the baby is good when she sleeps through the night and we can get to sleep too. So a bad bee would be one that a child would bring to a zoology class and the teacher would find that its wings are crushed or that it is too small to exhibit. It is a bad specimen.

To have made the distinction between a bad bee and a bad little bee was a rather hopeless small protest. What I would like to do now is to question the whole procedure that made us go to the bees in search of some light on our moral life. I want to begin with our familiar picture that in our activities and endeavours we can roughly distinguish between our dealings with factual matters and with matters of value. What I want to attempt is to make a further distinction in the second field, in that field of our lives where we are grappling with values. In doing this I shall have to end up with some criticism of the way in which the distinction has been drawn between these two large fields. But to begin with I would like to say that its recognition has been very important and quite understandably it impressed us so much that we tend to regard other types of activities as only subdivisions or variations of these two main activities, of making factual statements and of making evaluative judgments. It is this further assumption, namely that all, or most, human activities are subdivisions or variations of these two, that has got moral philosophy entangled in the second of our great divisions. Quite understandably, if we can choose only between these two fields, the subject matter of moral philosophy is somewhere in the second field. Then usually this is what happens: we regard those features of these two fields that distinguish them from each other to be their general and typical characteristics, and so various philosophers arrive at various sets of characteristics as the general and typical characteristics of evaluative judgments. Then, since moral judgments are thought to be within this field, they too are first burdened with these characteristics and then, since in fact they are not at all like evaluative judgments, they are somehow distinguished from evaluative judgments.

Might it not be the case, however, that the field of moral philoso-phy differs from the field of evaluation just as fundamentally and radi-cally as the field of evaluation differs from that of description? Perhaps we place our moral judgments in quite unsuitable company and spend most of our energies on working out how to extricate them, when they should not have been there to begin with.

We begin our moral philosophy by describing how we choose fire-extinguishers and cricket bats and then say that moral choices are like this except that in moral choices we do not choose between things like fire-extinguishers and cricket bats. Or we begin by describing how we evaluate functional objects and then say that moral decisions are like this except that in moral decisions we do not, and should not, regard people as functional objects. These are like the story of the boy who asked his father what a telephone was. He was told: 'Imagine a long snake with its tail in Edinburgh and its head in London. If you tread on its tail its head will move in London.' 'I see, but what about the wireless then?' 'Well, it is exactly the same, only without the snake.'

Our philosophical literature has good runners-up to this story, like the stories of the social contract, of natural law, non-natural qualities, or when you are asked to listen to the voice of your heart or obey commands that you addressed to yourself. So we are asked to observe the good bee and the good fire-extinguisher. They are good because they do what they are supposed to do. The good man is exactly like this, except that we, unlike these other objects, can choose to do or not to do what we are supposed to do, and also we do not know what we are supposed to do. This is exactly our problem.

There are many activities that we can properly describe as evalua-tion. Some of them are of quite recent origin, as when we evaluate the results of a survey or evaluate data. We must not ignore these if we want to understand ourselves. Here I want to outline what is the most ancient and widespread of these activities, when we make an evalua-tive judgment on this or that as a good something or other. This is not only the most ancient type of evaluative activity but the most ancient activity altogether. I would be tempted to say that it precedes the use of language as we know it, except for the fact that as we know this activity *now* it cannot exist without language.

Our language did not begin with some cave-men, say, seeing some large floating objects on the sea and thinking: how interesting, they all look very similar, let's abstract their essential characteristics and form a general concept of them. Then we could call them by one word, say, 'boat,' and wouldn't it be convenient for communication? No, when they went down to the sea there was nothing there but fish and they thought it would be nice to be able to go after them. First came the final cause of what later was to be regarded as a boat, then this brought about its formal cause, namely the idea of the sort of thing that would do the job. Then some of the cave-men became the efficient causes by providing the material causes in the shape of wood. If the first of their constructions didn't quite do the job, they thought that this was not what they intended, this was not quite what they had in mind, this was not ... well, let's help them and say, this was not a good boat.

What enables us to evaluate things is that our descriptions of things are standards; they embody the purposes and intentions that made us form the notions of those things to begin with, and they are all capable of being exemplified by many particulars in space and time. We evaluate particulars that fall under a certain description as they more or less come up to the standard of what they are supposed to be or regarded to be. If anyone defined what a boat was purely in terms of the characteristics of any of those visible objects that we call boats, he would commit the naturalistic fallacy in the sense of identifying a standard with something which is not a standard but is made to approximate to it, and he would logically prevent us from producing better and better boats in the future, in fact he would prevent us from evaluating boats.

When something is not good as a boat it could still be good as a container on dry land or good for firewood. In each case one has to complete the phrases 'good as' or 'good for' with a description. The phrase 'good as' indicates most clearly that we bring the object in question under some heading, under a description. These phrases are like levers shifting the objects from under one description to under another. We can say that something is not good as this but it is good as something else or good for something else. But we do not use the phrase 'good for' when the object *is* for what we want to judge it good for. Not because it is not good for it but because this is what it is for. This further indicates how descriptions are standards. We do not say that needles are good for sewing, except when we first explain to someone what they are at all. 'Good at' and 'good with' are used to evaluate skills and here again we can observe the same pattern. If the skill in question can be described by the use of one word or one phrase we can evaluate someone's skill by saying that he is a good such and such, e.g. that he is a good carpenter. In the absence of such a word or phrase, e.g. 'firelighter,' we say that he is good at lighting fires. Incidentally, it is for reasons like this that I was tempted to say that this sort of activity of evaluation may precede in a sense the formation of our language because only after continued recognition of things being good for this or that do we begin to form terms for this or that. But of course we cannot for long recognise that something is good as this or that without some notion of this or that.

I used to think that the phrase 'good to…' when followed by a verb also falls into this same pattern, as when I was thinking of examples like 'good to eat'. What is good to eat is good as food or as nourishment. But there is a sense of 'good to…' followed by a verb which is not used for evaluating but for what I shall soon call 'valuing,' as when your dentist advises you that it is good to chew, or when someone questions your beating the carpet and you say 'it is good to beat it'. We mean in these cases that it is a good thing in the *1066 and All That* sense of a 'good thing'. The other 'good to…' phrase when it is not followed by an infinitive but is used meaning 'good towards' (as when the stepmother was not good to Cinderella) is a notable exception among the phrases using the word 'good'. This is the only one of these phrases which is used for talking about human relationships and which could be used in a moral context.

Before I turn to the consideration of what I want to call 'valuing' as against 'evaluating,' I would like to consider two connected objections to what I have said so far.

It could be argued that I have been unfair on two counts in taking functional objects as my examples. First, it could be said that I made it too easy for myself to illustrate what we do when we evaluate by taking functional objects, professions and skills as my examples when there are many other objects and human performances as well. Secondly, it could be said that by taking functional objects or professions and skills as my examples I was not giving examples of what could be called, strictly speaking, descriptions.

With regard to the first objection I would like to ask what other examples could one use to illustrate evaluation? These *are* the things we evaluate. If I were to investigate, say, the concept of 'growth,' it should not be objected that I am making my job easy by taking as my examples organic matter and human institutions instead of other things. Similarly I am not just making my job easier by taking functional objects and human skills as my examples of evaluations. I am showing the examples where we evaluate. This is the main burden of my paper, to argue against the view that we are evaluating all over the place, including our moral life; and that in order to introduce what we do in our moral life we first take 'easy' examples like the evaluations of fire-extinguishers and then proceed to the more difficult ones like deciding whether to tell a lie or not. This way we make our job not only difficult but impossible or, insofar as it is possible, misleading. Of course we shall find it more difficult to find out how we evaluate in our moral life if the first thing we are asked to observe is that there we are not dealing with functional objects nor with skills; nevertheless we are evaluating on the same pattern (it is the same you know, without the snake). Why not just talk about evaluation and then take functional objects as our examples, not because it is easier but because these *are* the sorts of things we evaluate. And when we turn to moral philosophy why cannot we recognise that there we are dealing with quite different problems, and I mean quite different.

Even outside the field of morals, however, there are cases where evaluation is rather difficult, or more complicated than in the case of functional objects. How would we evaluate pebbles for instance? Well, we don't. We could make use of them as ballast but then we evaluate them as ballast, under a different description. We employ one of these phrases that will shift them under a different description and say 'these are good as ballast but those are not,' or 'this is good for ballast'. But where we do *not* evaluate, do not ask how we evaluate there, but say that there we do *not* evaluate. Especially we should not make the mistake of thinking that the 'easy' examples are not genuine cases of evaluation, but that the real examples are those where it is hard to think how we could possibly evaluate something. On this view the 'real' example of evaluation is when we evaluate pebbles. Here there is no given standard but we, as collectors of pebbles, make up some standard of our own. So the real case of evaluation occurs when the description of what we evaluate cannot give us any help, but we provide the standard by our own decision. This may be the genesis of our prevailing distinction between evaluation and description into which I do not want to inquire now directly. Let me just say that this is carrying my snake story really too far by assuming that the real and genuine cases of what is illustrated by the snake are exactly those where there is no trace of a snake. Let me also repeat that the collector of pebbles evaluates them as geological specimens, as semi-precious stones or as beautiful objects, not as pebbles. In turn we can evaluate him as a collector and, if he is not good at his standards, he is not a good collector. But let us not pursue the collector any further because he cannot serve as an introduction to moral philosophy, not even if we make him say 'I hereby resolve to collect stripy pebbles; do so as well'. The collector of stripy pebbles is not deciding on his standards but on a description of something which he is going to collect *good examples of.*

I have mainly answered by now the second objection as well, which is this: my examples of descriptions are not examples of genuine descriptions. Genuine examples of description are those that do not help us with evaluation, like describing some objects as pebbles. Instead of saying that certain objects are boats, which is cheating, I should have said that some pieces of wood are arranged in a certain way and nailed together. This is what they are, not boats. How could I evaluate this, or how could I move from this to an evaluative judgment? My answer is again simply that we do not evaluate this and we cannot move from this to an evaluative judgment. But if we want to illustrate how we evaluate something we have to take examples of those things that we do evaluate. We can of course say that this construction is good for floating on and to go out fishing in and then we are right back in the stone age and soon we shall be creating some such simple word as 'boat'. The person who says that the object in front of him is not a boat but pieces of wood arranged in a certain way and nailed together does not only make evaluation impossible, he does not know how to describe the object, he does not know what the object is. To test this we should observe whether he can follow a rule in recognising other objects as being the same or not the same. In the next object on the water the pieces of wood are arranged differently and they are not joined by nails, and the one next to it is not even made of wood. If he keeps to his original statement then he cannot regard the second and third objects to be the same as the first, nor of course the first to be same as the second and third; therefore he does not know what even the first object was; he has no notion of a boat. Let us not ask, therefore, how someone who has no notion of what a boat is will evaluate boats in the hope that his resolution of this problem (e.g. adopting his own principles) will shed some light on the problems of moral philosophy.

There is a use of the word 'descriptive' according to which to describe something as a boat (or an act as stealing) is not a good example of description but to describe it as pieces of wood nailed together (or to say that he moved an object that makes the noise 'tick-tock' from one pocket to another pocket) is a good example of description. I want to say this to people who use the word 'descriptive' in this latter sense: this use of the word itself is not a descriptive use in their sense of 'descriptive' but only in mine because it is used as a standard, it was formed from a certain point of view, it was formed for a purpose. Its purpose and function is simply for use in certain types of moral philosophies to illustrate terms that are of no use or little use when we evaluate. Because the term 'descriptive statement' is itself used as a standard and used for a purpose in philosophical system-construction, it enables those who use it in this way to make evaluations. They can say, for instance, that the statement 'he put marks on the paper' is a good descriptive statement and the statement 'he signed the document' is a bad one.

But I have to turn now briefly to what I want to call 'valuing'. Here I am handicapped by the interesting fact that the word 'valuing' has not one single opposite, nor is there what I would really want for my purpose, a more general term that would include both 'valuing' and its many opposites. Let us keep this in mind when I want to point out the distinction between evaluating and valuing.

We value a good knife more than a bad knife but I suspect we do this because we value knives as such. We may admire or be fascinated by a good burglar more than by a bad burglar, but we do not value him more, because we do not value burglars. We can evaluate both things that we value and things that we do not value. (And by 'do not value' I mean the opposite of valuing and not simply the absence of valuing.) In both cases the good one is the one that comes up to the standard of what it is supposed to be according to the description. But we do not decide what things we value as against those that we do not value by regarding them as instances of a higher description, and those that come up to the standard of the description we value, and those that do not come up to that standard to the same degree we do not value. So valuing is a different type of activity from evaluating. As I was trying to say, we evaluate particulars as they fall under a certain description but valuing is what governs the formation of our descriptions.

I would like to suggest that our moral life is more akin to valuing and is not at all like evaluation.

When I have to make a decision whether to be honest and go to jail or be dishonest and allow an innocent man to be put in jail instead, I am not trying to choose between several honest acts, some of which are better than others insofar as they are honest, nor do I regard both honesty and dishonesty as instances of something of which one is a better instance than the other. (Of course we can find better *examples* of honesty, if we want an illustration, as some Renaissance paintings are better than others. But the honest man's job is not to try to perform better and better examples of honest acts as the Renaissance painter's job was not to paint the best example of a Renaissance picture. As the moral agent is not conducting a class in moral philosophy, the painter is not compiling a selection of illustrations.)

When I say that when we decide whether we should be honest or not we do not choose between several possible honest acts, and that when we are praised for being honest we are not praised for having done the best honest act but simply for being honest, I am not saying that each honest act is unique as against boats of which there are many. In a sense every act is unique but insofar as we judge an act to be honest it is not unique. In our moral life we are interested in an honest act insofar as it can be described as honest and not insofar as it may approximate to honesty. It must have been very puzzling, even for Plato, why the subject matter of moral philosophy, like the subject matter of mathematics, should be in the upper half of the Divided Line. But we must not think that the reason for it is as mysterious as the Divided Line and all that system would suggest.

In our moral life we are interested in the description under which our action falls and in the relevant facts that justify us in regarding our acts as falling under one or another description. The facts we are interested in are not *qualities* that make a particular a good instance of something but those facts of the situation and circumstances that make what we are doing one act rather than another. The very facts that are in the running for being relevant are of different types in the case of evaluation and in the case of our moral decisions. So as an introduction to moral philosophy, instead of taking clues from how we evaluate, we have to take clues from how we describe. To defend myself from the accusation that I incite you to commit the naturalistic fallacy would require another paper in order to outline what it is to describe, how we form the terms by which we describe, and why we form terms at all in order to describe our acts in certain situations. I just remind you how I laboured earlier in the paper to indicate that our intentions, purposes and standards are part and parcel of our descriptions. This is even more so when we turn away from the inanimate world and become not only the describers but also the subject-matter of our descriptions.

In conclusion I would like to mention three problems that complicate my thesis.

The first is the case of decisions that one makes as part of certain types of long-range attitudes or policies like wanting to be kind to someone. This is different from the choice between being honest or not; here we have a choice of different acts, all of which can be described as kind, and I have to choose between them, as in the story of the boy whose name was Jim whose friends were very good to him:

> They gave him tea, and cakes, and jam
> And slices of delicious ham,
> And chocolate with pink inside,
> And little tricycles to ride,
> And read him stories through and through,
> And even took him to the zoo...

Here is an ample choice of kind acts to choose from. There are many reasons for choosing one kind act rather than another but I do not think one could make up a case for saying that we choose the one which is better as a kind act. The kindest act is not the one which approximates in a scale of kind acts to what a kind act is supposed to be.

The next problem I want to throw up equally briefly is the problem of the good Samaritan. It looks as if this were a problem for me because here is the word 'good' used in a moral sense. But to indicate briefly how this judgment differs from the usual pattern of evaluation let me draw your attention to the difference between the good burglar, who is good as a burglar and does his job efficiently, and that other good burglar who is so bad as a burglar that, when he discovers the old lady resting in the house, he makes her a cup of tea. If a policeman investigating the burglary does the same for the old lady, then he is a good policeman in the sense in which the burglar was good in the first case and not in the second. The good Samaritan is like the burglar in the second case. The operative word is 'Samaritan,' and again the story would not have the same moral if it were the story of the good ambulance man.

My last problem really is a case of evaluation that should be of interest to moral philosophers. The problem is really in the field of what is usually called cultural or anthropological relativism, but it could be the problem of a moral agent either during a period of social and moral change or when the agent has to choose between different societies. Let me illustrate this by a simple account of how one might justify the institution of revenge in a certain society. There is no police force or effective judiciary in that society. Now if a strong bully would want to murder someone in that society, he might run over the following points in his mind before he would attempt the murder. He might think that although he is stronger than his intended victim, the victim's two brothers are a rather formidable team. And even if he were to join the crusades after the murder, those brothers might kill off his family. Our potential criminal today would think about the police force this way and he would even check on the laws of extradition before he would plan to fly off to modern Istanbul. Of course, if today the brothers of victims would kill murderers or their families, we would say, among other things, that they should not take the law into their own hands. But what about a society where there is no law to take into your own hands?

Now what enabled me to make the comparison between these two cases is that one does recognise something in the two cases which is the same in spite of all the differences, even though we might not be able to say before lengthy consideration what it is that is the same. What I want to say is that if someone is looking for evaluative problems in the field of moral philosophy then this might be it. One could argue that one of my examples is a better manifestation of something than the other. This is more like the case of evaluating boats, when we compare primitive constructions with other developments that are designed to serve a purpose. As in the case of boat-building we have to take into account the available material and human sophistication, so in our cultural and moral development we have to look at our human resources and available institutions, but nevertheless I think we could make evaluative judgments here and say that one arrangement is better than another. But here we are dealing with institutions and arrangements and with whole moral systems and not with the problems confronting moral agents within any of these systems, though perhaps today these larger problems confront us more and more even as individual moral agents.

Against the Ritual of 'Is' and 'Ought'

However much the preoccupations and problems of moral philosophy have changed in the last decade or so, we retain, with a ritual observance, a basic conceptual framework. Apart from a few bold spirits who disregard the ritual, most moral philosophers, before they can say anything, have to re-enact the moves of trying to justify how they dare to move from description to evaluation, while others, opposing them, claim that they have disregarded sacred texts and violated the most sacred of ritual moves.

Some, and I would like to count myself among these, would like to argue that the whole ritual is unnecessary, misleading, confused and confusing, and even detrimental to moral philosophy. It is most difficult to argue for this, because, as I said in a brief postscript to *Moral Notions*, in our arguments we have to make use of a terminology which is not neutral but embodies the very theory one is arguing against. But added to this conceptual handicap is the probability that the effort of replacing this terminology with a more profitable one will be misunderstood as a subtle way of moving from 'is' to 'ought'. Thus the effort of replacing a framework is thought to be a move within the framework.

In my *Moral Notions* I was using, as I said, the terminology of contemporary moral philosophy as Wittgensteinian ladders that I was trying to throw away surreptitiously on the way, but some of them I had to use right to the end. Only when I finished that study did I realise that the whole of it should be thrown away in order to start doing moral philosophy properly. I still think it is good as a moral philosophy game but otherwise I think of it as Marx and Engels thought of their *German Ideology*—the work in which they settled their accounts with the Young Hegelians and with their own former philosophical consciousness, but otherwise did not want to publish any more. (Only, without immodesty, I do think that my book is not so thoroughly bad as theirs.)

John Searle left the ladder—the throwing away of which was the main point of one of his articles—ostentatiously in his title when he called it 'How to Derive an "Ought" from an "Is".'[1] This is some excuse for reading his article as an attempt at 'a feat which many before have thought to perform;' that is, deriving a moral judgment from statements of empirical fact.[2] I am not taking such chances with the title of my paper and I want to make it clear that this is not another attempt to derive an 'ought' from an 'is.'

There are many reasons for wanting to do away with the whole ritual. In this paper I shall try to give three such reasons. First, I want to indicate that the dichotomy is a thoroughly amorphous family of problems. Secondly, I shall indicate that the dichotomy is not the result of a neutral philosophical analysis but is an ideologically motivated doctrine. My main concern will be the third reason, which is that our preoccupation with this ritual completely distorts what moral philosophy is about and misdirects our attention as to what constitutes moral life.

The Amorphous Nature of the Dichotomy

Hume and G.E. Moore are thought to be the two who pointed to the dichotomy most succinctly, though others before them were thought to have seen 'it' before. The fact that the one talked about deducing an 'ought'—in some sense of 'deduce'—and the other about defining 'good'—in some sense of 'define'—does not seem to worry many people who invoke them indiscriminately in support of a set of modern theories that neither of them had in mind. The phrases 'as Hume has pointed out' and 'as G.E. Moore has pointed out' are used almost interchangeably. In fact the only similarity between Hume and G.E. Moore is that both of them thought that certain value terms *are like* colour words, but there the similarity ends, because they thought they were like colour words for diametrically opposed reasons. Hume thought that virtue and vice are like colours, sounds, heat and cold, which according to 'modern philosophy' are not part of the furniture of the world but are our contributions to the description of what the world is like, and G.E. Moore thought that his little indefinable good is like yellow because, like other innumerable indefinable simple objects, it is part of the basic furniture of the world. If these views are put back into their context then they are even further away from anything said by contemporary moral philosophers whose views acquired initial prestige by invoking the names of Hume and Moore. One cannot see how the views of either of them are even dimly related to statements such as: only a command can be an answer to the question 'What shall I do?' or that our moral life should be regulated by nothing else but universal imperatives which by definition are made to have the force of a command addressed to oneself. True, these views are not presented as something that either Hume or Moore have actually said, only as the only solution to the otherwise inescapable problem they presented to moral philosophy. But what solution is offered indicates what the problem was thought to be. Most of us can offer half a dozen different versions of what the naturalistic fallacy or an evaluative–descriptive dichotomy is supposed to be, and these are not merely different formulations, but drastically different versions.

What is detrimental in all this to philosophical reasoning is that when one argument for the supposed dichotomy is discredited or disputed, then it can be countered that the argument was directed only against a misunderstanding of the dichotomy, and so on over and over again about each and every argument. And when all the reformulations of the dichotomy have been discredited or disputed, it can still be assumed that there is an unassailable dichotomy, and only inadequate formulations have been picked on by philosophers who can even be blamed for misunderstanding the dichotomy. In this way the dichotomy can take on an independent existence, not depending on any one particular argument. I am not saying, of course, that it is supported by the cumulative force of all the arguments rather than by any single one of them, rather that it is sustained by the assumption, each time an argument fails, that there is, indeed there must be, *another* argument for it. This is largely responsible not only for the continued deferential treatment accorded to the dichotomy, but also for the assumption that its origin is to be found in Hume and Moore. This move has been applied to them in the first place. 'There is indeed,' wrote Hare in his *Language of Morals*, 'something about the way in which, and the purposes for which, we use the word "good" which makes it impossible to hold the sort of position which Moore was attacking, although Moore did not see clearly what this something was.'[3] I am suggesting that 'this something' has a mystique like the emperor's new clothes.

The Ideological Nature of the Dichotomy

That the problem is so amorphous is partly due to the ideological nature of the dichotomy. It is characteristic of ideological beliefs that their truth is upheld independent of the arguments for them, and the arguments are looked for and produced in support of beliefs already held independently of arguments, and for other reasons. When it was found, for instance, that the proletariat did not bring about the renewal of creation, this was not regarded as confounding predictions of the imminent renewal of our condition, but another agency was looked for to bring it about. Though the original claim was made because of the nature of the proletariat, the claim itself acquired such an independent existence that by now some can allege that those who made the original claim did not quite understand what would bring about that transformation when they said that it would be the proletariat. There are many other examples in other religious or political theories of a claim becoming detached from the origin which gave it its first impetus and acquiring a life and force of its own.

Another feature of ideological thinking is that the believer creates a position for his ideological opponents within his conceptual framework. Often his opponents, by trying to argue against him, take up that prearranged position, thereby accepting his system by occupying a place *within* it. It is sad to think how many moral philosophers took up the role of being naturalists because they were trying to argue against some theory of an anti-naturalist; how many of them tried to derive value judgments from brute empirical facts because they wanted to argue against the theory, say, that we make our values by our decisions.

But I want to say more than that the arguments about the dichotomy exhibit some of the features of an ideological belief. The dichotomy is animated by ideological beliefs.

Professor Hare, at the end of his article in reply to Searle, offers his own answer to the question why one ought to keep promises, and ends the article by saying that his answer 'needs no "is"–"ought" derivations to support it—derivations whose validity will be believed in only by those who have ruled out *a priori* any questioning of the existing institutions on whose rules they are based'.[4]

One would fall into the ideological trap either if one took up the role assigned by Hare for those who wanted to derive an 'ought' from an 'is,' or if one tried desperately to protest that one did not wish to be such an authority-oriented personality. But I cannot forbear adding to these reasonings an observation which may, perhaps, be found of some importance, which is that the author proceeds for some time in the ordinary way of reasoning, quotes the *O.E.D.* and makes use of some morally neutral rules of logic, when all of a sudden one is surprised to be saddled with a particular moral and political position.

But to my mind one of the most revealing and instructive articles that has appeared about the evaluative dichotomy is Montefiore's reply to Philippa Foot's paper on 'Goodness and Choice'.[5] Montefiore presents there the doctrine of what he calls an 'individualist,' whose freedom and very existence as an individualist is threatened by the fact that our language provides us in most cases with criteria of evaluation. What his individualist has to do in order to have his ideal existence is to eliminate all 'criteria-setting' terms from our language, such as 'knife' or 'pen,' and operate only with the category of 'object'. Montefiore considers the possibility that even to categorise something as an object already carries with it 'some peculiar even if as yet unknown function'. Though he rejects this possibility, he thinks that if it had been so 'we should clearly have had the greatest difficulty in ever conceiving the individualistic project of stating all the facts about pens in some overtly non-functional, non-evaluative way'.[6]

The individualist, however, has another problem as well. 'The category of "object" cannot be pressed into service for the defunctionalisation of all functional or similar terms.' 'Farmer,' 'trap,' 'writing,' 'puzzle,' 'appeal' are his examples that cannot easily be categorised as objects. In such cases the individualist's solution is that of Hare's horse, which, I think, should be as well known by moral philosophers as G.E. Moore's horse. Hare's horse refuses the description of himself as a 'charger' in case he may fail to be a good charger, and redescribes himself as 'a solid-hoofed perissodactyl quadruped, having a flowing mane and tail'.[7] As long as the individualist can redescribe himself, his action, or the objects he wants to choose, he can retain his freedom. While this escape route is open his obligations are only hypothetical. But if he cannot redescribe his objects or actions his obligation is categorical. The strangeness of this view will become clearer when, towards the end of this paper, I shall outline how moral obligations are different from evaluations. Philosophers who *would like* to derive our obligations from the type of considerations which show that terms like 'pen' or 'farmer' provide us with criteria of good pens and good farmers, would probably very much like to know how Montefiore thinks that categorical obligations follow from having such words in our language as 'pen' and 'knife'. The third section of my paper will argue that the problems of moral life are quite unrelated to the humdrum affair of evaluations.

But more is at stake for the individualist than his freedom. The very possibility of evaluation seems to be at stake if we have 'criteria-setting' terms, for Montefiore claims that 'he alone evaluates who creates or chooses his values for himself.'[8] It is very difficult to make sense of this claim, but I think I see why he says something like this; he tries to make the individualist's position secure by this attempted definition. In the paragraph to which this is a conclusion he asks in what sense of 'must' one must not try to force the individual to accept values that he does not freely accept for himself. The reason for it cannot be that it would be wrong to do so because this would refer to 'standards of extra-individual value'. The only answer is that it is impossible to do so and thus he tries to make his individualist's position follow from the very definition of what it is 'to evaluate'. I should quote at length what Montefiore has to say a few pages earlier:

> To face him [the individualist] with values that were given to him as facts would be to restrict his freedom on the issues that were most important to him; it would be self-defeatingly to concede that what is of supreme importance is in some instances at least after all above and beyond the creative control of individuals as such. It is for this reason that a fully rigorous version of the doctrine of no 'ought' from an 'is' becomes an essential feature of any such thorough-going individualism. Its acceptance is the only guarantee that there can be no observations of fact by which the individual valuer might be committed one way rather than another.... When the individualist incorporates it as a principle of the very logic of his language he rules out any would-be non-individualist system of values as strictly unintelligible as such.[9]

If the 'descriptive words' that an anti-naturalist claims to be irrelevant to evaluations were the 'descriptive words' of our ordinary language, then the individualist would not need to worry about our description of the world because it would be irrelevant for his evaluations. Montefiore does not only agree that such words as 'pen' and 'farmer' are 'criteria-setting' terms without any decisions of ours; he fundamentally assumes that the description of the world is of the most vital relevance for our moral life, and this is why his individualist desperately wants to change the description of the world. He does not want to leave the world as it is: he is trying to derive an 'is' from an 'ought'. He does not choose or create values irrespective of the facts, he eliminates the facts. Montefiore even conflates facts and values when what he is concerned about is that his individualist will be faced with 'values that were given to him as facts.'

Now there are many things wrong with Montefiore's individualist, but again one should not, by way of criticism, try to defend an 'authoritarian' or an 'other-directed personality,' nor should one anxiously try to show that one is just as good an individualist as he is. It would be easy to show that an individualist could not exist in a world where we operated only with the category of 'object' (nor could anyone else for that matter), not only because he has to eat before he could be an individualist, a point to which I shall return later, but because an individualist can exist only in societies that have attained a certain level of conceptual development. Indeed, I am not sure that Montefiore could have made his point without describing the person he is talking about as an individualist. A role, however, that he cannot avoid is that of a chooser, and an analysis of what would make him a good chooser would be very instructive. In a criticism one should also show that the way of life the individualist is recommending is incoherent, or that if it came true, his aim would be defeated because in a world where *everyone* operated with the category of object, he could not show how different he is from the common run of people who have pens and knives.

The nature of man that is presupposed by the various anti-naturalist theories deserves a special study of its own. Here I shall say a few words, not about Montefiore's individualist, to whom I shall return briefly in the next section, but about Hare's individual whose life is governed by universal principles that have the force of commands.

Though one usually associates Hare's ethical theory with the closing paragraph of Part I, Section I of Book III of Hume's *Treatise*, far more helpful passages for understanding why Hare's man would respond only to commands are some of those where Hume distinguishes between passions and reason, and claims that 'reason is perfectly inert, and can never either prevent or produce any action or affection.' Because Hare replaced Hume's passions with imperatives and put them not into one's breast but into major premisses, we tend to mistake a psychological theory for a logical one. Of course Hare would be the first to deny that his is a psychological theory; this is indeed why he replaced Hume's passions with imperatives. But what I am saying is that it is Hume's *passions* that he has replaced with his imperatives, assigning to them the role of moving men to act, while leaving reason 'perfectly inert.'

The imperative is then made to move us by definition. 'I propose to say that the test, whether someone is using the judgment "I ought to do X" as a value-judgment or not is, "Does he or does he not recognise that if he assents to the judgment, he must also assent to the command 'Let me do X'?" Thus I am not here claiming to prove anything substantial about the way in which we use language....'[10] But now one cannot give *reasons* for acting on one imperative rather than on another, or for not acting on some of them, because reason is inert. An 'active principle' cannot be opposed by an 'inactive principle'. But if we universalise whatever we want to act on then it will entail not only 'let me do X' but also 'let X be done to me,' and this is something I might not want. There could indeed be no reason why I should not prefer the destruction of the whole universe to the scratching of my little finger, except that the destruction of the whole universe would entail the destruction of my little finger, which I very much want to scratch. Not even this is a *reason* for not wanting the destruction of the universe but here an active principle opposes another active principle.

It is strange to think that views about the questioning of institutions, about the individualist's way of life, about the role of reason in human life, are fought over in terms of good strawberries, good knives and good farmers. Neither the anti-naturalists, nor the anti-anti-naturalists (who are not necessarily naturalists) leave alone the arguments about good pens and knives as irrelevant to morals. The anti-anti-naturalists too know that there is more at stake in these arguments than the fear that someone might decide that a blunt knife is good for cutting. It is the desire to show that it is possible to give *reasons* for value judgments, and that values are not as random as they apparently fear that others might think, that keeps some of them arguing about good knives however otherwise unrelated such arguments are to the problems of morals. The arguments about evaluating artefacts are like elaborate tournaments with set rules fought in place of and away from the real battles.

The Difference Between Evaluating and Moral Life

My main grudge about the descriptive–evaluative dichotomy is that it takes our attention away from the subject matter of moral philosophy to areas which might not even be connected with it, or if they are connected, it is only by convention that they are. To argue against a well established convention is hard, but nevertheless I shall try to do this.

The convention is that moral life falls on the evaluative side of our dichotomy, and this looks plausible enough if we place brute facts on one side and values on the other, and if there is nowhere else to put them. But I want to argue that there might be an even greater difference between evaluation and the problems of morals—not just a gap to be bridged but a complete difference—than there is usually thought to be between description and evaluation. The problems of moral life do not constitute a subsection of the evaluative side of the descriptive–evaluative dichotomy. I want to come back here to a theme that I dimly came to see towards the end of my *Moral Notions*, which is that no light is thrown on the problems of values, nor, which is yet a further problem, on the problem of obligations, by considering what we do when we evaluate.

I want to emphasise that moral judgments are not a subsection of evaluations because the assumption that they are has led philosophers to look in the wrong place to find what makes a judgment a moral judgment, and to attribute as a chief characteristic of moral judgments that which is not their characteristic at all. Of course we all know that moral judgments are different from evaluations of artefacts and skills. But if we assume that they are alike, only different in some vital respect, then we will think that we have found in that vital respect a defining characteristic of moral judgments.

The activity of evaluation very often needs tremendous skill and knowledge, sensitivity and discernment, but its logic is simple. The whole secret of evaluation is the basic fact about our world and life that whatever we find interesting or important enough to bring under a term or description is exemplified by many instances, none of them fully embodying or exemplifying that for the sake of which we took an interest in bringing them under a term or description. There are not many, if any, objects in the world like the standard metre in Paris. The reason for this is not, as the Neo-Platonists thought, that there is some recalcitrance in matter which resists the reception or embodiment of forms. It is not that the potentialities of nature are aiming at the fulfilment of various forms without ever quite achieving those aims. It is we, human beings, who have aims, intentions, needs and purposes. Our aims and purposeful activities are prior to evaluation, and the activity of evaluation could be said to be prior to our language, except for the fact that we could have only very limited aims and purposeful activities without language. When we want something for some purpose we look around to see what would do the job. So we start looking for things that would be *good for* our purpose. There is nothing mysterious in the fact that the objects the cave-man found for the purpose of cutting or for the purpose of piercing did these jobs only more or less efficiently. Ever since, even the specially made objects only more or less fulfil their functions.

Montefiore's individualist would have to eliminate not merely the terms of our language; he would have to cease to perform any activities that we have to choose or to perform. If he wanted to catch animals for his food, he would have to start looking around for implements that would help him in this. Though he would have as yet no words for knives, projectiles, or spears, nor would there be any ready made, he would nevertheless have to choose objects that would do the jobs better than others. And when he lost or broke one of the implements he used for cutting, in looking around for another one, he would not look at the broken one as an exemplar, but, like Plato's carpenter, he would think of that which does the cutting and would look for whatever would exemplify it or embody it. He would think, without the word 'cutter,' that one object was better than another for..., and then sooner or later he would have the terms 'cutting' and 'cutter'. It is in this sense that evaluation is prior to our language.

Even when we have the terms that incorporate our aims and purposes in performing an activity, the term we use to identify something is only one piece in the jigsaw puzzle of an activity or situation, all of which we have to understand in order to be able to evaluate. Furthermore, the term itself is not always fully developed from the point of view of the function of the activity or the purpose or aim for which we engage in the activity, or the use of the object which is identified by the term. Nor can we change the term too easily to include our aims and purposes fully, for there are many other demands on our terms at the same time. Answers to tax declarations or statistics, as well as past history and technology, will influence the development of such terms as 'professional,' 'housekeeper' or 'coin'. Very often there is not even one single term that we can use to refer to an object or activity that we want to evaluate. These are the occasions on which we have to use the various *good* phrases such as 'good at...,' 'good for...,' or 'good as...' followed by an explanation in place of one term. We also use these phrases when we want to evaluate something under a description other than the one by the help of which we identified what we want to evaluate. I say this not so much to plug the loopholes where someone might claim that a term by itself does not provide us with the criteria of evaluation, but to indicate that our *activities* are prior to evaluation and, indeed, to language.

The individualist may say, however, that all he wants is not to be compelled to do the things we normally do, he just wants to be free to do his own thing. But he will still be confronted by the fact that whatever he wants to choose will be exemplified by a number of objects or in a number of ways, and whatever he wants to do, he will be able to do in a number of ways. He will have to cease aiming at all or wanting to do anything at all, in order to escape standards or criteria of evaluation. Fully to explore this problem we should investigate the nature of man presupposed by Montefiore's individualist, a task at which I hinted earlier. My aim is far more limited here. Let us just remember that the individualist was worried that 'to categorise something as an object carries with it the assumption that it must have some peculiar even as yet unknown function.'[11] The assumption here seems to be that by contemplating the notion of 'object' one might or might not excogitate a function. It is at times like this that one can see the poverty of the type of linguistic philosophy which ignores the fact that language is part of human activity. It is not the case that if the *O.E.D.* tells us what an object is for then we just quote what others decided to use it for, and if it does not tell us what an object is for then we are free to create our own criteria. Even if I know the meaning of a clearly functional term like 'fishing rod,' I do not know how to evaluate fishing rods if I have never been fishing or learnt about that activity, and even if as yet we do not have a term like 'fishing rod' in our language, we will still have to choose one rod rather than another as better for the activity of fishing. As I said earlier, though the logic of evaluation is a simple affair, the activity of evaluation often needs great skill and knowledge, sensitivity and discernment.

We do not enter the world at the level of brute objects. We enter the world as intending people and *make use* of brute objects. It is for this reason that we do not 'move' from 'facts' to 'values' or 'derive' them from 'facts'. By the time we have described the world it is not 'brute'. For whatever was good for cutting before we had the term 'cutter' can now be said to be 'a good cutter' and whatever is not good for cutting cannot even be *described* as a cutter. I shall come back to this briefly when, discussing our moral life, I shall want to say that in the same way as I do not first find that I can shout 'help' and then decide to shout for help, but find that I need help and make use of shouting to get it, we do not first keep uttering sounds like 'I promise to pay you' and then make a decision about keeping promises, but first find the need for the institution of promising and then make use of words to make promises.

We are now in a better position to see why it is often argued that the essential feature of moral judgments is that in the case of moral judgments we decide on the criteria of goodness. It rests on the following simple blunder. It is characteristic of evaluation that we evaluate according to criteria of goodness. Moral judgments are (thought to be) evaluations, so the characteristic that moral judgments share with the genus is that they are evaluations according to criteria of goodness. It is an established fact that the family of terms that one might call functional terms provides the criteria of goodness. But moral judgments are not like judgments of functional goodness. Therefore the characteristic feature of moral judgments is that in their case we have to provide the criteria of goodness.

The idea that moral judgments are not evaluations does not even occur. When we make a moral judgment we do not evaluate according to criteria of goodness, therefore in the case of moral judgments we do not provide the criteria of goodness.

This is how the tournament about evaluation is being fought away from the battles of moral problems. It is thought that this tournament can decide the fate of the battle. The anti-naturalists think that they have to demonstrate that even in the field of evaluation the criteria are not always given, and then claim that moral judgments are like that. The anti-anti-naturalists want to show that in the field of evaluation the criteria are given, and then claim that moral judgments are like that. The battle has to be fought out in this substitute tournament because it cannot be fought over examples from moral life—because in moral life we do not evaluate.

When in the previous paragraphs I tried to indicate that the lack of criteria given by a term does not mean that there are no criteria, only that they are not given by a term, I did not do this in order to show that in our moral life the criteria of evaluation are given because the criteria are always given. I did it partly to indicate what sort of activity evaluation is, in order to contrast it briefly with moral judgments and partly to show that the anti-naturalists would lose even in the tournament.

Just one more example of evaluation might be instructive. In answer to Geach, Professor Hare gives 'a good sunset' as his example to show that here is a case where the 'standard is not even hinted at in the meaning of "sunset," let alone in that of "good".'[12]

Now where we do not evaluate there we do not evaluate. I do not think we have occasion for waiting for the sunset, day after day, in expectation that the next will be a good one. There are, however, beautiful sunsets and Hare in fact gives us a description of a beautiful sunset: 'it has to be bright but not dazzling, and cover a wide area of sky with varied and intense colours, etc.'

Let us observe that an interesting feature of judging something beautiful, as against judging something good, is that in order to know in what manner something could be beautiful one has to be familiar with the appearance of the actual physical object, rather than what the object is supposed to be. Take a leaf for example. Knowing what a leaf is would enable an expert to say what a healthy leaf is (the nearest to judging a leaf a good one). But knowing what a leaf is does not enable us to know what shape a beautiful leaf would have: for that one would need to know how leaves do and can look. Then with discernment we would be able to choose one particular leaf as more beautiful than another. Such are the examples that are expected to help us solve problems of moral philosophy, but this example does not even show what it was meant to show about evaluation.

But now when we are confronted with a decision to be honest and perhaps suffer for it, or to tell a lie and get someone else into trouble, we are not confronted with several acts all of which are supposed to be honest but some more so than others. The choice before us is not between several honest acts some of which are better than others insofar as they are honest. I am not suggesting that we demand that one had better be honest or dishonest and there should be no half measure of just trying to be honest to some extent. I am suggesting that we are not presented with the *type* of choice with which we are when we are evaluating. Although in some manuals of moral life we might find several examples of, say, brave acts, and the manual might even suggest that one was braver than the other (though probably it will turn out to be a better example of a brave act, or perhaps a more difficult brave act but not a braver one); when we have occasion to be brave, we are not choosing from possible brave acts some of which are braver than others. Nor is it the case that honesty and dishonesty are instances of something of which one is a better instance than the other. We do not choose to be honest because honesty is a better instance of that of which dishonesty is a less perfect instance.

In our moral life we are interested in the description under which our action falls and the description of the situations in which and because of which we are confronted with choices. We are not interested in the qualities that make one of several things falling under the same description better than the others, but in the relevant facts that justify us in regarding our acts as falling under one description rather than another.

Compared to the problems of moral philosophy the logic of evaluation is such a humdrum affair that it is not worth the attention of moral philosophers. As we know by now, we evaluate particular objects or performances insofar as they fall under a description, when our knowledge of what the objects or performances are supposed to be indicates or provides us with the criteria of evaluation, a knowledge gained either by our experience or, if we are armchair evaluators, through good dictionaries. But there can be outrageous things and performances, or such that we would rather not have them, like poisons, lies, murders and tortures. And yet there might be people who aim at choosing a good poison if they want to murder well. We all know that a good poison for a good murder should not only be efficient but should not leave traces for easy detection, a quality not indicated by the meaning of the word 'poison'. Neither the activity nor the logic of evaluation gives us any clue or help as to whether we value or detest something, whether we ought to choose or reject a course of action. For the moral problem is whether to lie or not lie, and the philosophical problem is what constitutes a lie as against saying what is not the case, and why we should make such distinctions, and the problem is not the problem of a good liar who wants to lie well. Evaluation is quite neutral to morals. We can and do evaluate both what we value and what we detest.

Moral notions and judgments are not about objects 'out there' which we can *both* identify with a 'descriptive' phrase *and* evaluate as a good one of that sort, nor about ourselves insofar as we too can be evaluated along the lines of evaluating 'things out there'. Moral notions and judgments are about our life insofar as our life is constituted by these very notions, judgments, concepts and descriptions. Perhaps this is the place to say something about a paradoxical remark I made at the end of *Moral Notions*: 'Moral notions do not evaluate the world of description; we evaluate that world by the help of descriptive notions. Moral notions describe the world of evaluation.' By the 'world of description' I mean the world other than the world of our moral life, the world of tables, knives and farmers. It is not the case that while descriptive terms describe this world, with our moral notions we do 'the other thing,' we evaluate it. No, we evaluate that world with our descriptive terms because I can describe that world with such terms insofar as things and people in that world are supposed to come up to some standards and expectations. When we turn to our moral life we do not find that there is some raw material there waiting to be described and evaluated. For the sake of the paradox it was proper to say that moral notions describe the 'world of evaluation,' that is, the world of our moral life. But this should not suggest that there was something there waiting to be described. Our moral notions constitute that world, and without our moral life and notions there is nothing there to be described or evaluated. Montefiore's individualist would find it indeed impossible to reduce the description of our moral life to the category of 'object'.

To follow up this suggestion would not lead us outside the empiricist tradition of British moral philosophy. I cannot do more here than suggest that we would be well advised to pay more attention to some of Locke's ideas on what constitutes our moral life.[13] For after exploring our knowledge of nominal essences we find that there is a residue of substance which might correspond to Montefiore's object. But the mixed modes of our moral notions do not have such residue and ideally they are transparent because they are of our making.

It would be tempting to think that we could reduce moral descriptions if not to objects, then to something akin to objects, to movements, sound waves and similar happenings. 'Promising' could be reduced to 'saying something' and that eventually to sound waves. But the genus of 'promise' is not 'saying something'. We do not choose or pick out promises from the family of performances of 'saying something' as we choose or pick out cutters from a certain family of objects, or chargers from the family of horses. This is even more obvious in the case of 'appeal,' an example mentioned by Montefiore. In whatever senses of the word 'appeal,' if I want to appeal or make an appeal I would have to do something, most often I would have to put it in certain words. But an appeal is not a sub-class of the manner in which I appeal.

But why should the individualist or anyone else accept that what he made was a promise and not just saying something? Why should he be described in certain cases as a liar and not as someone who said something? Why should he accept that he stole a watch and not merely removed a round object that made the noise 'tick-tock'?

I would like to distinguish now four different types of redescriptions: the evaluative, the ideological, the diluting, and the substantiated redescription.

Evaluative redescription should be familiar to us by now. This is when we employ the various 'good-phrases' to shift an object from under one description to under another description. Though we do not evaluate pebbles as pebbles we might find that some of them are good for paving, that is, by the phrase 'good for' we shift them under the description 'paving material' and we say they are good paving material. Or an object which is not good as a knife might be good as a screwdriver: the phrase 'good as' shifts the object from under one description to under another. The individualist could use even a good knife as a decoration around his neck if he thought it might be good for his purpose which might be to *épater le bourgeois*. But in all these cases the individualist would not be happy yet because he would have to be observing objectively given criteria in working out whether something would be good for one thing rather than for another. Not everything around your neck would show that you are different from others rather than that you have bad taste or that you are ignorant. Perhaps what the individualist wants is to redescribe his activity in order to avoid appearing bad at something merely by the description attributed to his action. Thus, if someone else assumes that he is trying to cut down a tree and he is doing it rather badly, he might want to be free to claim that he is only patting it.

Ideological redescription is a very important problem for moral philosophy, but here I will not say anything about it except to contrast it with other redescriptions. When the Nazis redescribed their murder as the 'final solution' it was not because they were not good at murder but better at final solutions. Though the other two redescriptions also differ from the evaluative redescription, the ideological differs from them in involving a distorted conceptual framework, an ideology or a mythology, the nature of which cannot concern us here.

Examples of diluting redescriptions are redescribing 'lying' as 'saying something' or 'murder' as 'killing'. What happens in diluting redescriptions is that an attempt is made to deny or ignore a morally relevant fact which would distinguish the act from a morally neutral family of acts. Again, such attempts are not made because someone might not be good at lying but better at saying something, or not a good murderer but rather good at killing.

Both Hare and Montefiore talk about redescription in the context of evaluation, and they seem to want the freedom to redescribe a thing or an action in order to get rid of the criteria that enable us to evaluate the particulars falling under a certain description; but in fact all their examples are of the diluting type, and one does not know what they would say to the ideological redescriber. But let us turn now to the substantiated redescription.

In response to a claim 'it was a murder' we might ask for a description of what has happened. What we are requiring when we are asking for a description of what has happened is not a different description: we are asking for the relevant facts that would substantiate the original description. This is a normal procedure in all our life, not only in our moral life. If someone claims that a certain substance is poison we might ask for a description of the substance. What we want is not a diluting description, for example that the substance is a greyish liquid, but we want a description which would establish the correctness of the original description. Similarly, in the case of murder, we are not asking for the substitution of a different description, for instance 'he moved a piece of steel very fast and the other person became motionless,' but we ask for something that would substantiate the original description. Only if the claim cannot be substantiated can we demand a *different description.*

In moral life and appraisal we are interested in substantiated descriptions and redescriptions, and no light is shed on the problems of these by the ritual arguments about description and evaluation or about the dichotomy of 'is' and 'ought'. Even just to indicate what the problems of morally relevant descriptions are, cannot be our concern here. But I have been saying more than that we should not rule out *a priori* any questioning of the existing philosophical orthodoxies that are based on the assumptions of the 'is–ought' dichotomy. I have been saying that we must forget that dichotomy if we want to give our attention to the philosophical problems of our moral life.

Descriptions and Reasons

It might seem unfair to take as my point of departure an isolated argument from Professor Perry's *Moral Reasoning and Truth*, but although I
make some critical comments on that passage I make them in order to
continue the struggle with the difficult problems Professor Perry there
presents rather than to show imperfections in it. In fact Professor Perry
does mention in a footnote that my comparison of judging an object to
be a table and an action to be a murder is similar to the one he presents
there, so my critical comments are intended more as a further contribution to the clarification of a problem that interests us both.[1]

Professor Perry points out, I think rightly, that the appropriate analogy of a moral judgment in the world of objects is not with contingent
generalisations, explanations or predictions, but with empirical classi-
fications. 'More concretely, statements like "That action of Jones (of
which we are otherwise fully informed) is wrong" should be compared
with statements like "That other object before us is a table" or "That
object before us is a person," and not with statements like "That table
will still be in the room tomorrow" or "That person will never marry"...'
He wants to use this analogy to cast light on the question whether a
particular action, say a particular sadistic killing, would still *be* what
we now call wrong even if practically everyone who considered it from
a moral point of view would say it is *not* wrong. And to do this, he first
considers this imaginary case: suppose that practically everyone who
is in a position to observe and use English normally, no longer calls
even paradigmatic tables, 'tables'. Would they still *be* tables?

If the object we pointed to had the same *uses* as what we now call
table, then whatever other word we used in place of our present word,
it would have the same meaning as our present word 'table,' 'for it is
the uses of a thing which determine the meaning of the words we use
to refer to it'. But if the object did not have the same uses then it would
be a 'useless object, or perhaps a device for warding off evil spirits, or
just some curiously arranged wood we can build a fire with'.

It is in the application of this theory to moral judgments that I find some ambiguity in Perry's argument. Coming to the question whether the sadistic killing of a human would still *be* wrong even if practically everyone who might consider it from the moral point of view would say that it is not wrong, this is how Perry formulates his answer: 'Yes, it would still be what we now call wrong if the people who take the moral point of view towards things continued to have the same "uses" for it: that is, if they continue to have the same evaluative response to the sadistic killing of humans'. Although the 'it' refers to the sadistic killing of a human, we do not hear of its 'uses' at all but instead we are asked to envisage a different moral judgment of it. This is far from what Perry intends to say, rather it is almost the opposite of what the whole machinery of the comparison was meant to show; nevertheless something went wrong, for this is what he goes on to say: 'But if they would not so characterise it with a synonym of "wrong," but would use some value term of an entirely different meaning—one expressing mild approval, for example—then under this more radical supposition it *wouldn't* still be wrong, just as this table I am now writing on wouldn't still be a table under the corresponding radical supposition.'

I cannot blame Perry for some ambiguity here, for the problem he has attacked is very complex and subtle, and furthermore, our philosophical habits of thinking have hardly prepared us for handling it. I am not sure that I can clarify the problem, but I would like to attempt it for I think it is a very important one.

The main problem is, of course, what is parallel to what; what should be compared to what in judging physical objects and judging moral acts. But before we can map that, we should clarify an important point. The operative concept is not that of *using* something, but is a higher or more embracing concept, of which using is an instance in the case of tables and bicycles. We have to ask something like 'what is the place of that something-or-other in our lives' or 'what is the point of having something-or-other in our lives,' or even 'what was the point of forming the idea of and then making and maintaining certain objects'. It just so happens that the answer to such questions in the case of tables is in terms of their use.

It is strange to ask for the uses, even in a very broad sense of 'uses,' of a sadistic killing of a human. We should look for the appropriate comparison in terms of the point of selecting certain features of human actions for special recognition, which in the case of actions is not their 'use'.

Perry suggested that to continue to have the same 'uses' for it is to continue to have the same evaluative response to the sadistic killing of humans, and to change its use is to have a different response to it, perhaps one expressing mild approval. My further objection now is not only that this should not be discussed in terms of 'uses,' nor that its 'use' in a broad sense of it is perhaps different from what Perry suggests. The whole logic of the problem and the whole point of drawing the parallel are distorted here. As Perry presents the case it looks as if the very same action, the sadistic killing of a human, could be right or wrong, *everything else remaining the same.* I am sure this is not what he would have liked to say, but by presenting the *judging* of the action to be right or wrong as the parallel to the *use* of the table, he has destroyed his parallel, with drastic consequences. To reverse the parallel: it is as if the use of tables consisted of judging them to be tables.

Now in the case of actions (though less so than in the case of making and doing) one must bring about some observable movements or interfere with the world in some way, but those movements or interferences are not the equivalents of observable objects that we have in the case of tables. In the case of actions we have only descriptions, or if this offends anyone, we have only specifications. So the parallel to the use of tables should be something like the reasons for selecting certain features of our lives, actions and situations for special recognition.

The elusive nature of our problem is such that it is very easy, or natural, to make two mistaken and diametrically opposite assumptions at the same time. This can happen because the comparable levels or elements of the parallel are shifted but at the same time there *is* a parallel, so the two mistakes are due to a sort of distorted double vision. Incidentally, I believe that it is at the heart of so much of the cross-purpose arguments about 'description' and 'evaluation,' and this is why I said that our philosophical habits of thinking have hardly prepared us for handling this problem.

Since in the case of actions there is no observable object such as we have in the case of tables, we easily fall into the assumption that a wrong act continuing to play the role that wrong acts play is to be continued to be judged wrong, and *at the same time* to assume that since in the case of objects there is something observable even when their use and their role in our life have changed, so in the case of actions there must be as it were some residue of the action which remains the same. In the process the most important element in the comparison, the very element which the comparison was meant to bring out and spotlight, was conjured away: namely that there is something in our moral life comparable to the roles which objects play in our lives. What the parallel intended to show was that in the same way as we cannot succeed in judging a table other than a table as long as it continues to play the role tables play in our lives, so we cannot succeed in judging a wrong act other than wrong as long as that act continues to play the role wrong acts play in our lives.

The philosopher who came nearest to seeing what is happening is Locke in his analysis of mixed modes. Moral notions for Locke are mixed modes, and mixed modes are made by the understanding. They are not copies of real existing things in the world but 'are the creatures of the understanding, where they have a being as subservient to all the ends of real truth and knowledge as when they really exist'.[2] The names of mixed modes always signify the real essences of their species. 'For, these abstract *Ideas* being the Workmanship of the Mind and not referred to the real Existence of Things, there is no supposition of anything more signified by that Name, but barely that complex *Idea*, the Mind itself has formed...'[3] In mixed modes the real and nominal essence is the same. The examples of mixed modes are moral notions, and he does call them notions. There is a reason for forming these notions. 'But though these complex *Ideas*, or *Essences of mixed Modes*, depend on the Mind, or are made by it with great liberty; yet they *are not made at random*.'[4] Now of course the reason why we select certain features of our lives, actions and situations into one notion and describe them by one term is because certain such configurations have moral significance. Taking away that reason is like taking away a king-pin, and the whole configuration will fall apart and the bits and pieces will take their place in other, not necessarily moral, configurations, or just remain as scattered pointless pieces. And those features of our lives that are features because of their moral significance will cease to be features at all. Here is the equivalent to tables turning into useless objects or perhaps devices for warding off evil spirits.

We see now another reason why Perry made that slight mistake in his analogy, but we can also see now a further consequence of that mistake. If the point of bringing together certain configurations into one notion is their wrongness, then it is easy to mistake this role of these notions in our lives for *judging* them wrong. But by conflating the two—their roles and judging them—Perry has let slip from our attention the point that the *reason* for judging a notion wrong is the role it plays in our lives.

Locke's views on mixed modes are hardly made use of in moral philosophy. Such views as these are put down to his rationalist side, and his analogy with 'Mathematicks' makes him a bit of a curiosity in the history of moral philosophy. It even seems incredible that anyone could compare the practical affair of morals with such theoretical study.

Before we go further I just want to mention one of Locke's examples, an example I look on as one looks on past battles or skirmishes, the different outcome of which could have changed our whole subsequent history. Here is one of Locke's examples with which he illustrates how mixed modes have no natural articulations corresponding to them in nature from which they could be derived. 'What Union is there in Nature,' asks Locke, 'between the *Idea* of the Relation of a Father, with Killing, than that of a Son, or Neighbour; that those are combined into one complex *Idea* and thereby made the Essence of the distinct Species *Parricide*, whilst the other make no distinct Species at all?'[5] This is indeed the question Hume asked later, and as we know, Hume's answer was not that it is our mind and understanding that creates such mixed modes and creates them for good reasons. He looked for the answer in his breast and we know what consequences it had for moral philosophy, while Locke himself went on to make the unfortunate analogy with mathematics. A few chapters later he says '...I am bold to think that *Morality is capable of Demonstration*, as well as Mathematicks: Since the precise real Essence of the Things moral Words stand for may be perfectly known, and so the Congruity or Incongruity of the Things themselves be certainly discovered, in which consists perfect Knowledge'.[6] No wonder Hume treated Locke's question on parricide in the same chapter in which he argued against Wollaston.

There is an interesting philosophical tradition where we find the constant recurrence of the partly helpful but also rather misleading analogy of our knowledge of what we have made with our knowledge of mathematics and geometry. The analogy is usually invoked to show the superiority and completeness of the maker's knowledge. Vico, for instance, claims that God knows the world as we know mathematics, not because the world is mathematical, but because God made the world as we made mathematics, and concludes that since we made history, we should have a divine knowledge of history and adds that the historian should have divine pleasure in contemplating history. Hobbes also draws the same analogy: 'Geometry therefore is demonstrable, for the lines and figures from which we reason are drawn and described by ourselves; and civil philosophy is demonstrable, because we make the commonwealth ourselves.'[7] Earlier still, Maimonides made use of the idea in order to show the difference between God's complete knowledge of the universe and our incomplete understanding of it. He makes use of the example of a water clock which is known by its producer according to the principles by which he made it but which others know only by observing it as an object. This is how he contrasts God's perfect knowledge of the world with our poor understanding of it.[8]

Interestingly, we find the same idea in Lukacs' interpretation of Marx: throughout history we make the objects of our knowledge, nature and society, more and more intelligible by transforming them. Finally in the proletariat this social reality becomes completely rational and knowable, and at the same time this subject matter is the knower, so in the proletariat the knower and the known become one, as God is described in some theories.

Locke, in his theory of mixed modes, gives, I think, without mystification and without megalomania, a very helpful account of what is involved here. In our knowledge of substances like gold or cabbages, the nominal essences never really exhaust, do not really coincide with, the real essences. However much we know them there is always a residue beyond what we know or what is knowable. But, as I said, in mixed modes the real and the nominal essences coincide.

The claim that maker's knowledge is divine knowledge is of course an admission that we have not got that knowledge; and the mathematical analogy is a very misleading attempt to indicate something which is true about our moral and social life, namely that in studying it we have to chart out and explore intricate structures of conceptual relationships. But knowing this is not like knowledge of our intentions and in fact it is even more difficult to know than the physical world. The embodiments of our intentional endeavours in our language and culture are not the making of an individual agent, and yet only individuals can know, so however much that world is in a sense our creation, the maker and the knower are not the same. This is what is partly behind the prescriptivist's objections that on the descriptivist's account our moral decisions are, at least in part, made for us by others. But of course it is not our *decisions* which are made for us by others, but what we make our decisions about, the world in which we make our decisions, the world which includes the reasons why we have to make decisions at all. As others cannot know for us, our decisions cannot be made by others, only what we know about or make decisions about can be made by others. But as some Husserlian phenomenologists fear that our knowledge is falsified as soon as an intentional object is described, some prescriptivists have similar fears about the embodiments and expressions of our decisions in moral terms. Such terms can only be a descriptive corpse without a vital element. We can see also in the views of the prescriptivists another way in which the tradition of maker's knowledge went wrong. We meet here again the Promethean temptation of a world where I *make* my own values, and values not made by me confront me like *objects* made by others: they appear to me as *descriptions.*

We are further handicapped in our knowledge by the moral world's differing from that other branch of the subject matter of maker's knowledge, from the world of artefacts. As Locke so clearly argues, the mixed modes of our moral notions, unlike complex ideas of substances, do not have references to substances existing in the world; they come to exist only when by our actions we instantiate them.

We just have not got the models and the vocabulary to chart properly this world of conceptual structures, their multiple interrelationships and the patterns of structural and other changes within it. I am not referring to problems of methodology developed and argued over by philosophers and social scientists. Our handicap is inherited from our pre-academic development and perhaps from our pre-intellectual development, from the time when we developed primarily as visual observers.

Even Wollaston, who came very near to saying that by our actions we instantiate concepts and propositions which are appropriate or inappropriate in relation to other instantiated concepts, retained a correspondence theory of truth, appropriate to propositions we use in talking about the physical world. For this Hume rightly criticised him by arguing that in all his arguments 'there is an evident reasoning in a circle'. To make a false statement by my action presupposes a moral world *about* which my action makes the false statement. It is very difficult to express the idea that my action is not a statement *about* a moral world but in a sense constitutes it.

Others who borrow from the models of the visual world to express the fact that they are not talking about the visual world postulate non-natural qualities or other invisible entities. What should strike us about these is not the implausibility of such qualities or entities but that in trying to talk about our moral life they only extend the furniture of the physical world.

But the most prevalent way in which we borrow models from our dealings with the physical world is when, in order to draw the distinction between talking about the physical world and talking about our moral life, we first draw it *within* the ways in which we talk about the physical world and then transfer that model to our moral life, without the objects in connection with which we made the distinction. We are all familiar with those introductions to moral reasoning which begin by saying that there are two sorts of things we can say about strawberries or tables: one sort is to say that they are sweet or round, the other sort is that they are good. Then, in order to have a reason to choose, we have to add that I like strawberries. I have argued elsewhere that the difference between these two is not as great as that between both of these types of statements about objects and our statements about our moral life.[9] We must not assume that out of the two ways—among many others—in which we can talk about *objects*, one of them provides the pattern for talking about objects and the other provides the pattern for talking about our moral life.

I want to bring out by the help of an absurd-sounding example the difference between the two worlds. The difference is not that in one case we say that this is a table, or that it is round, and in the other we say that it is a rather good table. To envisage our moral life we have to envisage *ourselves* as instantiating a table. If I want myself to be described as a table I have to be careful not to wobble, and whenever I see that the occasion demands it I would have to bend down sufficiently low so that the appropriate people could write on me or place objects on me.

Let us observe the completely different relationship between description and action on the pattern I am suggesting. On the model of choosing *objects* we are choosing from already existing objects and we choose the one which comes up in a sufficient degree to what the object is supposed to be under that particular description. On my pattern I am not choosing the best instance of different particulars, for there are no particulars there to choose from. The connection between description and action is that I am *instantiating* by my behaviour the description. I choose, if I can, what description I want to instantiate, or choose actions falling under different descriptions. I choose an act not because it is the best instance of something under a certain description but because I want to instantiate that description—or I refrain from doing something because I do not want to instantiate that description.

Of course, in the slave market I might be chosen because I am a good instance among other slaves of a sturdy physical specimen. But I am being chosen as an object; the choice is not a moral choice. The moral choice is choosing to choose you under that description, and what is more, it involves *treating* you under that description. We can see that there is a connection not only between the description I instantiate and my behaviour but also between that and the behaviour of others: both I and the slave owner enter into a world of conceptual relationships. And now we can see that the absurd-sounding example was not quite so absurd after all. The absurdity is only in our repulsion at thinking of a man as a table, to think of him and to treat him as what he is not. As Wollaston said: 'To talk to a post, or otherwise treat it as if it was a man, would surely be reckoned an absurdity, if not distraction. Why? because this is to treat it as being what it is not. And why should not the converse be reckoned as bad; that is, to treat a man as a post...'.[10]

We can work out, for instance, as a theoretical exercise, what is implied in the notion of a friend. In analysing the concept we work out what is entailed in being a friend, what behaviour we expect from friends, with what intentions they do what they do, and so on. And when I am a friend, I have to act out in my life the implications of the concept. When someone reproaches me by saying 'I do not mind you doing that but do not call yourself a friend' he is pointing to the logical incompatibility of my action and my describing myself as a friend. Of course if I have reason to take on a different description I can cease to regard myself as a friend. But my description of myself needs justification just as much as the description of anything else. Moreover, changing my self-description is itself an action, just as much as resigning from a job, marrying or divorcing, or joining the resistance movement are actions.

I am not giving in this paper an account of moral obligation; nevertheless I want to mention some reasons why we cannot lightly take on or abandon descriptions, reasons that are connected with my limited objective in this paper.

One is the inter-relatedness of whole webs of connections in such a way that I have to consider a whole set of consequences—and I do not mean utilitarian but logical consequences—in renouncing or taking on a description. During the height of the student unrest in the early 1970s a student handed in to me a sheet of paper at the time when essays were due. On the paper was a drawing of a steam engine with a flower in its funnel and with big bold letters the inscription: 'I expressed my freedom but you academics do not care about it.' With my limited artistic ability I drew a little pussycat in the corner of that paper, the sort children draw, with whiskers, and handed it back to the student next day. He came to me fuming that I had penalised him, that he was right to say that I did not care about his freedom to express himself. I did my best to look puzzled and asked him in what way he was penalised. 'You did not give me a mark.' — 'I cannot mark your expression of freedom. If you expected a mark then perhaps what you submitted was an essay.' 'You just want to treat me as a student, you don't treat me as a human being.' 'In that case my giving you a mark is even more incomprehensible. I cannot mark you as a human being. But if I treated you as a human being I would certainly ask you not to intrude on me and not to take up my time. For as a human being you are disagreeable, and I don't want to talk to you. But insofar as you are a student I would have to give you a distinction if you produced good work. In this case it is not because I do not like you that I did not give you a mark but because I took your paper as an expression of freedom and not as an essay. So instead of a mark I just expressed my freedom and do not know why you are so upset about my expression of my freedom.'

This was regarded as bourgeois formalism. I don't think that young man had worked out the implications of opting out of certain descriptions. Notions like relevance, fairness, corruption and a whole host of vital moral notions come to life and into prominence as relevant concepts logically connected even with such a simple case as this.

Another type of consideration that one might have for not wanting to get rid of a description is the recognition that the aspects of our life that it carves out and brings together into what Locke calls a mixed mode, and other aspects that it leaves out and sharply distinguishes itself from, are important and worthwhile distinctions. To use again my example of a student, we have to realise what conceptual transformations were needed to separate out and to create the notion of student as distinct from the notion of disciple. In marking the essay of a *disciple* it would be relevant to consider whether he is reproducing *my* thought and whether he is furthering the cause I am dedicated to. In considering the value of having such a description as being a student, again we have to trace and chart a whole set of relationships with other concepts with which our concept is connected and of which it forms a part. But without such a description one might not be able to be a student at all.

This illustrates also the reverse relationship between description and action. Very often when people are told that moral distinctions are man-made they are not only shocked but think that moral distinctions cannot be very important—if they are only man-made. But this is all the more reason for their importance and we cannot take it for granted that they will exist by nature. If we value some concepts we have to exemplify them and instantiate them by our actions in order to keep them alive. I do not mean 'exemplify them' in the sense that by our example like a living advertisement we shall propagate them. I mean that only by us being instances of it can the concept stay alive, for this is its mode of existence.

I think, incidentally, that Locke could have dealt with the connection between the conceptual relationships of moral notions and our actions in a similar fashion. 'If it be true in Speculation, i.e. in Idea, that *Murther deserves Death*, it will also be true in Reality of any Action that exists conformable to that *Idea of Murther*'.[11]

Someone might object that this shows how wrong Locke was, and say that most people would dispute that murder deserves death. The point is, however, that we do work out 'in Speculation' whether murder deserves death and if we come to the conclusion that there is no such implication then 'it will be true in Reality of any Action that exists conformable to that Idea of Murther'.

But the problem still remains, even supposing for the sake of argument that murder deserves death, why should I *do* anything about it. This would depend on my description, or on what idea I instantiate, and how I am related under the appropriate description to the rest of the situation which consists of a configuration of other appropriate descriptions. If it be true in speculation that judges should sentence criminals and I am the judge then I should be doing the sentencing. If I am the murderer then I should think of myself as deserving death. But however much murderers deserve death, if I am not the executioner and he has not yet been condemned, then if I killed him I would be described as someone who took the law into his own hands, and that has yet further implications. If, however, there is no appropriate legal system in the land and I am the murdered person's brother, I could not be described as taking the law into my own hands, there being no laws that I could be supposed to take into my own hands. This last example also shows how an act of revenge could change its role, which would help to illustrate Professor Perry's discussion of actions which could play different roles in our lives.

If, on the other hand, I am not in a situation, that is, if I am not related conceptually to the other concepts in question, all I might be expected to do is *merely to make a moral judgment.* Versions of the fact/value distinction which locate the distinction in the gap between describing something and doing something suffer from a systematic confusion because we have not worked out the difference between moral judgments and moral decisions. Let me just say here that the occasions for making judgments, and along with them the reasons for making judgments, are quite different from the occasions and reasons for making decisions. I am making a moral decision when I *have* to make one, and I have to make one when I am in a situation. I am in a situation when I lock in, under a certain description, to a conceptual field, *as one of the elements of that interlocking conceptual field.*

So the connection between a description and an action is not like the connection between describing something and judging it a good object of that sort; nor is it like the connection between describing it and choosing it, when the connection has to be supplied by our liking it or wanting it or making a decision about it. In a situation I have to choose because I *have* to choose; that is what puts me in a situation. And my reasons for choosing are in the descriptions under which the alternatives present themselves.[12]

Principia Ethica Re-examined:
The Ethics of a Proto-Logical Atomism

I

One of the questions that any future history of British moral philosophy in the twentieth century should investigate and document is how it came about that G.E. Moore's *Principia Ethica* was appropriated by what we can call the Humean tradition of moral philosophy.[1] I shall not trace the development now but only argue that there was no excuse or justification for it.

That evaluative words and expressions do not conform to the pattern of descriptive expressions has been noted in one way or other by practically all philosophers writing on morals ever since Plato.

Moore, in order to refer to a special doctrine of his own, coined a perhaps unfortunate, but very handy term: the naturalistic fallacy. This expression proved to be so handy that moral philosophers after him took it over to refer to the family of problems peculiar to evaluative language, to a family of problems that had no common name until our time. Owing to this misuse of the expression 'naturalistic fallacy,' when we go back now to read the *Principia*, our mind is preconditioned to find there something which is not there, or to regard what *is* there as an old-fashioned expression of what we *now* regard as the naturalistic fallacy.

That the problems peculiar to evaluative language have not received a common name until this century is not at all surprising, for there is not *one* problem to be referred to, but a whole family of problems. I shall call these problems 'evaluative errors,' and I shall use the term 'naturalistic fallacy' strictly only to refer to Moore's doctrine, as he intended to use this term.

It is not my intention to argue whether the naturalistic fallacy is a fallacy or not, or what this 'fallacy' should be, nor to decide what these evaluative errors are. I am not going to break new ground in the field of evaluative language, but to investigate *Principia Ethica* as if we were reading it for the first time, without any preconceived ideas as to what the naturalistic fallacy ought to be.

If we use as our paradigm, in the Kuhnian sense of this term, the set of problems to which the notion of naturalistic fallacy has been assimilated by more recent moral philosophy, then in reading the *Principia* we constantly come across unexplainable odd arguments, irritating passages that do not fit into our paradigm. Such a reading of the *Principia* misses the whole point of the book and can only regard even the very formulation of the naturalistic fallacy as an inadequate formulation of that fallacy. All these oddities lead us to take up a rather patronising attitude to Moore, attributing to him an important discovery that he himself did not know how to express.

If however we take as our paradigm Moore's ontology that he developed in his criticism of Bradley, especially in his 1898 paper on 'The Nature of Judgment,' and his ontology and terminology as they continued to develop and change slightly at the beginning of this century, then most of what used to look odd and out of place will become intelligible and will acquire meaning and significance. To be sure, there will still be perplexities in reading the *Principia*, but these perplexities can have quite natural explanations which fit into our reading of the *Principia*. One is the fact I have just mentioned, namely that Moore's thinking about his ontology and the terminology in which he expressed it was changing slightly during these years. An obvious example of this is that in place of the term 'concept' he talks in the *Principia* of 'that object or idea' that we have before our mind, or of 'simple object of thought' or of 'notion' or 'quality'. The only place where I find him still using the term 'concept' in the *Principia* is in the Preface where he claims that Brentano appears to agree with him 'in regarding all ethical propositions as defined by the fact that they predicate a single unique objective concept'.[2] Interestingly, in his review of Brentano in the same year, he writes that 'we are immediately aware that "true" and "rightly believed" are two distinct concepts, one of which, "true," is an unanalysable property belonging to some objects of belief'.[3] The slightly changed terminology of the *Principia*, however, expresses the same ontology.

We must also keep in mind that in the *Principia* Moore's aim was not to expound his ontology, but to make what he believed to be a revolutionary break with both the idealist and the nineteenth century utilitarian moral tradition in favour of a more noble and elevated utilitarianism, just as revolutionary as his earlier break with idealist logic and ontology. He formulated this break with the help of his new ontology, and although in the *Principia* he does not argue for it, what he thought to be his revolutionary move in ethics presupposes it and is inseparable from it.

What one especially would have liked to see from a fresh explanation of his ontology in the *Principia* are (a) an explanation of how the newly-introduced indefinable atomic object of thought *good* is related to other indefinable atomic objects of thought or concepts such as *existence* and *truth* that we are familiar with from 'The Nature of Judgment,' and (b) how the distinction between empirical concepts, those that exist in time, those which are related to the concept of *existence* in 'The Nature of Judgment,' and those that have being in some other sense, coincide with the distinction between natural and non-natural properties or objects in the *Principia*. The change from the distinction between what exists in time and what has being in some other sense to the distinction between natural and non-natural qualities or objects is another terminological change in the *Principia* without a change in ontology.[4]

As it is, Moore introduced his indefinable object of thought *good* without any qualifications as another object on a par with other objects in his ontology. As we shall see, he even explicitly rejects the view that it might be an object of will and not cognition, by regarding its status as a problem of epistemology.

II

There is indeed one superficial similarity between Moore and Hume but this similarity is rather ironical. As I have said elsewhere, both Hume and Moore thought that certain value terms *are like* colour words.[5] However, the similarity ends here because they thought they were like colour words for diametrically opposed reasons. Hume thought that virtue and vice are like colours, sounds, heat and cold, which according to 'modern philosophy' are not part of the furniture of the world but are our contribution to the description of what the world is like, and G.E. Moore thought that his little indefinable good is like yellow, because, like innumerable other simple objects, it is part of the basic furniture of the world.

The two claims that are most important for Moore both in his 'The Nature of Judgment' and in his *Principia* are that the objects of our thoughts have a being independent of our mental states and that the basic constituents of what has such an independent objective being are atomistic. He calls these atomistic constituents of the world 'concepts' or 'meanings' in 'The Nature of Judgment,' and 'notions' or 'object or idea' in the *Principia*. In spite of this terminology, these concepts are not formed or abstracted, nor are they in any other way dependent on our mind. They are found, discovered or intuited, but their being in no way depends on their being known or discovered. What applies to what is known also applies in the *Principia* to what is desired or willed or commanded. There is an interesting passage where Moore draws an explicit parallel in this respect between the independence from a mental state of what is known and what is willed. Out of many passages I refer to this one partly because it is convenient for Moore himself to draw the parallel, and partly because the context is Moore's argument against a simplified Kant, insofar as Kant's views are shared by modern prescriptivists; and it is the prescriptivists who are the worst offenders in misreading Moore. My concern here, however, is not to argue against the prescriptivists by pointing out that they commit what Moore thought to be the naturalistic fallacy, except insofar as they invoke Moore's name in vain as their authority. There can be other arguments for prescriptivism and there can be good arguments against Moore's views. In fact if my reading of the *Principia* is right, an argument *for* prescriptivism should involve an argument *against* Moore. But my main concern is to outline pointers to the proper reading of the *Principia*.

'Kant also commits the fallacy'—says Moore—'of supposing that "This ought to be" means "This is commanded". He conceives the Moral Law to be an Imperative. And this is a very common mistake' (*PE*, 127–128). Then further on he says:

> But this assumption seems to owe its plausibility, not so much to the supposition that 'ought' expresses a 'command,' as to a far more fundamental error. This error consists in supposing that to ascribe certain predicates to a thing is the same thing as to say that that thing is the object of a certain kind of psychical state. It is supposed that to say that a thing is real or true is the same thing as to say that it is known in a certain way; and that the difference between the assertion that it

59

is good and the assertion that it is real—between an ethical, therefore, and a metaphysical proposition—*consists* in the fact that whereas
the latter asserts its relation to Cognition the former asserts its relation to Will.
    Now that this is an error has been already shown in Chapter I....
[N]or can I add anything to that proof. (*PE*, 128–129)

To show this to be an error was already one of Moore's main preoccupations in 'The Nature of Judgment'.
    For similar reasons he also claims that propositions in no way de-
pend on, or have reference to, the world. In opposition to Bradley,
Moore argues that the truth of a proposition does not depend on its
relation to the world: 'a proposition is constituted by any number of
concepts, together with a specific relation between them; and according to the nature of this relation the proposition may be true or false.
What kind of relation makes a proposition true or false, cannot be
further defined, but must be immediately recognised' (*NJ*, 180).
    We cannot stop yet to compare this with what Moore has to say
about the concept *good* in the *Principia*. First we have to go on briefly
to see why truth cannot consist in the correspondence of a proposition
with reality. In a sense there *is* no reality more ultimate than the world
of concepts. 'A concept is not in any intelligible sense an "adjective,"
as if there were something substantive, more ultimate than it. For we
must, if we are to be consistent, describe what appears to be most
substantive as no more than a collection of such supposed adjectives:
and thus, in the end, the concept turns out to be the only substantive
or subject, and no one concept is either more or less an adjective than
any other' (*NJ*, 192–193). In this world of equal concepts some concepts combine with or are related to the concept of existence. Such
combinations of concepts do not thereby become ontologically more
fundamental or more substantive. Existence itself is a concept.
    One of Moore's examples is the proposition 'This paper exists'. If
this is true, 'it means only that the concepts, which are combined in
specific relations in the concept of this paper, are also combined in a
specific manner with the concept existence. That specific manner is
something immediately known, like red or two' (*NJ*, 180–181).
    Four years later Moore will add, in the same manner, not to red and
two, but to yellow and two, the concept of good. In the *Principia* when
we talk about *that* which is good, the proposition 'this complex is good,'

if it is true, means only that the concepts, which are combined in specific relations in an organic whole, are also related in a specific manner to the concept good, and this is immediately known like yellow or two.

Moore's world of propositions, which comprises his ontology, consists of ultimately simple unanalysable concepts of equal ontological status. These propositions are independent of any minds or of psychic states, they do not depend on being stated or asserted or willed or desired. Nor is their truth or falsity dependent on a relationship to some world to which they might or might not correspond, for there is no other world 'beyond' them to which they can be related. What exists is only a subclass of propositions, all of which, even when they do not *exist* in space and time, even when they cannot be picked up and moved about, have a being. That subclass is the class to which the concept of existence is related. It seems that the concept of existence itself does not *exist* but this does not mean that it has not got the same ontological status or being as whatever does exist, that is, to whatever it is related; it only means that it is not related to itself.

It is into this world that Moore introduced that 'object or idea' that the word *good* 'stands for'. 'By what name we call this unique object is a matter of indifference, so long as we clearly recognise what it is and that it does differ from other objects' (*PE*, 21).

Over and over again Moore rejects the investigation of the proper *use* of words. He regards these as verbal questions, 'properly left to writers of dictionaries and other people interested in literature' (*PE*, 2). 'My business is not with its [*good*'s] proper usage, as established by custom... My business is solely with that object or idea, which I hold, rightly or wrongly, that the word is generally used to stand for. What I want to discover is the nature of that object or idea...' (*PE*, 6).

What Moore discovered about the nature of this object is that (a) of the two sets of alternatives, good is not a complex but a simple object, that is, it is unlike a horse and like yellow, and (b) of the ontologically equal objects of thought it does not belong to that subclass which exists in space and time, that is, in this respect, it is more like the number two than yellow.

(a) It is because good is a simple object that it is incapable of definition in what he regards as the most important sense of definition.

> The most important sense of 'definition' is that in which a definition states what are the parts which invariably compose a certain whole;

and in this sense 'good' has no definition because it is simple and has no parts. It is one of those innumerable objects of thought which are themselves incapable of definition, because they are the ultimate terms by reference to which whatever *is* capable of definition must be defined... There are many other instances of such qualities. (*PE*, 9–10)

Definitions of the kind Moore is asking for are possible only when the object in question is complex in the logical atomist's sense of 'complex'. A horse or a chimaera can be defined for they are composed of parts (*PE*, 7). 'But yellow and good, we say, are not complex: they are notions of that simple kind, out of which definitions are composed and with which the power of further defining ceases' (*PE*, 8). As he says in 'The Nature of Judgment,' 'a thing becomes intelligible first when it is analysed into its constituent concepts' (*NJ*, 182).

Incidentally, it can often be instructive to note the recurrence of a philosopher's examples, to make use of what one could call the archaeology of philosophical examples. On page 179 of 'The Nature of Judgment' Moore uses two examples: 'This rose is red' and 'This chimaera has three heads'. Of them he says: 'What I am asserting is a specific connection of certain concepts forming the total concept "rose" with the concepts "this" and "now" and "red"... Similarly when I say "this chimaera has three heads," the chimaera is not an idea in my mind, nor any part of such idea. What I mean to assert is nothing about mental states, but a specific connection of concepts.' The recurrence of a chimaera in the *Principia* as an example of a complex object should be an indication of where to look for the context of its significance. And one does not need to be a very subtle archaeologist of philosophical examples to recognise a few pages later the example 'this orange is yellow'.

We shall see later that in a different context Moore can give definitions of a different kind as well, definitions which tell us how a word is or should be used. But when he argues for the impossibility of defining *good* he does not talk about our use of the word; he argues that the object good is a simple object in the world. If we wanted to give a complete enumeration of all that there is in his world 'out there,' we should mention good beside yellow and red and beside the four legs and the livers of horses and the goat's head growing from the middle of the back of a chimaera. He argued for the possibility of Ethics against a logical atomist type of denial of its possibility, against a type of theory which might say that *in* the world there are no values, *not* by changing such a type of theory of language, but by adding another object to the content of such a world. 'Good' is meaningful not because words may have other functions beside standing for atomic simples, but because there is also a logically simple object to which the word 'good' refers. 'Good' is meaningful for the same reason and in the same way as 'yellow' is meaningful. The following passage states the essence of what I want to call proto-logical atomism.

> In fact, if it is not the case that 'good' denotes something simple and indefinable, only two alternatives are possible: either it is a complex, a given whole, about the correct analysis of which there may be disagreement; or else it means nothing at all, and there is no such subject as Ethics. (*PE*, 15)

Moore at this time seems to have operated with an ontology and theory of language which later became fully developed in logical atomism. In the very last sentences of 'The Nature of Judgment' Moore says: 'From our description of a judgment, there must, then, disappear all reference either to our mind or to the world. Neither of these can furnish "ground" for anything, save insofar as they are complex judgments. The nature of the judgment is more ultimate than either, and less ultimate only than the nature of its constituents—the nature of the concept or logical idea' (*NJ*, 193). As the term 'logical idea-ism' sounds uncouth I prefer the term 'proto-logical atomism' at the risk of being somewhat anachronistic.

Moore did not argue for the possibility of Ethics by rejecting an ontology and theory of language according to which 'good' either denotes a simple or a complex or is meaningless. Rather he made room for Ethics *by increasing the number of objects in the universe by one.* 'By what name we call this object is a matter of indifference, so long as we clearly recognise what it is and that it does differ from other objects' (*PE*, 21).

(b) Moore's famous method of showing that good differs from other objects is not used by him to show that we can ask an evaluative question of almost anything we describe, and that as soon as we use an evaluative word or expression as if it would merely describe, we could then ask an evaluative question about that description in turn. 'Even if it were a natural object, that would not alter the nature of the fallacy, nor diminish its importance a whit.' In fact good is a non-natural object, but what Moore intends to show is that good differs from other objects *on the same level.* One can see from the examples he uses that he is arguing against a Bradleyan theory of judgment. If when I say 'I am pleased' I meant that 'I' was exactly the same thing as 'pleased' it would be the same fallacy (*PE*, 13). Or if by judging an orange both yellow and sweet we would think that 'yellow' means 'sweet' it would again be the same fallacy (*PE*, 14).

Moore is preoccupied by the nature of judgment, not by the nature of value; he is interested in the distinctness of the constituents of judgments, not in the distinctness of value judgments. Any confusion of any atomic simple with any other would amount to the fallacy but Moore is not really as clear on this or other vital matters as his style or reputation for clearness would suggest. One often gets the impression that the further distinction between natural and non-natural objects is parallel to the distinction between the subclasses of existents and the rest of objects that have being; and the naturalistic fallacy is a subclass of the fallacies that confuse any logical simple objects, that subclass in which one confuses an object which has being with one that exists.

But the overall impression I get in reading the *Principia* is that Moore's two-pronged argument in 'The Nature of Judgment' against those who think that either the empirical world or the mind is more ultimate than propositions—the two-pronged argument he summed up in the last few sentences of 'The Nature of Judgment' that I quoted above (*NJ*, 193)—is the foundation of the naturalistic fallacy. Pages 124 and 125 of the *Principia* are very instructive in this respect for there he brings his two arguments together when he brings together his objections to the empiricists and the metaphysicians.

The paradigm statements of empiricists are statements where 'the grammatical subject and the grammatical predicate stand for something that exists'. The metaphysicians 'still think you must mean, somehow or other, that something does exist, since this is what you generally mean when you say anything... Every truth, they think, must mean somehow that something exists; and since, unlike the empiricists, they recognise some truths which do not mean that anything exists here and now, these they think must mean that something exists *not* here and now'.

What Moore is trying to object to here can be misleading for two connected reasons. One is that one would have thought Moore himself was at pains to say the sort of thing he is here and elsewhere accusing the metaphysicians of doing, namely of asserting that propositions have some sort of existence other than empirical existence. But what Moore is objecting to is not the assertion of the type of being he attributes to all his concepts that comprise his world of propositions. He is objecting to the postulation of an existence, empirical or otherwise, to which propositions could be related in order to qualify as true or false.

Not realising or fully understanding what Moore means by existential propositions when he claims that ethical truths do not conform to this type, some philosophers might misunderstand him as saying that moral judgments do not conform to descriptive statements. There could be nothing further from Moore's mind here as throughout the *Principia*. He is labouring the point here, as elsewhere, that good, like many other objects, though being on the same ontological level, is different from objects that exist in space and time. In the passage we are considering Moore complains: 'But philosophers suppose that the reason why we cannot take goodness up and move it about, is not that it is a different *kind* of object from any which can be moved about...' (Moore's italics).

Although the empiricists are really the naturalistic philosophers, the metaphysicians, as we saw, 'still think you must mean, somehow or other, that something does exist...' 'They are as unable as the empiricists to imagine that you can ever mean that $2 + 2 = 4$'. After rejecting the empiricists' account of $2 + 2 = 4$ in exactly the same way as he does on page 180 of 'The Nature of Judgment' he goes on to say that metaphysicians 'have no better account of its meaning to give than either, with Leibniz, that God's mind is in a certain state, or, with Kant, that your mind is in a certain state, or finally, with Mr Bradley, that something is in a certain state. Here, then, we have the root of the naturalistic fallacy.'

This root of the naturalistic fallacy is what we find in the last few lines of 'The Nature of Judgment' in which he sums up that article. But let us turn now to see what ethical theory Moore presents to us in the *Principia*.

III

The recognition of the simple unanalysable object is only the first step for Moore in building up his ethics. His main object is to find *that* which is good, to find *the* good. 'It is just because I think there will be less risk of error in our search for a definition of "the good" that I am now insisting that *good* is indefinable' (*PE*, 9).

The good is that to which good is attached. When Moore says that good belongs to a thing he does not mean that it is predicated of a thing or that we judge the thing to be good. His language clearly indicates that he is talking about two *objects* being related to each other when we say 'x is good'. He had the vocabulary to express himself otherwise if he had wanted to. At the top of page 9 he can talk about the 'substantive to which the adjective "good" will *apply*' (italics mine). At the bottom of the page he explicitly speaks in a different language: '"Good" then, if we mean by it that quality which we assert to *belong* to a thing, when we say that the thing is good...' (italics mine).

We separate and recognise this unique object, so that we may be able to find the good, by finding out to what thing or things this unique object belongs.

A natural quality may or may not belong to a thing; natural qualities enter into contingent relations with things and with each other. But 'good,' being a non-natural quality, is 'a different *kind* of object from any which can be moved about' (*PE*, 124). *The* good then, if it is good at all, if this unique object is attached to it at all, must be such that this unique object is always and necessarily attached to it. '"The good," "that which is good" must therefore be the substantive to which the adjective "good" will apply: it must be the whole of that to which the adjective will apply, and the adjective must *always* truly apply to it' (*PE*, 9).

It happens very seldom that our simple unanalysable object is attached to or belongs to something. As we learn in the last chapter of the *Principia*, it happens in only two cases, in the case of certain aesthetic experiences and in the case of friendship. There is no other instance of the presence of this unique object. When we judge an action or a motive or a human character to be good, this unanalysable non-natural quality is not at all present in that action, motive or character. And still, the word 'good' in these judgments does *refer* to this non-natural quality. In fact 'words which are commonly taken as the signs of ethical judgments all do refer to it; and they are expressions of ethical judgments solely because they do so refer' (*PE*, 21). This sounds very puzzling indeed: there is an object which belongs to a thing *only* when it always belongs to it, and this happens only in two cases; and still all the words that are commonly taken as signs of ethical judgments refer to this object.

The solution to this apparent puzzle is that Moore uses the word 'refer' in just as strange a way as he is using such words as 'definition,' or 'object'.

> [A]lthough all such judgments do refer to that unique notion which I have called 'good,' they do not all refer to it in the same way. They may either assert that this unique property does always attach to the thing in question, or else they may assert that the thing in question is *a cause or necessary condition* for the existence of other things to which this unique property does attach. (*PE*, 21)

Whenever we make a value judgment we always refer to this simple object. But we may refer to it in two different ways, and two ways only. If this simple object is always attached to a thing, we refer to this object directly by judging such a thing to be good. The only other way of referring to this object, and the only other possible use of value words is to state that the result of this action is a thing such that this simple object is attached to it. 'To praise a thing is to assert either that it is good in itself or else that it is a means to good' (*PE*, 171). What we ought to do 'introduces into Ethics ... an entirely new question—the question what things are related as *causes* to that which is good in itself... Every judgment in practical Ethics may be reduced to the form: This is a cause of that good thing' (*PE*, 146). 'What is "right" or what is our "duty" must in any case be defined as what is a means to good...' (*PE*, 167). '[S]o far as definition goes, to call a thing a virtue is merely to declare that it is a means to good' (*PE*, 173).

Evaluative errors can be committed by giving definitions of this sort, and on the other hand we are not saved from evaluative errors by not giving definitions of the sort that Moore regarded as the most important sense of definition.

Whenever I say 'X ought to be,' I mean—according to Moore— that a simple object is attached to X. Whenever I say 'I ought to do this' or 'This action is good,' I mean that the end result of this action is a thing such that a simple object is attached to it. All value words refer to this object ('by what name we call this unique object is a matter of indifference') in one way or another, and this reference is the criterion of their being value words. By the strict rules Moore laid down we are prevented from making any other evaluations, or rather we are prevented from making evaluations at all.

It is not even the case that when we judge an action to be good that action will be good insofar as it is the cause of that which is good in itself. For what possible meaning could the phrase 'good insofar as...' have? Can I mean by this 'good' that the action has that unique object attached to it? Clearly not. The only other possible use of 'good' is to say that this action is the *cause* of that to which this object *is* attached. So to say that 'This action is good insofar as it is the cause of that which is good in itself' is to say—according to Moore—that 'This action is the cause insofar as it is the cause of that which is good in itself'. And to say that 'This is good in itself' is to make a descriptive judgment about the necessary connection between an unanalysable object and a complex analysable thing.

One can hardly think of any other moral philosopher who would invite us to make such evaluative errors as Moore would want us to make. First he claims that 'good' is the name of a simple object. Then in effect, he defines all our value words and expressions by giving very strict rules for their use. These evaluative errors are called nowadays naturalistic fallacies.

IV

Moore sets the stage for the whole of his Ethics in the Preface of his *Principia*. There he distinguishes between two questions, as the most important distinction in Ethics. 'These two questions may be expressed, the first in the form: What kind of things ought to exist for their own sakes? the second in the form: What kind of actions ought we to perform? I have tried to shew exactly what it is that we ask about a thing, when we ask whether it ought to exist for its own sake, is good in itself or has intrinsic value; and exactly what it is that we ask about an action, when we ask whether we ought to do it, whether it is a right action or a duty' (*PE*, viii).

We must notice first of all that these two questions separate 'things' from 'actions,' and so whatever Moore will say about the nature of each of these questions, one will apply only to things, the other only to actions.

Then Moore goes on to say what kind of evidence or reasons are relevant as arguments for or against any answer to these questions.

For answers to the first question, no relevant evidence can be adduced at all; we know what is good in itself only by intuition.

In order to be able to answer the second question, 'evidence must contain propositions of two kinds and of two kinds only: it must consist, in the first place, of truth with regard to the results of the action in question—of *causal* truth—but it must *also* contain ethical truth of our first or self-evident class' (*PE*, ix).

By now we can recognise where this will lead us. *The* good, that which is good, will be the answer to the first question. When we answer the second question, our judgment will refer to *the* good via a causal relation. And since, according to Moore, we cannot have certain knowledge about a causal claim, we cannot say about any action whether it is or is not always good. Hence actions cannot qualify as that which is always good.

The whole of the *Principia* can be regarded as an elaboration and explanation of the difference between these two questions distinguished in the Preface. Moore, besides explaining his own theory, argues against two main types of ethical theories, both of which are fallacious because they do not recognise the different natures of these two questions. These two types of theories are: (a) 'The Intuitionists proper' (by this Moore means intuitionists other than himself and Sidgwick) and (b) theories based on the naturalistic fallacy.

(a) 'The Intuitionist proper is distinguished by maintaining that propositions of my *second* class—propositions which assert that a certain action is *right* or a *duty*—are incapable of proof or disproof by any enquiry into the results of such actions. I, on the contrary, am no less anxious to maintain that propositions of *this* kind are *not* "Intuitions," than to maintain that propositions of my *first* class *are* Intuitions' (*PE*, x).

Prichard's and Moore's intuitionisms are entirely different. Moore is doing what Prichard says we should not do: Moore intuits a self-evident first principle of morality from which every other moral judgment can be deduced. 'The Intuitional view of Ethics consists in the supposition that certain rules, stating that certain actions are always to be done or to be omitted, may be taken as self-evident premisses. I have shewn with regard to judgments of what is *good in itself*, that this is the case' (*PE*, 148). Of course intuitionists like Prichard would not claim that when they intuit an obligation they regard it as a premiss, but the quotation clearly indicates that Moore does regard *the* good as a premiss from which all other value judgments follow.

According to Prichard, whenever we have to decide whether we should do an act or not, first we have to take into account all the relevant facts, and then we just see whether we ought to do the act or not, and there is no more to it. There is no more question why I ought to do it. Moore on the other hand is looking for the first principles of morality, and he intuits these first principles, for the 'fundamental principles of Ethics must be self-evident' (*PE*, 143). In the case of Prichard we always have to use intuition, all through our life, whenever we are confronted with a moral decision. But according to Moore, we may settle by intuition what thing or things are good in themselves once and for all, sitting in our armchair. For the rest of our life then, we have to use induction and investigate causal connections whenever we are confronted with a moral decision.

I hope it is evident from Moore's language and system that it is not the simple unanalysable quality that we intuit; we intuit only that it is attached to something (or, what it is attached to).

(b) While the Intuitionists over-emphasise the role of intuition in Ethics—according to Moore—theories that commit the naturalistic fallacy ignore intuitions altogether.

Moore goes into battle with the naturalistic theories over the question what *the* good is, what is good in itself. No argument is relevant to show what *the* good is, and still moral philosophers tried to adduce proofs or arguments to establish their conclusions to this effect. So these arguments must either be irrelevant, or, if they seem relevant, involve a definition somewhere.

Moore discusses Bentham's theory in paragraph 14 of the *Principia* as the first illustration of the naturalistic fallacy. Bentham seems to imply that the word 'right' means 'conducive to general happiness'. 'This by itself need not necessarily involve the naturalistic fallacy.' The word 'right' can be appropriated to actions that are means to the ideal. 'This use of "right" as denoting what is good as a means ... is indeed the use to which I shall confine the word.' But first Bentham should have 'laid down as an axiom, that general happiness was *the* good, or (what is equivalent to this) that general happiness alone was good'. In this case 'it might be perfectly consistent for him to *define* right as "conducive to the general happiness".' But Bentham, by saying that the greatest happiness is the right end of human actions, 'applies the word "right" ... to the end, as such, not only to the means which are conducive to it; and, that being so, right can no longer be defined as "conducive to the general happiness" without involving the fallacy in question' (*PE*, 18–19).

What worries Moore, however, is not that defining the word 'right' takes away its evaluative force. The fallacy consists in the reasoning adduced to show what *the* good is; whereas it should be laid down what *the* good is 'as an axiom'.

'I do not wish the importance I assign to this fallacy to be misunderstood. The discovery of it does not at all refute Bentham's contention that greatest happiness is the proper end of human action...,' provided that this is an intuition and is regarded as an ethical principle. 'That principle may be true all the same... What I am maintaining is that the *reasons* which he actually gives for his ethical proposition are fallacious ones so far as they consist in a definition of right' (*PE*, 19).

The value of avoiding the naturalistic fallacy is that 'if ... we once recognise that we must start our Ethics without a definition, we shall be much more apt to look about us, before we adopt any ethical principle whatever; and the more we look about us, the less likely are we to adopt a false one' (*PE*, 20).

In Chapters II–IV Moore argues against several naturalistic theories, 'theories which offer us an answer to the question "What is good in itself?"' All his arguments centre around *the* good, that which is good, and not around the simple unanalysable object called 'good'.

In the last chapter of the *Principia* Moore offers us his own answer to the question what *the* good is, what is that for the sake of which we ought to perform our actions, if those actions are to be moral.

'No one, probably, who has asked himself the question, has ever doubted that personal affection and the appreciation of what is beautiful in Art and Nature, are good in themselves...' But 'what has *not* been recognised is that it is the ultimate and fundamental truth of Moral Philosophy. That it is only for the sake of these things ... that any one can be justified in performing any public or private duty; that they are the *raison d'être* of virtue ... the rational ultimate end of human action and the sole criterion of social progress: these appear to be truths which have been generally overlooked' (*PE*, 188–189).

Theological Papers:
Introduction

Selwyn Grave

The papers in this section, 'Marxist Ecclesiology and Biblical Criticism' (published in the *Journal of the History of Ideas* in 1976) and 'Some Philosophical Aspects of Demythologising' (written between 1976 and 1979 but never published), reflect between them the primary concerns of Kovesi's theological thought. These were with various tendencies which emerged in the Catholic Church in the wake of the Second Vatican Council, and with the notion of a demythologised Christianity. Striking among the tendencies within the Church after the Council was one towards a Protestantising of the Catholic mind—not only as regards specific doctrines but in general attitude, part of this being a desire to undo the development of Catholicism and get back to the beginning. An associated tendency was towards the production of 'saints'—not saints of the traditional kind, but of the kind envisaged by the Puritans when they demanded 'the rule of the saints'. Another tendency was towards the evolutionary optimism of Teilhard de Chardin.

I don't know who originated the idea existing in the circle of Catholic academics to which Kovesi belonged, that an understanding of the Reformation had become possible in our time that had not been available since the time of the Reformation. (Not available to Protestants because the Reformation came about within the Catholic Church, and not available to Catholics, for whom the thing was unimaginable until they saw it taking place among themselves.) But the opened-up possibility of a psychological understanding of the sixteenth century phenomenon suggested nothing to us that might throw explanatory light on its present recurrence. Kovesi tried harder to reach an explanation than the baffled rest of us, I think. I don't think he got very far.

The Protestantising tendency to go back to the beginning, and the tendencies towards the production of 'saints,' and towards Teilhardism, are noticed in 'Marxist Ecclesiology,' the primary intention of which is to exhibit the working of the ecclesiological mind, whether its church is the Catholic Church or the Marxist-Leninist ecclesia. Some of these themes were light-heartedly satirised in *Trialogue*, a spoof theological journal 'for the exchange of ideas—for something else'. Kovesi brought out two issues in cyclostyled form at the end of 1970. Satirised also in *Trialogue* is the affirmation of highly-placed ecclesiastics, which especially angered and dismayed Kovesi, that nothing was going wrong with the Church. Their attitude influenced the choice of a name for *Trialogue*, and its declaration of editorial policy. Heralding an advance on an 'age of dialogue' contented with double meanings, *Trialogue* aimed at 'infinite ambiguity'. Everything it published, regardless of content, would be (in a phrase Kovesi had encountered) 'patient of an orthodox interpretation'. With a glance at the radicalising clergy themselves, the editorial continues:

> But of course this applies only to matters of faith. On all matters of opinion we are the only ones who know what is the Christian teaching.

Trialogue carried a satirical review of 'Progress's Pilgrimage':

> This is a book about Man come of age. As the great Teilhard de Chardin says, man is nothing else than evolution become conscious of itself.

In the course of Christian's journey, the journey of Modern Man towards the Ultimate, he is befriended by Relevance, who invites him to the house of Dialogue, where, to his dismay, he is told that God is dead, and that there is therefore no point in continuing the journey to meet Him. A cheerful prophet, however, explains to him that:

> On the contrary, God is not dead. He has not yet achieved full existence. He is becoming, in fact, He is He who is becoming.... The further [Christian] goes, the more he is realising the Absolute Consciousness, and at the end of his journey he will meet—himself: for it is he who becomes the Absolute. This is the Absolute End.

Primitivist aspirations and demythologising were brought together in a news item describing an Ascension Day Mass 'in a corridor darkened and painted to represent a catacomb'. The sermon declared that Ascension Day was

> a triumphalist festival, irrelevant to the concerns of the pilgrim post-Christian-catacomb church. It is not important whether Christ actually ascended into heaven or not. What matters is the significance of the Ascension story for our common life. All we have to believe is that Christ was no longer seen.

Attention needs to be directed to the bearing of contentions in the Demythologising paper on a position taken up in the Marxist Ecclesiology paper. One of the parallels drawn between the Catholic Church and its Marxist 'counterpart' is that both are said to originate 'in response to a crisis':

> To ask whether Marx intended a Party is as futile as to ask whether Christ intended a Church.... A Church is a response to a crisis: what happens if the predicted imminent end of the old dispensation and the ushering in of the new era does not materialise? One response could be to regard this as an empirical refutation of the promise. The alternative is to find an embodiment of the promise, a Body in which the promise is already fulfilled, which already belongs to the new era and yet has to live in 'the world' which has already been judged.[1]

The demythologiser's account of the Ascension, in the Demythologising paper, does not turn it simply into a 'non-event'. But that nothing actually happened outside the ordinary sense of things is presupposed by his account of it, according to which the Ascension becomes a glorifying response to the life and death of Jesus. The failure of Christ's imminent return to eventuate and, as a result, the exaltation of a mere community into a Church, looks very like that account of the Ascension, and equally to commit a Catholic believer endorsing it to the 'potato chip fallacy' illustrated at the end of the Demythologising paper. In this illustration of the fallacy, a potato chip on the ground that had been mistaken for an exotic butterfly, is still looked upon as having been wafted up from Brazil, even though it is now recognised to be only a potato chip.

Kovesi was uneasy about his parallel between the Catholic Church and its Marxist counterpart. That he could draw such a parallel is an indication of his own state of angry estrangement from the Church at the time he wrote the article. Kovesi had a strong sense of the intellectual contemptibility, not, of course, of the rejection of Christian belief, but of the rejection, in theological deliquescence, of the content of that belief. For him the Church, which claims that its teaching comes from God, had taken on the appearance of being willing to allow theological dissent to transform doctrines beyond recognition. He gave up the practice of his religion, but returned to it eighteen months before he died.

Marxist Ecclesiology and
Biblical Criticism

My theme is not Marx. I intend to outline the conceptual framework of a large variety of attitudes towards Marx, which in spite of their variety share a common set of characteristics. These attitudes towards Marx have acquired over the last hundred years just as much historical reality as the life, activities and writings of Marx himself, and thus deserve to be subject matter in the history of ideas just as much as the analysis of Marx's writings themselves. My thesis is that if we want to understand the religious dimensions and aspects of Marx's achievement we have to take into account the peculiar nature of these attitudes towards Marx as much as, and perhaps even more than, Marx's writings themselves. The common characteristic of the attitudes I am considering is an ecclesiastical framework, and the varieties are varieties, reforms, or rejections of an ecclesiastical framework. I have to extend my observations to a kind of biblical criticism (perhaps the kind which used to be called 'higher criticism') as well, because once one is within an ecclesiastical framework then the study of Marx takes on the form of this criticism. Even the rejection of the ecclesia takes the form of an appeal to the Bible.

I have to distinguish the attitude of mind of those who move within an ecclesiastical framework from others that offer superficial similarities. The study of great philosophers and thinkers is done not just by detached observers, but in order to find in them insights and ideas that we can accept as true, and to assimilate their ideas into our further thinking about the world and ourselves. Sometimes schools come into being where followers of a great master not only argue about the correct interpretations of his ideas but develop them further, perhaps even arguing for an orthodox or unorthodox interpretation and development of his thought. One could have such a relationship even towards Marx's ideas and yet not move within an ecclesiastical framework. Nor would an emotional devotion to a master, a willingness to propagate his ideas, or a desire to spread his teaching suffice to qualify as a distinctive feature of moving within an ecclesiastical framework. Unfortunately, many alleged similarities between Christians and communists have been these subjective ones of dedication and devotion. These are symptoms but do not adequately distinguish the conceptual framework I wish to outline.

I shall indicate first that there is a special reason why those who move within an ecclesiastical framework are dedicated and committed to it, and secondly, I shall point to the paradoxical nature of their acceptance of the teaching that originally gave rise to the ecclesia. People move within an ecclesiastical framework if they understand its doctrine as applicable not only to themselves but also to all others. The only teachings that can give rise to ecclesiastical movements are those that can be interpreted as an all-inclusive universal drama within which people can understand themselves as engaged *participants*.[1] This is why their commitment should not be described merely as a devotion to an idea: rather, they act out the roles of ideas when they, as it were, personify (individually or collectively) roles in a world drama and regard others as personifications (individually or collectively) of other parts in the drama. Commitment, zeal and action follow from these kinds of dramatised roles rather than as the result of an emotional attachment to an idea or person. Because of this lack of separation between people and their ideas, an ecclesiastic mind has a propensity to eliminate or neutralise or change the role of those who disagree rather than to *argue* against their ideas; if others express different views, raise objections, or show incomprehension, then this is what is *expected* of them as players of different roles in the drama. Ideas, views and arguments are not treated as ideas, views, and arguments for which there can be good or bad reasons independently of those who express them: the very fact of the existence of different ideas and views is explained from within the system; an explanation is given for the existence of differing ideas, how they arise, what causes them, what roles they play in the overall drama; and most of all, an explanation is given why others do not accept the only true ideas, why they have eyes but do not see, ears but do not hear.

A second feature of an ecclesiastical framework, mentioned earlier, is the paradoxical nature of the treatment of the original teaching that gave rise to the ecclesia. On a superficial look one might think that the person who lives within an ecclesiastical framework treats the writings that gave rise to his movement with greater respect than that shown by scholars towards the author they study and perhaps even follow. While there is a truth in this impression I want to point to a paradoxical aspect of this truth. After all, what makes a student of Plato a scholar is precisely his respect for the text, his thorough knowledge of it, his ability to understand and explain it, and the high standard of precision with which he treats his texts. The writings of Plato, Aristotle, or other great thinkers are studied by a large number of scholars, and have given rise to an extensive continuing literature, but in these cases the continuing studies and movements are an extension of the original literature's life, while in an ecclesiastical framework the original writings themselves become part of the movement's life. Surprisingly, the ecclesiastical mind, as against that of the scholar, can treat the literature that gave rise to the ecclesia more as an *incident* in the life of the movement. We shall consider later the interesting case of George Lukacs who supposed that all of Marx's propositions could be disproved by modern science without damaging Marxist orthodoxy. The paradoxical nature of this problem is interesting: the ecclesiastical mind can treat its literature as incidental precisely because it regards the revelations of its literature as more important than any other piece of writing. Its literature points beyond itself: it *reveals* the truth about the universe and about history; it reveals the great drama in which we are supposed to be participants. So the appearance of the writings themselves becomes part of this universal drama and the drama they reveal is what gives them their importance. A scripture can be thought to be inspired only by reference to that larger universal view that the scripture reveals; or a body of literature can be thought to be the voice of, or at least the key to, the true consciousness, only by reference to that larger universal view that the literature itself reveals. In this context we meet again an ambivalent attitude towards *reasoning.* While for the scholar earlier and later literatures than those that he studies will be relevant insofar as they help him to understand the arguments of the works he studies, for the ecclesiastical mind earlier and later literatures will be relevant only by reference to the drama. Earlier literatures, for the ecclesiastical mind, are a preparation for the decisive event and later literatures are further developments in the drama. The relationship of the writings of Lenin and Stalin to Marx is not like the relationship of the continuing literature on Plato or Wittgenstein to Plato or Wittgenstein, nor like the continuing interpretations of Marx by Marxian scholars to Marx's writings. They are further events in the drama which Marx's work is supposed to be about and their 'orthodoxy' is determined by reference to the continuing events in that drama.

We can also approach our problem through the difference between what I call a 'closed system' and an 'open system'. As Voegelin pointed out, when we reflect on social reality we find symbols and concepts in which the subject matter finds its articulation and self-understanding. Some, but not all, of these symbols and concepts can be used by the observer to describe the social reality he tries to understand; at the same time, however, the people who are the subject matter might not always accept the observer's description of themselves.

> If a theorist, for instance, describes the Marxian idea of the realm of freedom, to be established by a communist revolution, as an immanentist hypostasis of a Christian eschatological symbol, the symbol 'realm of freedom' is part of reality (part of the self-understanding of the subject matter): it is part of a secular movement of which the Marxist movement is a subdivision, while such terms as 'immanentist,' 'hypostasis,' and 'eschatology' are concepts of political science. The terms used in the description do not occur in the reality of the Marxist movement, while the symbol 'realm of freedom' is useless in critical science.[2]

In the light of what we have said so far we can develop Voegelin's point by saying that if I described myself as working for the realisation of freedom which is to be established by a communist revolution, I would not be a historian of ideas but rather a convert to communism. If, however, a communist described his beliefs as an immanentist hypostasis of a Christian eschatological symbol, he would cease to be a communist and would become a historian of ideas. Similarly, if St. Paul had reported in one of his letters that the story of the resurrection was a mythological way of expressing that Jesus is the Lord, that it was a symbol created by his contemporaries in reaction to a crisis situation, St. Paul would not have been a Christian, let alone an apostle, but some kind of anthropologist. If an anthropologist were to describe the resurrection in these terms he would have to describe St. Paul as someone who would reject such an interpretation; while if the anthropologist accepted what St. Paul believed to be the nature of the event he would become a Christian.

But are all observer–observed relationships of this nature? Is it always impossible for an observer also to be a participant in what he is observing? I think it is impossible only in cases where what we are observing is what I call a 'closed system'. In these cases to become a participant is to be converted, and to become an observer is to break the magic circle of the 'closed system'. On the other hand, as an example of an 'open system' one could imagine oneself trying to tell Plato what one thinks Plato is trying to do, and in this case it would hardly be possible to distinguish between the roles of the observer and the participant. Or, which comes to the same thing, we could remain an observer by fully participating in the activity and remain a participant by being an observer. If Plato did not accept the description given by a scholar of what Plato was trying to do, both would, in discussing the problem, be joint participants and observers of the activities of both of them. (There is of course also *a* Marx with whom we could be joint participants and observers, otherwise there could be no Marxian scholars but only Marxists.) This is what I would call an 'open system' of ideas which is nothing more mysterious or special than the continuing rational thinking of people who treat ideas and arguments at their face value, as ideas and arguments for which there can be good or bad reasons or evidence. In this activity ideas or arguments are proved, established, or eliminated, and not *dramatis personae*.

In order to explore now what type of literature could give rise to an ecclesia I begin first with an imperfect model which contains some but not all of the ingredients of such a literature. Let us take Plato again as an example, put to a different use. Someone could understand himself as the Philosopher King and others as the spirited or appetitive elements of the society. In this case, if others objected to or questioned his views, he would not, and from his point of view should not, take their objections at their face value, as arguments, but as expressions of the society's appetitive element—and since reason should rule in society, this element should be silenced. Rousseau's work also could almost give rise to an ecclesia, and indeed some people during the French Revolution understood themselves as expressing not their own will but the General Will. If I understand my views only as *my* views, for which I need to give arguments, then I have to take the views opposing mine seriously and try to argue about them, and certainly I have no right to impose my views on others if they are *only my views.* But if I understand my views as the expression of the General Will, and others disagree with me, the disagreement is not between two persons' views, but a case of some individual trying to assert his own particular will against the General Will. The very fact of his disagreeing with me is the proof of his not possessing the General Will, and I am not surprised at this because I know that most people, unlike me, tend to express only their particular will, and I can explain this by reference to the theory in terms of which I understand myself. But my megalomania here is just too obvious, and it would be similarly obvious if I understood myself as the Philosopher King.

Before we ask what is missing from my oversimplified model of theories that could generate an ecclesia, let us observe an element which makes them potential candidates for such a role. Such a theory enables you to substitute for yourself something greater than yourself, and makes others less than they are. Again another paradox: it enables you to combine the greatest possible humility with the greatest possible arrogance. It enables you to say, in effect, something like this: 'It is not I who am speaking; if this were merely my thought I would have no claim on you; but what you are expressing is something subjective and partial, arising from your particularity and *divergence* from what is universal, objective and true. While my personality disappears and I am expressing the truth, your idiosyncratic personality is asserting merely itself.'

What is missing from my simple model is that element of *drama* emphasised earlier. The systems of both Plato and Rousseau are static, they do not reveal a movement in history which enables people to understand themselves as participants in that drama without appearing to be too obviously megalomaniac. The mechanism of the drama will *appoint you* and identify you, as the spokesman of that which is greater than yourself. What Marx reveals is such a drama. I would like to give first an example of an intermediate stage between a system in which one could be only a self-appointed spokesman with all the appearance of megalomania, and the sort of drama which points to you as the spokesman.

The work of Teilhard de Chardin reveals a drama where the love of God and faith in the world will eventually converge. At the end of his *Le Christique* he claims that this is already 'in the air' though rarely, as yet, combined in one person. Then he goes on to say:

In me, by the chance of temperament, education and environment, the proportion of the one and of the other are favourable, and the fusion has spontaneously come about—too feebly as yet for an explosive propagation—but still in sufficient strength to show that the reaction is possible and that, some day or other, the two will join up. A fresh proof that the truth has only to appear once, in a single mind, and nothing can ever again prevent it from invading everything and setting it aflame.[3]

In this passage we find an excellent example of the simultaneous combination of the greatest possible 'humility' with the greatest possible megalomania. While scholars, scientists and philosophers work hard and achieve something as a result of their own thinking, Teilhard does not claim any such achievement. His own humble self disappears and Truth appears in him. With great humility he does not claim anything more than that Truth appeared in him, in a single mind. It is not on the pathology of this case that I wish to dwell, but rather to draw attention to the structure of the 'argument': only if it is the case that the drama of history is the convergence of the love of God and faith in the world is it the case that if this convergence appears in someone then Truth has appeared in that person. This convergence *is* what is meant by the appearance of the Truth in Teilhard. We have here a self-justifying circle; only if his theory is true did Truth appear in him. But if we observe the passage again we find that the appearance of truth in the single mind of Teilhard is itself an event in this drama, and this event is used as a *proof* for the Truth of his theory, namely, that this combination of love of God and faith in the world will spread from now on as the culmination of the drama of history.

We can now turn to Marx, who was not a megalomaniac. Though he thought that he revealed the true drama of history, he pointed to others as the heroes of his drama. Working in the British Museum he wrote to Kugelmann in 1857: 'I am working like mad all through the nights at putting my economic studies together so that I may at least have the outlines clear before the deluge comes'. But the deluge would come without him. Again a year later he wrote:

I have a presentiment that now, when after fifteen years of study I have got far enough to have the thing within my grasp, stormy movements from without will probably interfere. Never mind. If I get finished so late that I no longer find the world ready to pay attention to such things, the fault will obviously be my own.

I do not wish to add here to the expositions of and arguments about Marx's system and about the role of the proletariat in Marx's world-view. As stated earlier, my theme is not Marx. My concern is to show that Marx's system is capable of being interpreted by others coming after him as referring to them, as allocating a *role* to them in a drama. Marxism is in a sense a theory trying to prove that it is *not* a theory. It reveals what is happening before our eyes, if we have eyes to see. 'In the measure that history moves forward,' says Marx, 'and with it the struggle of the proletariat assumes clearer outlines, they no longer need to seek science in their minds; they have to take note of what is happening before their eyes and become its mouthpiece.'[4] Of course, Marx's claim that we should leave theorising behind and turn our attention to the real historical process, and the further claim that the real historical process itself will replace theorising are themselves theories. The subtle arguments behind these claims are the subject matter of Marx scholars. Some Marx scholars see theological patterns in Marx's arguments, but I am not basing my contention that Marx gave rise to an ecclesia on a theological interpretation of his writings. My argument is based on the fact that his theory is capable of being interpreted, and was in fact interpreted, by millions in such a way that they made themselves into an ecclesia by understanding themselves as the mouthpiece of the real historical process. 'Heralding the *dissolution of the existing order of things*, the proletariat merely announces the *secret of its own existence*.'[5] To ask whether Marx intended a Party is just as futile as to ask whether Christ intended a Church. It is interesting to note here that theorists like Saint-Simon or Rousseau who explicitly projected the formation of a new religion did not give rise to a new religion. The explanation for this might be that they themselves felt the need to add to their theories the demand for a new religion because the inner logic of their own theories would not have started one. Marx did not feel the need for forming a new religion: not only because he lacked religious experience but because of the inner structure of his thought. Whatever paradoxes I have already stated, I have to bring out another one now: had his promise and expectation come true there would have been no need for a communist ecclesia. A Church is a response to a crisis: what happens if the predicted imminent end of the old dispensation and the ushering in of the new era does not materialise? One response could be to regard this as an empirical refutation of the promise. The alternative is to find an embodiment of the promise, a Body in which the promise is already fulfilled, which already belongs to the new era and yet has to live in 'the world' which has already been judged. One consequence of this solution is that the Church does not understand herself as being like any other association, just as the Party is not thought of by its members as being like any other party: the Party acquires an ontological status in a cosmic history and struggle.

I know that there are serious objections to this account of the origin of the Christian Church, but I do not think they invalidate my *logical model* which calls for a characteristic response as a solution to a crisis. There can be and indeed have been several important theological variations in the response to the crisis. It is neither within my competence nor within the scope of this essay to outline these various models in St. Paul, Tertullian, Origen, the Donatist and Montanist solutions, culminating in the classical solution of St. Augustine which lasted through the Middle Ages.[6] Marxists equally had to struggle with various solutions to the problem: 'What holds it back?' Christians were not the only ones to argue about the correct identification of the fourth Beast of Daniel which is to be the last dominion; Communists and Marxists argue until the present day how to identify the fourth mode of production which is to be the last before the 'end of prehistory'. While for Marx this was capitalism, it had to be extended to imperialism as the last stage of capitalism and then to neo-colonialism as the last stage of imperialism, while, at the time of writing, cultural imperialism is the last stage of neo-colonialism. The doctrine of 'socialism in one country' is another explanation both for the non-appearance of the universal revolution and for the state not withering away, a solution which had more drastic consequences than the Christian ecclesiological theories that incorporated the Roman Empire as part of their solution. One would think that one solution which was open to the Christians is barred for the communists: namely, the transferring of the Kingdom to a spiritual realm and the creation of the 'two cities'. But a dualism is an essential part of communist ecclesiology, the dualism of the invisible and the visible Church. What good Catholic would give up his faith because of bad visible manifestations of the

Church? Similarly, there is no point in arguing with a communist or a fellow-traveller about the misdeeds and horrors perpetrated by communist states. Anyone who tries to argue by reference to such empirical facts stands condemned in the eyes of the believer for not being able to see beyond such things; moreover he is condemned for not even knowing what socialism is if he identifies it with such visible manifestations. In a certain type of ecclesiastical thinking, mainly among extreme reformers and puritans, we find also another dualism which is a variant of the distinction between the visible and the invisible Church. Whatever is wrong in the Church is due to the influence of the corrupt world in which the Church still lives, while on the other hand the Holy Spirit works also outside the Church and whatever is good there is due to his influence. Similarly, whatever is wrong in the Soviet Union or in Eastern Europe is due to the remnant of bourgeois attitudes or to the re-emergence of such pernicious influences, while whatever is good, say, in the United States, is due to 'the people'. Thus comparisons are not made between empirical realities: a cosmic struggle is going on between good and evil, and in this world good may be incarnated in an unattractive earthly vessel, while evil, as is its wont, appears in tempting garments.

Of course, bourgeois society *looks* good, so is 'the world' full of temptations that Christians have to resist. While in the nineteenth century such temptations were 'trade-union consciousness' and parliamentarianism, today other liberal institutions, including tolerance, are added to the list of temptations. According to the dualist ecclesiastic mentality, tolerance and liberal institutions not only hide the *real* nature of our civilisation which is *essentially* wicked, but these temptations corrupt us, they make some unwary people love what is essentially evil, they dull us into acceptance of this world and make us forget our task of staying pure and fighting evil. The task of the saint—and to engage in the enterprise makes one a saint—is to unmask the *true* nature of our society. You do not need to believe in a transcendent God in order to think in terms of a dualist ecclesiastic framework, in terms of a visible and invisible Church.

We are dealing now with patterns of thinking which do not belong to what historians consider as the mainstream of orthodox Christianity. This is not the place to distinguish all the patterns as they appear within Christianity and as they appear in secularised forms, though the task is not impossible because the spectrum of alternatives is limited. What complicates such a comparative study is that we do not have a single spectrum, with a belief in a transcendent God at one end and a complete secularised revisionism at the other: we meet almost the same spectrum twice over, both within Christianity *and* within a secular ecclesia like the Communist Party. Thus, after some terminological clarifications, we could describe some aspects of the liberalisation process in confessional states such as the Communist states as a process of *secularisation* confronting a 'secularised' ecclesia. I wish to indicate now only two interesting conclusions that such a study would reach: (a) What would be described as orthodox versions of Christianity and of Communism exhibit similarities to each other, and reformers and revisionists in each resemble each other. Consequently, the orthodox and the reformer/revisionist face the same problems in confronting each other within both Christianity and Communism. (b) While the orthodox on each side know their differences, the extreme reformers and revisionists of each camp merge into each other. While the orthodox express something totally different by the help of the same conceptual framework, the extreme reformers and the revisionists often say the same things in different languages.

The merging of the extreme reformers and revisionists also throws light on the phenomenon which baffles some people, namely, the existence of Christian atheists, on the one hand, and atheist believers, on the other. On each side there is some unwillingness to admit even the possibility of such phenomena within one's own side, while they are obvious to those on the other side, and of course to outside observers. Most Christians seem to be constitutionally incapable of comprehending that Christian atheists are atheists, and it is anathema for Communists to recognise the theological structure of their own thought. But the recognition of such states of mind in the other camp should logically enable the recognition of them in one's own. We noted earlier that one does not need to believe in the existence of God in order to think in terms of a dualist ecclesiastical framework. Now if Communists and their revisionists are capable of doing this, *a fortiori* a Christian can think in terms of his accustomed ecclesiastical framework. They of course would use a different vocabulary for the same enterprise. One way of showing, therefore, that ecclesiastical thinking can exist outside the Christian Churches is to show that ecclesiastical thinking can exist within the Christian Churches *without* a belief in God. The most striking and clear-cut example of this in recent years is in an article by

Father Giles Hibbert, O.P. in the Dominican periodical, *New Blackfriars.*[7] Father Hibbert offers there an analysis of the Christian claim which, he says, is 'at once materialistic and dialectical'. Though there is no dialectic in the analysis, it is certainly materialistic. His claim is that the Church has 'a richness, a "further dimensionality," which is in fact precisely what we should have been using the word God for all along. This "further dimensionality,"... this *spiritual element* embodies what is meant by God, and by heaven etc. [*sic*].' To illustrate what he means by a spiritual element he makes an analogy with a 'profound work of art' and its effect on a 'sensitive observer' and adds: 'but no one but a fool would suggest that this "spiritual quality" is something in a different sphere of reality to the work itself'. Since works of art, unlike their creators and observers, do not possess consciousness, he adds, as if in an afterthought, that the relationship between this 'spiritual quality' and its materiality is the other way around in the Christian Church. (As it is indeed, one should add, in *any* human society: as a first step in studying human society, one should surely make this elementary distinction between beautiful objects and social beings.) But, says Father Hibbert, 'these differences do not bring with them, however, any *danger* of a return to dualism and religion as long as the principles for the interpretation of Christianity, which we have outlined, are faithfully observed' [italics mine]. 'For Christians it is essential to nurture, cultivate and explore this "more," ... this cannot easily be done, nor can the claim effectively be pressed however, until the Christian Church has put its house into better order and made it look less like what Christ himself referred to as "a den of thieves".' Thus, we are offered an explanation why most of us have eyes but do not see, and have ears but do not hear; why most people within the Church do not 'faithfully observe' this Christianity, while others outside the Church presumably 'nurture, cultivate and explore this "more".' Now this is a very crude and simplistic view, but all the more does it illustrate the possibility of an ecclesiastic thinking without a belief in God.

On the orthodox end of the scale, let me illustrate briefly how an observer like Leszek Kolakowski, dealing with the problem of historical determinism, can recognise even the problems of predestination and grace as they reappear in Communist ecclesiology.

Marxist literature on the subject presents various motifs, usually revolving around solutions close to those of the Council of Trent: Actions that correspond to the desires of the historical absolute move within the framework of determination derived from that absolute. Nevertheless, there is not irresistible grace, and the individual bears responsibility for accepting or rejecting the offer of co-operation that the absolute extends to everyone. Redemption is available to everyone, yet on the other hand not all will take advantage of it, and therefore the human race is inevitably divided into the chosen and the rejected. This division is irrevocably planned by the absolute and all its consequences are pre-ordained; nonetheless, individuals freely enter one or the other category.[8]

It is far from me to say that this is the Marxist view, nor do I want to commit Kolakowski to any views he held at the time of writing this essay. But it shows that Marxists can understand themselves in these terms even if they cannot always articulate it with such historical knowledge and such precision as Kolakowski does in this paragraph. That Kolakowski was able to perceive so clearly a common feature between Marxism and Catholic theology is not merely a matter of intellectual ability. It also illustrates what I described earlier as a mind moving in an open system.

On the other hand, whatever were the intellectual abilities of Lukacs, he is a classic example of a mind caught up in a closed system of ecclesiastical thinking. One could not find a theologian in the entire history of the Church who has stated the infallibility of the Church in such unqualified terms as Lukacs did in his essay on 'What is Orthodox Marxism?' where he shifts infallibility from Marx to the proletarian Ecclesia.

Let us assume for the sake of argument that recent research had disproved once and for all every one of Marx's individual theses. Even if this were to be proved, every serious 'orthodox' Marxist would still be able to accept all such modern findings without reservations and hence dismiss all of Marx's theses *in toto*—without having to renounce his orthodoxy for a single moment.[9]

In order to understand what Lukacs is going on to say we must distinguish it from another Marxist view with which it is often confused, namely, the view that what characterises a true Marxist is the practice of Marx's *method*, not the acceptance of the *content* of his works. We would miss Lukacs' whole argument if we understood by 'method' a *theoretical* method, one which enables us to understand, analyse, and predict social movement and change. Method, or *praxis*, as understood by Lukacs, leaves theory behind; it *is* the real movement of history and not a theoretical method of understanding that real movement.

The argument of Lukacs' essay is that Marxism is not about Marx but about the real historical movement that Marx revealed. This movement is the dialectical development of the relationship between subject and object in the historical process. The resolution of the dualism between subject and object, between the knower and the known, is not a theoretical problem; it is being resolved in practice by the culmination in history of the unity of the knower and the known. This cannot be comprehended if we assume that the object of knowledge is some 'objective' reality existing independently of human beings. The object of our knowledge is the metabolism of nature and man as producer, and this 'object,' the subject matter of our knowledge, is itself developing until it finds its highest development in the proletariat; but this social reality, this subject matter, is at the same time conscious of itself, so in the proletariat the knower and the known will be one and the dualism is overcome in reality.

'To posit oneself, to produce and reproduce oneself—that is *reality*,' says Lukacs. There is an affinity between historical materialism and Hegel's philosophy because both conceive theory as the *self-knowledge of reality*. But, Lukacs goes on to say:

> Marx reproached Hegel ... with his failure to overcome the duality of thought and being, of theory and practice, of subject and object ... [I]n the crucial point he failed to go beyond Kant. His knowledge is no more than knowledge *about* an essentially alien material. It was not the case that this material, human society, came to know itself... [At the beginning of our social history] man finds himself confronted by purely natural relations or social forms mystified into natural relations. They appear to be fixed... In feudal society man could not yet see himself as a social being because his social relations were still mainly natural... Bourgeois society carried out the process of socialising society ... [T]he economic relations that directly determined the metabolic exchange between men and nature progressively disappear. Man becomes, in the true sense of the word, a social being.

Society becomes *the* reality for man. Thus the recognition that society is reality becomes possible only under capitalism, in bourgeois society. But the class which carried out this revolution did so without consciousness of its function... It was necessary for the proletariat to be born for social reality to become fully conscious ... [T]he proletariat is at one and the same time the subject and object of its own knowledge.[10]

Compared to this great drama, it is indeed unimportant whether Marx's statements are true or false; to be an orthodox Marxist is to be a participant in this great drama. Indeed, by reference to this drama it is not surprising if Marx's statements are not correct; after all, he lived at an earlier stage of historical development and his consciousness could not be at such a high level as the consciousness of those in the Kremlin who even condemned Lukacs. Lukacs himself said in this essay: 'Hegel was unable to penetrate to the real driving forces of history. Partly because these forces were not yet fully visible when he created his system.' Hegel, with all his ideas, was but an earlier event in the drama: 'the corpse of the written system remained for the scavenging philologists and system-makers to feast upon'. It is interesting to note how Lukacs looked upon his own work in the Preface of its 1967 edition. Claiming that it is no contradiction to assert the importance of his book in spite of its 'negative aspects,' he says:

The very fact that all the errors listed here have their source not so much in the idiosyncrasies of the author as in the prevalent, if often mistaken, tendencies of the age gives the book a certain claim to be regarded as representative. A momentous, world-historical change was struggling to find a theoretical expression. Even if a theory was unable to do justice to the objective nature of the great crisis, it might yet formulate a typical view and thus achieve a certain historical validity.[11]

We find certain similarities here with Teilhard's claim that it is not he who is speaking. A momentous, world-historical change was struggling to find expression in Lukacs' work. The fact that Lukacs does not appear here so obviously megalomaniac as Teilhard is due not to their comparative psychology, but to the nature of the system in terms of which they understood themselves. (For one thing, and in this Lukacs is a Marxist, he refers more to the objective conditions of history than to his own personality.) I hope I have been able to indicate this feature of the Marxist drama: it enables people *to be appointed* rather than to appoint themselves to world-historical roles.

Another similarity with Teilhard's logic remains. Lukacs claims that Truth appears in historical reality and not in theory, not even in that of Marx. But this is itself a *theory*, and only if this version of Marxist theory is true is it true that Truth appears as a historical reality in the most conscious elements of the proletariat, in the Leninist Ecclesia. At the same time the pronouncements of the Leninist Ecclesia are accepted as the yardstick to determine whether the world-historical movement did or did not find a correct theoretical expression in Lukacs. But I leave this problem to those who, no doubt, discuss it in sessions of Christian–Marxist dialogue.

The doctrine of the infallibility of the Church necessarily undergoes a drastic change when it is applied to a secular ecclesia. It is not just that Communists have never in fact worked out a limit to the infallibility of the Party decisions, as the Catholic Church has circumscribed the area of her competence. The difference is more systematic. It is not accidental that one of the areas excluded from the Church's infallible teaching is the area of empirical knowledge, where human judgment has both its competence and its failures; on the other hand, a secular ecclesia, *ex hypothesi,* does not make judgments on questions concerning matters of divinely revealed doctrine. The infallibility of the Party is about *this* world, and since competence in matters in this world strictly belongs to economists, historians, philosophers, artists and critics, and not to an ecclesia, a secular ecclesia becomes a totalitarian system. Indeed even the Church's behaviour within her own area of competence is justifiable only if there is a God who has revealed certain things.

When Lukacs' *History and Class Consciousness* was condemned, he submitted to the Ecclesia, though he could have gone from Vienna not to Moscow, but to California. After having outlined his ecclesiology, I would like now to argue briefly that his biblical criticism is that of the Left Hegelians. It was David Strauss who formulated the distinction between the left and the right Hegelians by reference to their attitude to the historicity of the Gospel narratives.[12] He gave the name 'Left Hegelians' to those who thought that the whole Gospel history was 'contained as history in the idea of the unity of divine and human nature,' while the 'Right Hegelians' denied that the Gospel history could be 'deduced as history from the idea'. What this amounts to is that if someone believes that our history, in terms of religious consciousness, is the realisation of the unity of divine and human nature, then he can claim that from this idea it can be deduced, without much need for historical records, that sometime or other during the history of our religious consciousness someone had to appear, Jesus, the first to claim this unity in his person. Jesus' appearance was an incident in the history of our consciousness and from the vantage point of our higher stage of consciousness we can understand the significance of that event even better than the early Christians who distorted and mystified it. According to this left Hegelian view we even know its significance better than Jesus did, simply by living at a higher stage of the history of our consciousness, after having overcome our alienated religious consciousness. The right Hegelians, however, based their belief on the historicity of certain events that cannot be deduced from the Young Hegelian drama about the development of our consciousness. It is in this sense that I regard Lukacs' view on the place of Marx in the history of the development of our consciousness as exemplifying the left Hegelian biblical 'higher' criticism. That someone like Marx with his ideas had to appear at some stage of our history can be deduced from the idea of the unity of the knower and the known, and from our vantage point of a higher consciousness we can understand the significance of Marx (or if one uses the terminology of liberal theologians, 'the Marx-event') better than his contemporaries or than Marx himself.

Lukacs, when he was confronted by those who condemned him in the Kremlin, looked beyond the visible manifestations of the True Consciousness. We noted earlier that the distinction between the visible and the invisible Church enables people to disregard harsh empirical facts, but there can be a point where the facts can no longer be ignored. The emergence of the New Left is a response to a new ecclesiastical crisis, when the pretence cannot be sustained and the distinction between the visible and the invisible Church cannot cope with the facts any more. One response to the crisis is again to regard the disappointment as an empirical refutation of the promise, and many tough-minded communists took this agonising step. Another response is to preserve your faith by claiming that you are right and the institution went wrong. The emergence of the New Left is comparable to the

92

Reformation. Ecclesiology is again connected with the Bible. By rejecting the Party the New Left rejected not only an institution but an intermediary between the original revelation and themselves. The unprecedented interest in the writings of Marx is, of course, partly due to scholarly interest following the publication of some of the most fascinating and intriguing writings of Marx; but perhaps to a greater extent it is due to a 'back to the Bible' movement and a desire for a private interpretation of the Bible where one finds a Christ according to one's own image and a humanist Marx concerned with the problems of present-day bourgeois youth.

One interesting way of grading the variety of movements that are grouped together under the term 'New Left' is to compare them with the varieties of Reformation opinion from the point of view of the answer it gave to the question 'Where did things go wrong?'[13] Was it only the selling of indulgences or should we also reject scholastic philosophy and go back to St. Augustine? Was it with Constantine that Christianity took a fatal turn? Should we reject the Church Fathers and the influence of Greek philosophy and go back to St. Paul? Though not many at the time of the Reformation went any further, present day Christian reformers try so hard to go beyond everything conceivable that one cannot help feeling that some of them would rejoice if in one of the Palestinian caves someone discovered Jesus' Early Manuscripts. On the Left some think that only the Cult of Personality ruined the true tradition and they would remain Marxist-Leninists, while others would go back to Rosa Luxemburg or stay with Trotsky, or regard the association of a world-revolutionary idea with a particular state-power in the Soviet Union as a tragedy comparable to what happened to Christianity through Constantine. There are of course scholars working on important and interesting questions like the difference between Engels and Marx and the difference between Marx's more mature works and his early many-sided speculations. But the New Left's interest in searching for the 'authentic Marx' is more like the interest in the Bible at the time of the Reformation.

All this crisis, however, has not eliminated the Marxist ecclesia: it has eliminated the visible Church and created an invisible association of Saints who refuse to be committed to or preserve anything in this corrupt world. This is not really a return to Marx but a return to the atmosphere of the Young Hegelians who realised that Reason was not incarnate in the Prussian State and were looking forward to the 'realisation of Philosophy'. Their disappointment in the Prussian bureaucracy did not shake their belief that as a result of historical processes Reason became perfect; nor did they give up the belief that the world was yearning to receive this pre-existent Logos. Hegel's mistake was only that he pre-dated the Incarnation. It is as if this one wise man mistook the Prussian state for the promised Child. One of the Young Hegelians, Moses Hess, began his *European Triarchy* with these words:

> German philosophy has fulfilled its mission, it has led us to full truth. What we have to do now is to build bridges which will again lead us from heaven to earth. What remains in separation, be it truth itself when it remains in its high distinctness, is untrue. Just as reality which is not penetrated by truth, so truth which is not realised, is imperfect.[14]

As the Young Hegelians, and liberal theologians, thought that Christianity was born of the consciousness and eschatological expectations of the early Christians, so we, in order to understand the origins of Marxism, have to understand the Young Hegelian '*Sitz im Leben*'. Marx also shared this atmosphere; he had no doubt about the fact that Reason only needed a material force in which it would take flesh. 'Revolutions require a *passive* element, a *material* basis... As philosophy finds its *material* weapons in the proletariat, the proletariat finds its *intellectual* weapons in philosophy.' He found the Suffering Redeemer in the proletariat which is, he says, 'the *complete loss* of humanity and can redeem itself through the *total redemption of humanity*.'[15]

But now the New Left are as disappointed in the proletariat as the Young Hegelians were in the Prussian state. No statement can express this eschatological predicament better than a quotation from Sartre: 'It is not the idea that overthrew us; nor moreover was it the condition of the workers ... no, it was the one *linked* to the other, it was ... the proletariat as the *incarnation* and vehicle of the idea.'[16]

But the Saints are still looking for the Incarnation and momentarily attach themselves to a hero or to a movement and anxiously ask: 'Art thou he that is to come, or look we for another?' And they say: 'Perhaps he is in the desert, perhaps he is in the jungle...'

Some Philosophical Aspects of Demythologising[1]

What I have to say has no exclusive reference to biblical scholars or theologians. Even most of the mistakes and fallacies I want to point to and investigate are shared by others who also operate in a theological frame of mind, such as members of eschatological or gnostic political movements which are characterised by the claim that their legitimacy derives from a special knowledge, teaching or message.

Otherwise the problems I want to raise are familiar problems of philosophy. They are problems we encounter in the philosophy of history when we distinguish between the actual occurrence and documentation of a happening, and the significance, meaning and interpretation of that happening; between establishing, for example, that someone did put an end to another person's life, and asking whether it was killing, execution, murder or sacrifice. Again we encounter similar problems in the philosophy of sociology or anthropology when we distinguish between observing and understanding, or ask what performances in societies different either in space or in time have the same meaning; when we distinguish between the content of a theory and its significance and message, and ask what theories with a different content have the same significance or message. On a smaller scale all these problems are similar to those we encounter when we distinguish between movements and actions or performances and their significance.

I emphasise that we are dealing with problems that are somewhere within this whole family of problems not just as a reassurance that I am not going to discuss some esoteric problems of biblical criticism. I must emphasise this because I think one of the reasons why some theologians commit some of the fallacies I am going to point to, and why others do not clearly see what they are confronted with when they are confronted with these fallacies, is that they think the problems are peculiar and special to them. In the study of Greek philosophy, for instance, we distinguish between the questions involved in first establishing the accurate reading, authenticity and date of a text, then its correct interpretation in the context of contemporary philosophical arguments, and finally the questions involved in the possible restatement of that philosophical theory in present-day terminology. The theologian or biblical scholar, however, when confronted with equivalent distinctions in his own field, is quite likely to regard the first type of question as one of historical science and the second and third as matters peculiar to believers who sometimes *are* believers or are thought to be believers because they do not stop at the first type of question. To go back to my previous example: only questions equivalent to whether someone in fact died at a certain date in a certain place are regarded as belonging to history; but questions equivalent to whether it was killing, murder, execution or sacrifice are often thought to be questions peculiar to believers, or questions to which certain answers would establish one as a believer. I do not wish to eliminate faith. There is plenty of room for faith even after all philosophical problems have been resolved or at least sorted out, but I do not want faith to interfere with or to be a substitute for tackling certain philosophical problems. In particular I think that the move from describing a happening to deciding what event it constitutes, or from describing a physical movement to deciding what action it constitutes is *not* an act of faith but is a matter of philosophical analysis. Although the problems raised by demythologisers are complex and interesting, they are quite ordinary problems.

Another reason why the entanglements I try to talk about may not at first look familiar to philosophers is that they are created by the kind of modern biblical scholars or theologians for whom it is important to preserve the legitimacy derived from or attributed to an original teaching, but who at the same time feel inclined or compelled to change that teaching.

I want now to explain briefly some philosophical tools or philosophical mini-theories that I shall need later.

One tool or mini-theory that we shall need is the distinction, and the one–many relationship, between movements and actions, or between what is given to sense experience and what an object or state of affairs is. This one–many relationship exists both ways: the same action can be performed by different movements, and the same movement can amount to different actions. This can be illustrated by the familiar example of the movement of your pen on the paper which can amount to writing your name or signing your name; again you can sign a document in a number of ways, and I do not mean that you can change the style of your signature, but if, for instance, you cannot write, you can sign a document by putting a cross in an appropriate place in the presence of a Justice of the Peace.

I want to add three small points to this.

(a) One is that one way of finding out what someone does in doing action A is to ask what else he would do instead, as an equivalent action, if for some reason he cannot do A. Thus, if we want to find out what someone who is trying to buy flowers is doing, we should ask what else would be appropriate if he could not find flowers. If he buys some coloured crêpe paper instead, then we can say that in looking for flowers he was looking for decorations. But if he settles for some chocolates instead, we should not be surprised by this unexpected alternative but understand that in looking for flowers he was looking for something to give as a present.

(b) The second addition is that this one–many relationship exists on a whole hierarchy of levels and not only between what is empirically given and what this amounts to—not only between observable movements and actions, or between observable properties and objects. Already in my example there were two actions, not mere movements, that fell under yet higher order concepts. Each of these higher order concepts is of course an instance of still other concepts: decorating a room can be either a way of earning one's living or of welcoming one's parents, and moving down again, there are a number of other ways of earning one's living. Similarly, giving a present could be an act of kindness, or an expression of respect, or of returning a kindness, and again each of these actions can be performed in ways other than by giving a present.

Let me now give an illustration of a more complex situation. We read in the Gilgamesh epic that Gilgamesh, having been given a leaf which was the secret of eternal life or at least of rejuvenation, while on his way home puts down this leaf on a lakeside while he goes for a swim. While he is under the water a snake comes, swallows the leaf and disappears. Isn't this, someone might ask, the same as the Genesis story of Adam and Eve being deprived of eternal life by a snake?

But what is it that we could substitute for the snake in the Gilgamesh story while retaining the meaning and message of the story? Of course we do not need to stick to the snake, it is not essential for the story. We could replace it with an earthquake which swallows up the leaf, or with a gust of wind which blows it away. If we substitute these I think the Gilgamesh story would remain the same story. But one could not substitute any of these for the snake in the story of Adam and Eve and still retain the same story. What we need to substitute for the snake there is another cunning, tempting or deceiving agent. Thus, by seeing what substitution we can make, we can see what the point and meaning of the story is.

(c) The third addition I want to make is that in order to perform an act at any of the levels of this hierarchy of concepts one has to make use of one or other acts of a lower level and then in turn, again, of a still lower level until one effects the appropriate interference in the world, which interference in turn will have to be interpreted or understood by others on the ascending conceptual levels so that the intended result would be achieved. One cannot just be *kind* without actually *doing* anything; one has to decide either to give a present or to do some useful chores; then in turn, if one decides on giving a present, to choose chocolates or flowers, or on the other alternative between, say, doing the shopping or doing the dishes; then in turn one has to make the appropriate moves towards shop or sink. But the choice has to be such that the movement will move up the conceptual levels again in such a way that it will be understood by the other person as an act of kindness.

Even God, if he ever wanted to communicate with us, would have to observe this conceptual requirement. This is not a limitation on his omnipotence but a logical requirement. If, according to the conceptual framework of a community, the devil usually speaks from the moon, then, although God has the ability to make any sounds or other signals come from the moon, he could not communicate with that community from the moon. Even his shouting 'I am God and not the Devil' would be understood as the Devil trying to deceive. If in that community's understanding God always speaks from a rosebush, then even God would have to communicate through a rosebush. But he would have to perform some interference in the physical world which could be understood as his communication. For instance, if after having been on earth he wanted to communicate that he was going to resume the ontological form and status appropriate to a Deity, he would have to use a spatial expression of this, appropriate to the people he wanted to talk to. In fact he would have to use a spatial expression in any case since he had abandoned his appropriate ontological form in order to assume a spatial-temporal existence. But he would further have to use the particular spatial expression of a particular community. Thus, in ancient Greece he would probably have to get into a chariot and disappear towards Mount Olympus. Outside Jerusalem he would have to go up on a hill and disappear behind the clouds. But he would have to do something of this sort if he wanted to communicate a change in his ontological status.

Now perhaps this is the place to make a very important point which is one of my main arguments about the demythologising project. It is one thing to say that when Jesus disappeared behind the clouds what he wanted to convey was that he had resumed his proper ontological status, not that from now on he would be somewhere behind a cloud; it is quite a different thing to say that the early Christians, *by saying* that Jesus disappeared behind the cloud, wanted to express that Jesus had returned to his heavenly Father, so we do not need to believe that he *did* disappear behind the cloud, since in fact nothing of the sort happened.

In this second case we have to express not what Jesus *did* differently, for he did not do anything, but we have to express what the early Christians expressed, by expressing it differently.

It is vital not to confuse the two, nor to slide from one to the other, which, it seems, it is easy to do in a pious frame of mind, or in a frame of mind anxious to avoid saying things that might sound embarrassing to the 'modern ear'.

To say that early Christians wanted to express that Jesus went to his heavenly Father *by saying* that he disappeared behind the clouds is to talk not about what Jesus did or wanted to express but about what the early Christians did and wanted to express. The point of the second alternative is that originally *nothing happened.* The report that there was a happening was the early Christians' expression of their beliefs, and it is *that* that we now have to express differently. The early Christians expressed their belief *by saying* that Jesus disappeared behind the clouds. This was just their way of saying that he went to his heavenly Father. But an alternative way of expressing this act of belief is not an alternative way of expressing that Jesus returned to his heavenly Father. We are required to give an alternative response. But a response to what?

To leave this as a rhetorical question should make its point but nevertheless we should consider several alternatives as an answer.

(1) Before considering the possibility that the early Christians' response was to a non-event or to a crisis of disappointment let us consider that there *was* some happening to which this expression of belief was an answer. There are two possibilities.

(a) Remembering that Jesus himself could have chosen a different scenario to inform his followers that he was returning to heaven, we might assimilate the second alternative (that we are dealing with a response) to the first alternative (that there was an original event): there was an event, only it was not a disappearance behind the cloud but some other occurrence which indicated what he was doing. There are two difficulties about this answer. First, that other event had to be something that the early Christians did clearly understand as meaning that Jesus was returning to heaven. If they did not, then their alternative way of expressing it was misguided. If they did, why did they have to express it differently to the very same people for whom, in their own idiom, Jesus expressed what he was doing? Secondly, this possibility would not be acceptable to the demythologisers. Returning to the heavenly Father is an extraordinary thing to do, and any expression of it must be some extraordinary performance. It would not fit into the demythologiser's programme to say that the early Christians, by saying that Jesus disappeared behind a cloud, expressed that another feat, equally extraordinary, was actually performed by Jesus.

(b) Let us consider the possibility that the response (which was the claim that he disappeared behind the cloud) was to an actual event or events in the life of Jesus, but not such extraordinary events that it would be embarrassing for a demythologiser to admit them. This is indeed, as we shall see, the position the demythologiser takes and we shall consider later what is wrong with this position after an outline and some examples of the demythologising project. For the moment I want to stress again that my argument is not against faith. For the objection I shall bring against this position, that *ex hypothesi* the events in Jesus' life are no reason for saying what the early Christians said about Jesus, is not regarded by the demythologisers as an objection at all, but on the contrary is turned, on theological grounds, into a virtue—the virtue of faith. What I wish to eliminate is not faith but plain irrationality. There is not only room for faith but a great need for it even when Jesus performed feats that can be interpreted as his wanting to communicate that he was returning to his Father. There is a need both for an intellectual and for a moral decision. To disappear behind a cloud does not necessarily mean that the person who does it is the Son of God about to return to his Father (though even the Son of God would have to do something of the sort once he took on human existence in order to reveal some extraordinary things). And along with an intellectual decision there is also a moral decision to make as to what to do when confronted by such a state of affairs. But one makes decisions when one is in a situation or when one is confronted by an occasion calling for a decision. What I am concerned with now is not the ethics of belief, that is, not with the question of the type and amount of evidence needed for different types of beliefs and decisions. I am pointing to something quite different: that to make a decision when nothing happened or to make a response when nothing happened is not foolish or immoral, it simply does not make sense.

(2) What does concern me on the second alternative, and what is part of my main line of argument, is this: what would count as *the same* action or response? Since on the second alternative we are not dealing with what Jesus did but with what the early Christians did, we have to find an alternative expression not of what Jesus did but of what the early Christians did. Since the actions are different, the alternatives that would amount to *the same* action will be different.

What is it of which we should find an alternative expression? It could not be the communication on Jesus' part. Even if it sounds blasphemous I must say, in order to bring home the point, it is only from Christ himself that the demythologisers can expect an alternative expression of *that*.

It is the making-of-an-alleged-factual-claim to which we have to find an alternative, for this is the occurrence we are dealing with, not with the disappearance-behind-a-cloud. Now we have to ask: what does this making-of-an-alleged-factual-claim amount to, and what are the alternative expressions of *that*?

The making-of-an-alleged-factual-claim could be an act of self-deception, or of deception, or a special characteristic response to a disappointment, or, among other things, a creative act of myth making. The demythologiser's contention is that of all the plausible alternatives—and it is the demythologiser's elimination of any extraordinary performances on Jesus' part that makes the alternatives very plausible—we have to opt for the claim that creating a myth was the early

Christians' way of expressing their faith. And it is this act of faith that we have to express differently now. The confusion is bewildering. For centuries Christians expressed faith *in* what is now said to be only one way of *expressing* a faith. In what?—one is compelled to ask again.

Now did the early Christians themselves believe the truth of their claim? If they did we can no longer have an alternative expression of a factual claim which was believed to be true but is now known *only to be thought to have been true*. The magic is broken. We are confronted not with an alternative way of expressing the Christian claim, not even with a fundamental reinterpretation of what Christianity is about, not even with a new religion, but with a new type of religion.

The term 'myth' can feature only in an observer's terminology, not in a believer's description of his belief. If we ask the elders of a tribe to tell us their fairytales, they would go on recounting them all night. If we asked them, however, to tell us their myths they would say they have none, but they would be willing to tell us the myths of all the other tribes. It is not that they want to keep their myths secret. The point is that if they described them as 'myths' they would not be their myths. But they have to describe what the other tribes believe as myths, otherwise it would not be the other tribe's beliefs but their own.

As far as I know this is the first time in the history of religions that we are told that the acceptance of a myth, knowing it to be a myth, is a virtue, by degrading the myth into one way of expressing that for which only the truth of the content of the myth could have been a reason.

To avoid the intrusion of piety into recognising what we are confronted with, let us imagine that we read in someone's diary that there was a volcanic eruption. If we discover that there was not one, or go out of our way to claim that there was no eruption, we should consider first the possibility that our diarist made up the story for some reason, before we would say that his description of an eruption was his way of saying that he was impressed. Now if we said that he just made it up, it would be disreputable to ask that in order to imitate him we should make up another story, more acceptable to modern geologists. Nor have we any reasons for asking others to do this. It is equally shameful and just as unreasonable, but this time less obviously so, to ask others to imitate him when we describe what he wrote as his way of being impressed. For describing it as 'being impressed' does give the impression that there *was* after all something there to be impressed by;

and being asked to be impressed does not sound as disreputable as being asked to imitate someone who invented a fiction. The move from an alleged factual claim to our making just a response instead of a factual claim is conjured away *by describing the original factual claim in the first place* as merely an expression of being impressed, so we ourselves are asked only to make the respectable substitution of a proper response for a deceptive response.

On what grounds then are we expected and even asked to be impressed ourselves? The reason cannot be that there was an eruption. That was only the man's way of expressing that he was impressed. The only thing we can go on is that he was impressed and *that* is the reason for us to be impressed. We should be impressed by that man's being impressed, and this is why we should express in different terms his saying that there was an eruption.

The pious frame of mind can often act as a cushion of air for a hovercraft argument. The above secular story shows up the rough terrain on which the demythologiser's hovercraft travels. Demythologisers, along with many 'modern' Christians, live on the capital of faith which was produced by the labour of earlier generations. But arguments are not like flywheels: if you take away the impetus of the reasons for a conclusion the conclusions cannot go on turning round under their own momentum.

I used as my example the story of the Ascension as recalled in the Acts of the Apostles, which is among those that have weakest textual support, and the authenticity of which might be among the least important for Christians. But I want to emphasise that I am not dealing with biblical criticism; I am not arguing about what should or should not be accepted as part of history. I am dealing with a *pattern of argument* the implications of which are not realised by Christian apologists. And I am critical of what I call a pious frame of mind only because, in a subtle way, it obscures the seriousness of the argument's implications.

But let me turn now to the actual project of and to a few actual examples of demythologising. The term was originated by Bultmann and was made current by the arguments about his project. The term is very misleading and the actual project of demythologising is really the opposite of what the term suggests, for two reasons. One reason is that far from demythologising the Christian story, the project in fact turns Christianity into a myth. The other reason why the term is misleading is Bultmann's actual intention. He is not doing what the liberal theologians were doing and what could be described with more justification as demythologising. He is not *pruning* the gospels of mythological elements leaving the hard core of historically reliable elements and the moral teaching like the parables. He is not denying in a simple way the divinity of Christ and the resurrection while keeping the story of the Good Samaritan. Bultmann *does* make the distinction between the historical life of Jesus and mythological elements in the New Testament account. He does not, however, prune away the mythological elements. Rather, they are the most important elements of the New Testament account, for the mythological elements express, in the language of factual statements—and it is this factual form which makes them mythological—the meaning of the historical life of Jesus. It is this mythological element which has to be restated in order to express the meaning of the life of Jesus for modern man.

But now there is an important point to notice here. Alleged events like the miracles, the resurrection, the ascension, are *not* part of Jesus' life, they are the early Christians' *expression* of the meaning of his life. The historical life becomes quite uneventful, by definition. For as soon as Jesus himself tries to perform something that would indicate the meaning of his life, that would be such an extraordinary event that it could not be part of his historical life but part of the early Christians' expression of what they thought was the meaning of his life. So one could say that by definition the early Christians had no reasons to produce those interpretations because as soon as one of those reasons cropped up it could not be part of the life of Jesus that they were confronted with, but could only be part of their interpretation of that life put in mythological terms, that is, *as if* they were part of the life of Jesus, like miracles and the resurrection.

I said earlier that Bultmann, unlike some liberal theologians, does not deny in a simple way the divinity of Christ or the resurrection. To assert that Christ has risen is to assert that the cross was not an ordinary event; it is the early Christians' interpretation of that part of Jesus' life, for the crucifixion was just part of history. Now to *deny* the resurrection would amount to denying that the crucifixion was more than an ordinary event, hence he does not deny the resurrection because he does not deny that the crucifixion was more than an ordinary event. In fact it *was* that. Nothing else *happened.* It was historically an ordinary crucifixion and historically no resurrection occurred afterwards, but by saying that there was a resurrection the early Christians expressed the meaning of the historical fact of the crucifixion. What is our reason for attributing meaning to the crucifixion? It cannot be the resurrection because that is the expression of the meaning, not what provides the meaning. Can the meaning perhaps be provided by the claims that it was the Son of God or the pre-existent Logos who was crucified, so that it was no ordinary person who was crucified? This cannot be so either, because the claims that he was the Son of God or the pre-existent Logos are other mythological expressions of the early Christians' interpretation of the meaning of the life of Jesus. Bultmann goes so far as to say that the resurrection cannot be a separate event, as if it were a proof that the crucifixion was a redemptive event, because that would admit that the crucifixion *was* an ordinary event which *needed* the resurrection afterwards.

Let us see some passages:

> Now, it is clear from the outset that the event of Christ is of a wholly different order from the cult-myths of Greek or Hellenistic religion. Jesus Christ is certainly presented as the Son of God, a pre-existent divine being, and therefore to that extent a mythical figure. But he is also a concrete figure of history—Jesus of Nazareth. His life is more than a mythical event; it is a human life which ended in the tragedy of crucifixion. We have here a unique combination of history and myth. The New Testament claims that this Jesus of history, whose father and mother were well known to his contemporaries (John 6.42), is at the same time the pre-existent Son of God, and side by side with the historical event of the crucifixion it sets the definitely non-historical event of the resurrection.[2]

The New Testament differs from Greek myths in that side by side with myth there is also an actual historical life. The resurrection however is not part of that historical life. The historical life ended in *the tragedy of the crucifixion.* Then Bultmann goes on to ask:

> We are compelled to ask whether all this mythological language is not simply an attempt to express the meaning of the historical figure of Jesus and the events of his life; in other words, the significance of these as a

figure and event of salvation. If that be so, we can dispense with the objective form in which they are cast.[3]

Bultmann is saying that the New Testament contains two types of statement. Both types are expressed as if they were events of history. One type apparently describes ordinary events like the crucifixion (let us call them 'O events') and the other type describes extraordinary events like the resurrection (let us call them 'E events'). One would think that one would need to understand the meaning and significance of both types of events, if they really occurred, and one would say, on the whole, that the meaning and significance of O events, if they occurred, would amount to the same sort of meaning and significance as the ordinary actions and performances in the lives of many other ordinary men; while the meaning and significance of E events, if they occurred, would require further thought: they would be candidates for interpretation as, for instance, the acts of some extraordinary man, perhaps of an extraordinary being, perhaps even of a saviour. Whether O events or E events did or did not occur is not my concern. The point I am making is that O events are *ex hypothesi* candidates for interpretation as acts of an ordinary life, as for instance Bultmann in our first passage regards the crucifixion as simply a tragic end to a life— while E events are *ex hypothesi* candidates for interpretation as acts of an extraordinary life, as, for instance, rising from the dead would call for some sort of extraordinary interpretation.

Not for Bultmann. Bultmann wants to say that E events are the interpretations of O events, expressed *in terms of events*, and that this form of expression makes them mythological. He wants to say that O events are not to be interpreted as acts of an ordinary life but as acts of an extraordinary life, though he does not give reasons why O events should have extraordinary interpretations. E events did not occur, but Christians have to affirm them because by affirming them they affirm that O events, quite ordinary events, are extraordinary events.

Bultmann's account of the resurrection deserves careful reading:

But what of the resurrection? Is it not a mythical event pure and simple? Obviously it is not an event of past history with a self-evident meaning. Can the resurrection narratives and every other mention of the resurrection in the New Testament be understood simply as an attempt to convey the meaning of the cross? Does the New

Testament, in asserting that Jesus is risen from the dead, mean that his death is not just an ordinary human death, but the judgment and salvation of the world, depriving death of its power? Does it not express this truth in the affirmation that the Crucified was not holden of death, but rose from the dead?

Yes indeed: the cross and the resurrection form a single, indivisible cosmic event. 'He was delivered up for our trespasses, and was raised for our justification' (Rom. 4.25). The cross is not an isolated event, as though it were the end of Jesus, which needed the resurrection subsequently to reverse it. When he suffered death, Jesus was already the Son of God, and his death by itself was the victory over the power of death.[4]

This is re-mythologising. 'Modern man' cannot accept the historicity of the resurrection, so instead 'modern man' is asked to accept that the crucifixion was an even greater extraordinary cosmic event with some tremendous mythological significance, and is asked to accept this *without* the credentials of the resurrection.

Let us now consider briefly a couple of examples from the Rev. J.C. Fenton, author of the Pelican Commentary on St. Matthew. Fenton argues in his Introduction that there are several things in Matthew's gospel that a twentieth-century reader cannot accept. But it does not really matter, because they are just Matthew's way of expressing his beliefs about Jesus, they are just the way he puts the interpretation and the meaning of his life. We can express these things differently and still believe what Matthew believed about Jesus. One of the things about which Matthew was wrong was his interpretation of what is now called (largely because of him) the Old Testament. He interpreted the Old Testament as pointing towards Jesus as the fulfilment of the Old Testament prophecies.

Modern study of the Old Testament does not support Matthew's understanding of it, nor the use he made of it when he was writing his Gospel. It is now seen that the Old Testament was not a collection of detailed foretellings of future events, which could only be understood centuries later.... We must, however, try to see what Matthew was saying by means of these fulfilments; because it may be that what he was saying is still capable of being understood and accepted, although his way of saying it is no longer valid.... Matthew and the Christians

who used this fulfilment-method were saying by means of it: Jesus is
not just an ordinary man, but a special person, the one for whom the
Jews have been waiting, one sent by God to Israel.[5]

Fenton's solution and suggestion is this:

> We might show how Jesus fulfilled other laws—moral and psycho-
> logical laws, for example; Matthew did not do so, because Matthew
> lived in the first century. But it is still possible for us to believe what
> Matthew believed about Jesus, without expressing it in the way that
> Matthew expressed it.[6]

This is again the characteristic Bultmannite move of regarding the
reason for saying something as being the interpretation or meaning of
an event *without* however that reason and without that event. Had
Jesus fulfilled the Old Testament prophecies it would have been one of
the *reasons* for saying that 'Jesus is not just an ordinary man, but a
special person, the one for whom the Jews have been waiting, the one
sent by God to Israel'. But if he did not fulfil the Old Testament law,
why should Matthew express that non-event by saying that he fulfilled
the Old Testament prophecies? Did he do something *else* which could
be a reason for saying that Jesus was not just an ordinary man but a
special person, which Matthew then expressed by saying that he fulfilled the Old Testament prophecies? If he did, it should have been
understood by his contemporaries and so Matthew could have expressed *that.* But only some extraordinary performance on the part of
Jesus could have been such a reason, and had Matthew reported that,
the Bultmannite would have to say of it that it is only a mythological
way of expressing something which did not happen and now we have
to express 'it' by saying something else.

Now turning from why Matthew should have expressed anything
to why we should express anything, we should ask why, if Jesus did
not fulfil the Old Testament laws, *we* should want to say that he did
fulfil other laws, or why indeed we would want to say *anything else* at
all? All we can go on is that for no apparent reason Matthew was so
impressed by Jesus that he set about representing him as if he had
been the one foretold in the Old Testament prophecies. Had he had
any genuine reasons to be impressed he would not have had to resort
to saying things about Jesus that we now know, according to Fenton,

not to be the case, but could have given us those genuine reasons. Why should we then believe what Matthew believed? With nothing more to go on, why should we in turn resort to expressing something by saying that Jesus fulfilled 'moral and psychological laws'?

I do not wish to dwell on the extraordinary suggestion that moral *and* psychological laws are alternative expressions to fulfilling the Old Testament law. The author of the Pelican Commentary on Saint Matthew should not be taken seriously on this. Even 'modern man' knows enough about the sort of thing that fulfilling the Old Testament law is supposed to be, to know that the suggested alternatives are not possible alternatives. And since the suggested alternatives are what 'modern man' can understand, *a fortiori* he would know that 'moral laws' and 'psychological laws' are not alternatives, nor can they be 'fulfilled'. But we should observe that Fenton began by confusing the fulfilment of prophecies with the fulfilment of the Old Testament law.

But to return to our main puzzle, someone might suggest that such other events in Jesus' life as miracles might have been what impressed Matthew so much that he presented Jesus as the one who fulfilled the Old Testament laws. Turning to miracles this is what Fenton has to say:

> Again, our best method is to ask what Matthew and the other Christian writers who recorded the miracles of Jesus were saying when they said that he performed miracles, and that he was himself the subject of supernatural activity (his conception and his resurrection). They believed that Jesus was the one upon whom God's Spirit had come (3.16), and that it was through this Spirit that he was able to do miraculous acts (12.28). This Spirit, they believed, would renew the whole of creation when this age came to an end. Jesus was therefore the one who was sent by God to declare the coming of the new age, and to demonstrate it by means of miracles. He was the bringer of the complete, full, and indestructible life—the life of the age to come.[7]

So far one assumes that Jesus performed miracles and this is how he demonstrated that he was sent by God, and the disciples understood that it was through the Spirit of God that he was able to perform miracles. But the passage continues:

> Here again we see that Matthew writes in the way he does because he belongs to the first century; and that this is not the way we should

write today. Nevertheless, it is possible for us today to believe what Matthew believed about Jesus as miracle-worker (i.e. that Jesus offers a full and indestructible way of living), without necessarily believing in the historicity of the miracles which Matthew records.[8]

Again, Fenton is not saying that *by performing miracles* Jesus wanted to communicate to us that he wants to offer us 'a full and indestructible way of living'. He did not perform miracles. We can see by now that he did not do anything else either which could have been a reason for Matthew to put any of his interpretations on the life of Jesus, interpretations that we are now requested to express differently.

Fenton's text is not the sort to be submitted to textual study; nevertheless it is worth pointing out how, in the first half of the passage I quoted, Fenton says that the early Christians believed that Jesus wanted to *demonstrate* something by means of miracles and that they believed that it was through the Spirit that he was able to do miraculous acts. Take away the miracles and we are still supposed to believe what Jesus wanted to demonstrate by means of them, and we are still supposed to have a theory as to the power through which he performed them.

In one of Schulz's delightful *Peanuts* cartoons, Linus and Lucy are looking at something on the ground. 'Well, look here!' exclaims Lucy, 'A big yellow butterfly!' 'It's unusual to see one this time of year, unless of course, he flew up from Brazil.... I'll bet that's it!' speculates Lucy in the next picture. 'They do that sometimes, you know ... they fly up from Brazil, and they ...' But Linus interrupts: 'This is no butterfly ... this is a potato chip!' 'Well, I'll be!' says Lucy. 'So it is! I wonder how a potato chip got all the way up from Brazil?'[9]

Only a Bultmannite could improve even on this. The Bultmannite would say that nevertheless we should still assert that it was a butterfly because only by asserting this can we assert that it was not an ordinary potato chip: Linus and Lucy expressed their response to the 'potato chip event' by saying that it was a butterfly, because this was their way of expressing that it came from Brazil, and we can now express this differently and still believe what Linus and Lucy believed about that potato chip.

Historical Papers:
Introduction

E.D. Watt

This group of writings consists of three items. 'Nature and Convention' was read at a residential symposium which used to meet annually outside Perth. Kovesi's English translation of *On the Essence of Money (Über das Geldwesen)*, by Moses Hess, and 'Moses Hess, Marx and Money,' his extended introduction to that extraordinary work, were written earlier, and intended to be published together, but that publication is taking place only in this present book.

Kovesi's students were constantly being urged to ask themselves (particularly when they encountered a line of thought that seemed to them bizarre), 'Why would anyone have wanted to say that?' The papers in this section illustrate that same interest in Kovesi himself. How is it, he asks in 'Nature and Convention,' that the concept of Nature 'can be played in almost any game as almost any card?' Not content with mapping the variety of ways in which notions of Nature have been pressed into service, Kovesi is also intent on showing that 'the confusing variety is not without rhyme or reason,' and that even ideas of progress touch upon some of the ways in which Nature has been thought of.

In 'Moses Hess, Marx and Money,' Kovesi explores the peculiar iconography shared by Hess and Marx in the early 1840s, and suggests that in reading Marx and Hess, it is to this iconography that we should attend, rather than to the men and events which form the ostensible subject-matter of their discussion. This, he argues, is because their thought-framework was so abstract, so remote from men and events, that it was not at all clear what, if any, empirical assertions they were making about men and events, or how, if disputes arose in applying these common thought-frameworks to actual human affairs, those disputes could, even in principle, be resolved.

Kovesi guides us through the maze of what he calls 'variations on the triadic theme' in Marx and the Young Hegelians during the first half of the 1840s, for there is not just a single 'triad' to be discerned in Marx and Hess but several. And both men had a vast capacity to theorise without touching the ground: to write about money with only the slightest reference to the ways in which money was actually used, and even of 'the Jews' (despite the Jewish origins that both men shared) in a way that has virtually nothing to do with what actual Jews actually did.

But, as Kovesi reminds us, Hess did not remain for the rest of his life at the heights of abstraction illustrated by *On the Essence of Money*. He considered that the débâcle of the revolutionary movements in 1848 was relevant to his theories of revolution, to the point of requiring him to revise those theories comprehensively, and he did revise them. He also returned to the Jewish religious practice of his upbringing, and so had the opportunity to supplement theories about 'the Jews' by regular interaction with some actual Jews. Marx did neither of those things. Contact with Judaism was one generation more remote for him than for Hess. As for revolution, Marx remained unshaken by events, and firm in his insistence that the worse things seem to be, the closer they are to radical transformation. No collapse of revolutionary plans and movements was conclusive enough to disturb Marx's confidence that the final social cataclysm was inevitable and imminent, or to interrupt his constant scanning of the economic and political skies for revolutionary portents.

This same line of thought on the symbolism of Marx and the Young Hegelians was the subject of the last thing Kovesi wrote, a paper for a European history conference that met at the University of Western Australia in July 1989, only a month before he died. He completed the paper but was not well enough to deliver it, and it had to be read to the conference by someone else.

Those who knew Kovesi will regret that he never published any of his original and challenging account of Plato's theory of ideas, a subject which interested him at least as much as did Hess and Marx. Kovesi wholly rejected the view that Plato thought there were two worlds: the chaotic physical world, in which things can be at once both like and unlike, both one and many; and the world of Forms, in which perfection, order and stability reign, and everything is exactly what it really is, and no Form can be anything but what it really is. This account, he held, leaves it unclear what purpose Plato had in postulating his world of Forms.

In Kovesi's view, Plato wanted to sort out the problems of talking about our ordinary world, not the problems of talking about an ideal world.[1] He was concerned not with the philosophers' so-called 'problem of universals,' the relationship between the concept 'table' and the many individual tables in the actual world, but rather with the way in which concepts relate to other concepts in our wrestling with moral and other issues. It is the entanglement of concepts that permits the sophists to argue that the one thing can be both good and bad at the same time, or the orators to argue at will that a certain policy is good but, when asked to do so, to argue equally that the same policy is bad. The true Form of a concept is discovered when it is disentangled from other concepts, not when it is separated from the physical world; and the point of seeking this true Form is to permit us to speak lucidly about our ordinary affairs.

Unfortunately, none of Kovesi's writings on Plato were sufficiently complete to warrant publication here.

Nature and Convention

Arthur Lovejoy quotes Friedrich Nicolai as saying: 'Der Begriff und das Wort "Natur" ist ein wahrer Scherwenzel'—the concept of 'nature' is the Jack of all trades of moral and political philosophy. This remark may serve as a warning against constructing yet another theory on this basis. However it is not a warning, but rather an invitation to take an interest in the very logic of this concept. My interest in and even fascination with this concept lies precisely in these questions: How is it that it can be played in almost any game as almost any card? How is it that it can be employed in almost any construction in almost any capacity? And how is it that, nevertheless, this concept retains its power and force and one can be sure that it will continue to do so? At present the notion enjoys great prestige; ironically, just at the time when so many moral theologians are dismantling their theories based on the concept of 'nature'. Its stakes are high not only among the environmentalists. The popular, widely but vaguely used notion of 'alienation' makes sense only if there is a real nature of man from which we are supposed to be alienated.

In this paper I shall first illustrate with a few brief examples the variety of uses this concept can and does have. My examples are very schematic, over-simplified references to otherwise complex theories, serving to illustrate not the theories but their varieties. Then I shall indicate that the confusing variety is not without rhyme or reason. For a fuller explanation of the logic of the term 'nature' and, incidentally, of many other terms, I shall have to explain my distinction between what I shall call an "insider's" and an "outsider's" vocabulary to describe various theories and practices. I shall end by saying a few words about the notion of 'progress'. This might sound unexpected, but the notion of 'progress' does tie up with what I shall try to say about the contrast between nature and convention.

We can base the necessity for social institutions on nature by claiming that without these institutions we would soon destroy each other, for the state of nature is a war of all against all, and we know that this life is nasty, brutish and short. Alternatively, we may claim that in the state of nature we are nice, benevolent and social, that is, we are by nature social animals and consequently our social institutions are based on nature. It does matter, however, which argument is used, because the type, I almost said the nature, of the institutions that one or the other would justify will differ greatly. The first type can be used by the sovereign, not by the subjects, by pointing to the consequences of not accepting some sort of political institution. The second type of argument can be more readily used by the subjects when they think the sovereign is not creating or supporting institutions that they think follow from or are intended by our natural social condition.

There can be further variations on and combinations of these two simple patterns. For St. Augustine, for instance, there was no need for a political state in our natural condition before the Fall. There must be a state now because we are in a fallen condition, and if this is the reason for its existence, then its function is to keep us up to what we were supposed to be before or without the Fall. The state exists to enforce the Divine Laws. This is an interesting combination of the above two theories: our natural condition is not a war of all against all, yet the state does not grow out of our natural sociability; its existence is called for by a Hobbesian condition. In the thirteenth and fourteenth centuries the newly-revived Aristotelian theory of the state challenged this, again by reference to nature. We are political animals, this is our very nature, and consequently the state and political institutions exist by nature. But if the state exists by nature then it has its own good, its own end, and should not serve an end outside its own, so it should not be subordinated to the Church.

Rousseau comes to mind, along with Hobbes, when one talks of the state of nature. Rousseau did not so much reject the Hobbesian description of the war of all against all; rather he placed it in a stage already removed from our original condition. Only if we have property can we be envious, only if we live in society (i.e., in the present ill-constructed society, not in the one where the General Will is to rule) can we hate each other. None of the Hobbesian characteristics can exist in our natural, pre-social condition; they are the results of living in our badly conceived society. We should note the similarity between this and St. Augustine's view. The difference is that the present condition of mankind—which, according to both thinkers, is an aberration—

is not the result of original sin for Rousseau, but of our social arrangements.

According to Rousseau we still preserve our Original Virtue but we cannot exercise it because of the System. The remedy differs accordingly. If our present condition is caused by an estrangement from God, then only grace or an eschatological event can heal the wound. But if the system is to blame then we have to change the system. This is the logical force of Rousseau's adding an idyllic stage of mankind before the Hobbesian stage. Its force is this: if the Hobbesian stage *were* the natural state of mankind, then the Leviathan is here to stay. The way to shake off the permanency of the Leviathan is, obviously, to say that it is not a permanent but an artificial device. Of course this is Hobbes' view also. But unless we postulate a previous state of nature, Hobbes' artificial device is a permanent artificial device, following from the very nature of things. For St. Augustine and Rousseau it is an artificial device, not following from the nature of things but from an aberration. (We shall see presently that the vitality of the concept of 'nature' comes from its being contrasted with what, in contradistinction, is described as 'artificial,' or in similar terms like 'man-made,' thus providing a powerful conceptual weapon for those who want to argue against, knock, or eliminate whatever they so describe in contradistinction to 'nature.')

Marx, in this respect, is also similar to St. Augustine. The political state did not always exist. Note how even just to say this much already reduces the importance and prestige of political institutions—at least for the unreflective mind. The present condition of mankind is that of alienation and division and the political state is at best an arbitrator and at worst the upholder of the interests of one side of the divided society. History is the history of the transmutations of the divisions in society until the transcendence of our alienation, which is the regaining of our real nature. Once we have regained our real nature 'the state will wither away'.

'Nature' can be used in arguments smaller, much smaller, than these cosmic or quasi-cosmic grand arguments. In the state of nature some of us would envisage our existence there with garlands of flowers around our necks and heads. Not Tertullian. When Tertullian argued against the pagan practice of wearing crowns of flowers on the head during pagan festivities, he claimed that 'the argument for Christian observances becomes stronger when even Nature, which is the first of all teaching, supports them'. Each of our senses has a natural object for enjoyment and there is no such *natural* pleasure as wearing flowers on our heads. 'With sight and smell, then, make use of flowers, for these are the senses by which they were meant to be enjoyed.... It is as much against nature to crave a flower with the head as to crave food with the ear or sound with the nostril. But everything which is against nature is deservedly known amongst all men as a monstrous thing'.[1] But, one might say, what an unnatural thing it is to smell flowers for enjoyment! Indeed, when St. Basil admonishes us not to read pagan literature for its enjoyment but for whatever value we can derive from it, he sets as an example to us the bees who are attracted by flowers for the honey and not for enjoyment.

In these and other contexts of moral and political arguments 'nature' is not a shorthand term for rivers, trees and birds. It belongs rather to the family of words like 'real,' 'authentic,' 'objective,' 'true,' 'genuine'. I do not mean that it is a synonym for any of these but that it behaves like them in two important respects. One is that we make a *claim* by using these terms; we are not merely describing but also prescribing by using these terms. Even, as we shall see, when this term is used to refer to some aspects of natural phenomena in the course of a moral or political argument, it refers to such phenomena as a recommendation, as a standard. This is much more the case when the term does not even refer to any natural phenomena but clearly sets up a standard.

The other respect in which 'nature' behaves like the terms mentioned above is that it lives on a contrast. The meaning of 'nature' can be understood only by completing the phrase 'as against...'. The sort of thing I have in mind is what J.L. Austin says about the logic of the word 'real'.[2] Sometimes 'real' means that the object in question is not a toy, at other times that it is not artificial; or it can qualify the size of an object, as for instance when a child wants a real bicycle. What complicates matters is that the term 'nature' can be contrasted not only with various different *concepts* like artificial, man-made, aberrant, alienated, contrived, and so on;[3] we should also look out for the specific contrasts within each particular sense of the concept. There are many ways in which things can be contrived or artificial; there are many different ways in which people can be alienated within each of the different senses of alienation.

I would like to say that the term 'nature' has such a great variety of uses because all human institutions, and not only institutions but the whole political, moral, and cultural life we live in is man-made, and consequently all institutions and human practices are liable to be contrasted to 'nature'.

By saying that all institutions are man-made I am not saying anything more shocking than when we say that language or science is man-made. I resist the addition of the qualifier 'only' to 'man-made'. I am not saying 'only man-made'. One of the reasons why I resist the qualifier will be clear in a minute. To the other reason I shall return at the end of this paper. Now I just want to say that everything is liable to be contrasted to 'nature' at different times, and the time for the contrast comes when people, or some people, begin to question some of our institutions or practices. While an institution is in accord with our living moral beliefs, while a practice is part of our moral life, we not only do not question them; we hardly even notice them, they are so *natural.* Institutions and practices become visible in proportion to our lack of belief in and natural acceptance of them. Our living moral life is transparent; this, incidentally, is one of the reasons why moral science is a difficult art.

No English gentleman would think he is formal. This is a French gentleman's description of him. For the English gentleman, on the other hand, the life of the Frenchman is full of formalities. The lives of both are not only visible and noticeable to each other, but by being described as formal they are claimed to be man-made and artificial: *only* man-made compared to how one 'ought' to behave. And when the whole notion of a gentleman is questioned we do it by asking: 'When Adam delved and Eve span, who was then the gentleman?,' that is, by implying that being a gentleman was not provided, at the start, by nature.

Now there is a special vocabulary for describing other people's beliefs and practices that one does not believe in oneself or has ceased to believe in oneself. If we asked the elder of a tribe to tell us the fairy tales of the tribe he would happily oblige. If however we asked him to tell us their myths he would say that they have not got any. This is not because he wants to keep them secret but because if he described what they had as 'myths' he would not have them any more except as stories he no longer believes in. Other tribes do have myths. Had he not described them as myths he would accept them as a valid account of the world. He would not describe any part of their living practices as magic either, or as only symbolic. The title of Mary Douglas's book *Natural Symbols* is an understandable anomaly, if not a contradiction in terms. In the book she laments the disappearance of so many of our living practices and beliefs, if for no other reason than that our lives are impoverished by their loss. She wants to assert that some of the symbols we are losing are not merely, or not only, symbols, but by the time we come to describe them as symbols they can no longer be resuscitated by being described as 'natural'. Most of her examples are from the impoverishment of Catholic life during the last couple of decades. As she puts it: 'the liturgical signal boxes are manned by colour-blind men'. And one knows how some of the clergy describe the adherence of some of the laity to what they themselves believed in some twenty years ago as 'adherence to magic,' and one knows their preoccupation with their conviction that modern man cannot accept myth any more. I am not concerned with the rightness or wrongness of their belief but with the analysis of the situation. It is not modern man who cannot accept myth; no man believes in myths; not even primitive men believed in them by the time that they came to regard them as myths. By the time the clergyman describes his problem in these terms I think the problem he describes is his own and not that of modern man. For he, too, the modern man, does not exist except as a description in the world of those who describe their beliefs as myths.

'Only man-made' belongs to the family of words like 'myth' and 'magic' and other terms which are part of an outsider's vocabulary to describe other people's practices and beliefs. This is why in saying that all our institutions and practices are man-made I did not want to say that they are *only* man-made. If I used that qualification I would be operating within one of the theories I am trying to analyse.

The strength of the term 'nature'—and of the various constructions like 'by nature,' 'according to nature,' 'natural,' etc.—comes from our continuing need to recommend something natural in contradistinction to other man-made beliefs and practices. Sometimes we can refer by this term to some aspects of our physical or biological existence, but even in those cases we select those aspects and use them as standards. At other times we use the term 'nature' to refer to concepts far removed from our physical existence. These latter are the more standard cases in natural law theories. We define the nature of an institution conceptually as when we define the nature of the political state, of a university, of marriage, or of a contract. I shall give two brief examples from the two ends of the scale, one from Antiphon, who is the only native Athenian sophist of any note, and the other from Marx, from his comments on the proposed Prussian divorce laws. 'Justice, then,' says Antiphon,

> consists in not transgressing the laws and customs of the city of which one is a citizen. It follows that the way for a man to be just with most advantage to himself is for him to respect the laws when in the presence of witnesses, but when he is alone and unwitnessed to respect the commands of nature. What the laws command is an extraneous imposition; what nature commands is a constraint that is part of our very being. The law is an artificial convention, not a natural growth; but nature is natural, not conventional. If, then, you transgress the laws, you are free from shame and from penalty—provided that those who participate in the convention do not know, but not otherwise; whereas if you seek to repress, beyond the bounds of possibility, what inheres in your nature, the resulting damage to you cannot be any the less for being kept private, nor any the greater for being made public because the damage is caused not by what people think but by what actually happens.
>
> The point to which these considerations are leading is this: that *many duties imposed by law are hostile to nature.*[4]

Here there is a clear reference to some of the physical aspects of our nature, but it is used as a recommendation, as a standard, in contradistinction to our man-made laws.

Eugene Kamenka, in his *Ethical Foundations of Marxism*, claims that it is hardly surprising that Marx should have begun his political activity by upholding natural law. It is not surprising because he moves in the Hegelian tradition where the nature of an institution is given by its concept and to appeal to a concept is to appeal to nature. As an example, this is what Marx comments on the proposed Prussian divorce laws:

> The dissolution of a marriage is nothing but the declaration: this marriage is a *dead* marriage, whose existence is a snare and delusion. It is self-evident of course, that neither the capricious will of a legisla-

tor nor the capricious will of a private person, but only the *essence of the matter* can decide whether a marriage is dead or not, for it is well-known that a declaration of death depends on the facts of the case and not on the *wishes* of the parties concerned. But if in the case of physical death you demand precise and unmistakable proofs, must not the legislator lay down *moral death* only after the most incontestable symptoms?

There is reference here to physical nature, to physical death, but it is only an analogy, rather highlighting the fact that the nature Marx is talking about is not physical nature. In looking for the symptoms of a moral death the legislator has to look at the *concept* of marriage, in contradistinction to the man-made proposals of the new divorce laws which reflect only the wishes of the parties concerned.

Between these two extremes, somewhere along the line, is St. Paul who referred to our ordinary moral life when he referred to what he called 'natural law'. He used the term 'law' because in his conceptual world what regulated his people's behaviour was the Law. When he observed that people who did not have the Law also behaved, he described this by saying that they have 'another law,' and, in contradistinction to the positive Divine Law, he described this other law as natural law. Otherwise there is no reference to nature in this usage; he is far from making a recommendation like Antiphon. All the characteristics he gives of this natural law are the characteristics of our ordinary morality. It would be an *extra* additional claim to claim that this morality consists in some conformity with nature in some sense of 'nature'.

The distinction and contrast between nature and convention, between *phusis* and *nomos* is one of the oldest distinctions and contrasts ever made. In a different context I would argue that this distinction signified the very beginning of our philosophical speculations. As a technical term in pre-Socratic philosophy *phusis* meant the intrinsic and qualitative constitution of things, or what things really were or were made of. But things did not appear to be what these cosmologists claimed they were 'by their nature'. Thus, when the distinction was made between what they claimed to be the intrinsic qualities of matter and those which were perceived by us, the term 'nature' was used to designate the former. The interesting thing to note is that not only was the term 'nature' borrowed by moral and political philosophers to draw the sort of distinction we are discussing in this paper, but the contrasting term of the moral philosopher, 'nomos,' was borrowed and used by the cosmologists to designate the subjective aspect of our experience. For instance Democritus says: '*Nomoi* things possess colour, *nomoi* they are sweet, *nomoi* they are bitter; but in reality there exist only atoms and the void'.[5] These are interesting pointers to the origins of the notion that what is objective and true is provided by nature and what is subjective and erroneous is provided by human beings. Though I mentioned one of the earliest cases of the parallel distinction, by 'origin' I do not mean origin in time but a conceptual origin. For the parallel distinction in both natural philosophy and moral philosophy persists through the centuries and I need only to remind ourselves of its succinct expression in the eighteenth century by Hume:

> So, when you pronounce an action or character to be vicious, you mean nothing, but that from the constitution of your nature you have a feeling or sentiment of blame from the contemplation of it. Vice and virtue, therefore, may be compared to sounds, colours, heat and cold, which, according to modern philosophy, are not qualities in objects, but perceptions in the mind: and this discovery in morals, like the other in physics, is regarded as a considerable advancement of the speculative sciences.[6]

This parallel is a very persuasive model. In fact Hume could not have read Democritus, at least not with this in mind, otherwise he would not have regarded his comparison as 'a considerable advancement of the speculative sciences'.

Is our language, then, permeated permanently with a distinction which is slanted against human achievement in spite of the fact that all our human life is a human achievement? Are we committed to describing only those aspects of our achievement that we suspect, question, or want to belittle or discard as human, and describing those aspects of it that we cherish, believe in, or are proud of by using some variant of the term 'nature'? Indeed, it seems that it is very difficult to praise and recommend anything by describing it as man-made as long as we use the conceptual framework of the nature–convention distinction. But do we need to be inside it? Here we should again recall the distinction between the insider's and the outsider's vocabulary. If I use the term 'man-made' inside the conceptual world of the nature–convention distinction then inevitably the qualifying 'only' will be attached to or understood to be attached to the term 'man-made'. In order to be able to praise anything by saying that it is a human achievement, we have to go outside this conceptual framework to become non-believers in it, as it were. It is the notion of progress that provides that other conceptual framework which enables us to speak of human achievements with praise. This is how, surprisingly, the idea of progress is connected to the idea of nature in the complex logical tug-of-war of ideas.

The type of mini-argument presented by the question 'when Adam delved and Eve span, who was then the gentleman?' can only be answered by the type of claim made by Xenophanes: 'The gods did not reveal to men all things from the beginning, but men through their own search find in the course of time that which is better.' This remark of Xenophanes is often quoted as one of the very first expressions of the idea of progress. Since then the idea of progress has had a complex and chequered history, as complex, if not more complex, than that of the concept of nature. When, in conclusion, I want to put in a good word for progress I am far from giving a blank endorsement of the idea. I am following the intellectual pilgrimage of Robert Nisbet who was and still is one of the most acute critics of the idea of progress. Indeed, most of our woes are due to the triumphant progress of the idea of progress. But now when our civilisation is so much under attack by knockers and levellers who would present what is most primitive as not only equal to but better than our hard-won, fragile, man-made fruits of civilisation, one begins to value one aspect of the idea of progress, an aspect which reaffirms our respect for our past rather than our confidence in the future. When people are dismantling and throwing out treasures of our culture and giving no better reasons than that 'this was added only in the nineteenth century' and 'this was added only in the middle ages,' then one does want to reaffirm Xenophanes' claim.

I would like to end by quoting the last few paragraphs of Gertrude Himmelfarb's long review of Nisbet's *History of the Idea of Progress* in which Nisbet gave his guarded support to the idea.

> It is not so much that Nisbet has changed his views as that history has given them an ironic twist. In *The Sociological Tradition* he explained how the ideals of the Enlightenment had become perverted, democracy issuing in a 'tyranny imposed by the mass,' liberty in a 'morbid

isolation' of the individual, reason in a 'rationalisation of spirit,' secularism in 'sterile disenchantment'. It was this perversion which Burke, Tocqueville, Burckhardt, Weber, Durkheim, and the others in the great tradition were responding to and which made them impatient with any theory of progress....

We are now witnessing one of those 'deep moral crises' that have periodically assailed us, only this time so deep that it may signal the end of Western civilisation. (As a small symptom of this, Nisbet cites the reversal of the role of the Western and non-Western worlds. Where once it was assumed that the West would serve as a model for the developing nations, ours being the condition toward which they were developing, we are being increasingly confronted with the claim that the Third World, with its peculiar, and peculiarly despotic, varieties of socialism, is the model for the future.) It is in this situation of 'disbelief, doubt, disillusionment, and despair' (one can go on with these negatives—a distrust of ourselves, a discontent with what we have achieved, a disrespect for our principles and institutions, a debasement of our culture) that Nisbet calls for a return to the idea of progress, perhaps not so much to signify our faith in the future as to reaffirm our faith in ourselves—which is to say, in our own past and present. Only by re-establishing the continuity can we prevent ourselves from being engulfed by a new 'wave of the future' that is not our future at all.[7]

Moses Hess, Marx and Money[1]

I

The aim and scope of this discussion is limited. I wish to explore a few themes within the Young Hegelian conceptual framework, in order to place within it Moses Hess's essay *On the Essence of Money*. However, I prefer to talk of a 'triadic framework' instead of the 'Young Hegelian conceptual framework,' for several reasons. The phrase 'the Young Hegelian conceptual framework' is very vague while it pretends to be specific. Consequently, while it gives only a rough indication of my subject matter it can invite criticism: one might justly ask what is meant by 'the Young Hegelian conceptual framework' and be lost for an answer.

To talk of a 'triadic framework' also gives some unity to the themes I am exploring, while not limiting me to its specifically Hegelian version. Triads do crop up in the writings of the Young Hegelians and it would be a mistake to see them either as corrupt versions of their classic appearance in the Hegelian system or just as oddities that can be ignored. There can be two different kinds of variety in the triadic pattern. One kind of variation is when the patterns themselves have different logical forces and serve different functions. In the other kind the pattern is the same but is filled with different contents, the assumption being that the logical force of the pattern will be transmitted to the new contents.

We shall see examples of both kinds of variation and combinations of them. The first kind, for instance, is that between (a) the triadic pattern of three succeeding ages of mankind, and (b) the triadic pattern of original unity, fallen or alienated existence, and return to unity on a higher level. We shall see both of these exemplified in Hess's writings. The first is his *Sacred History of Mankind* with the ages of God the Father, God the Son and the coming age of the Holy Spirit; the second is in his present essay where he argues that money is our alienated essence and that mankind will achieve a higher level of unity by overcoming this alienated state. We shall also briefly analyse a third type of pattern, the triad of head, heart and stomach, a symbolism which recurs in the writings of the Young Hegelians. Its decipherment throws an interesting light on the similarities and differences between the views of Hess and Marx about the role of the proletariat.

The above three are different types of triadic patterns. It is in connection with the second kind of variation, when the same type of triadic pattern is filled in with different contents, that we shall see the great significance of Hess and especially of his present essay. Even the title of his essay echoes Feuerbach's *The Essence of Christianity*. Hess placed a different human essence in what he understood to be Feuerbach's pattern of human alienation: it is not our consciousness of the infinite, that is, the consciousness of our infinity, which is projected into a Divine Being, but it is our co-operative productive work and exchange which, as our essence, is projected into an alien object, into money.

One of my brief critical comments later will concern the question whether, quite apart from the truth or falsity of the story, this triadic pattern has a power or logical force only with something like its Hegelian content, or whether its power can be transmitted to new contents. At present I just want to note that the significance of *On the Essence of Money* within the whole kaleidoscope of the Young Hegelian pattern of ideas is that it replaced the content of a powerful model that dominated the Young Hegelians. In another article Hess himself describes this move more succinctly than anywhere in the present essay:

> Money in the practical life of alienated men is just as all important and ever present, just as much the source of blessedness and grace as God is in our theoretical life. Why did not Feuerbach follow up this important practical consequence of his principle? The essence of God, says Feuerbach, is the transcendental essence of Men and the true study of the divine essence is the study of human essence: theology is anthropology. This is true but not the full truth. The human essence, it must be added, is the social essence, the co-operation of various individuals for the same cause, for exactly the same interest, and the true study of mankind, the true humanism, is the study of human society, that is, anthropology is socialism. It is self-evident that the essence of God and the essence of money are identical in the same way, in the sense that it is in the same way man's transcenden-

tal, practical externalised essence. But Feuerbach did not come to this practical consequence.[2]

Another concise statement of how Hess's achievement was understood in his time is found in the third section of Marx's *The German Ideology* dealing with the True Socialists:

> Feuerbach only partially completed, or rather only began, the task of anthropology, the regaining by man of his estranged nature...; he destroyed the religious illusion, the theoretical abstraction, the God-Man, while Hess annihilated the political illusion, the abstraction of wealth, of his activity ... that is, he annihilates wealth. It was the work of Hess which freed man from the last of the forces external to him, and made him capable of moral activity....[3]

In our time great claims have been made for Hess's essay on money. David McLellan emphasises the influence which Hess had on Marx's two articles 'On the Jewish Question': 'Many of the themes of this article ["On the Jewish Question"], particularly that of money and the Jewish–Christian relationship, are taken directly from an article by Hess entitled "On the Essence of Money".'[4] In his earlier work, after outlining shrewdly-perceived parallels between the two articles, McLellan concludes: 'These parallels between the two texts are more than enough to justify the statement that Marx copied Hess's ideas at this stage.'[5] Then after quoting Professor Silberner who describes this essay as 'one of the most important publications of early German socialist literature' he goes on to say: 'but it took a louder and more persistent voice to convey its message,' meaning of course the voice of Marx.[6] Silberner, in his authoritative work on Hess's life, speaks even more strongly of the inspiration Marx gained from Hess, and he in turn quotes Cornu who described Hess as 'une influence profonde' on the young Marx.[7] Tucker also emphasises the influence of this essay on Marx's articles 'On the Jewish Question,' claiming that the reasoning there 'turns wholly on Hess's thesis'.[8] Julius Carlebach disputes the hypothesis that Hess influenced the articles 'On the Jewish Question': 'If anything, it is possible to argue a much stronger case to show that the "Economic and Philosophical Manuscripts" of 1844 show signs of Hess's influence,' and he goes on to draw parallels in the two texts.[9] But Carlebach very wisely reminds us of several other influences working here.

Perhaps the widest claim for Hess's essay is made by Lobkowicz. After outlining some of the ideas in Hess's essay, Lobkowicz claims that what Marx does in the 'Economic and Philosophical Manuscripts' is 'to articulate Hess's ideas just sketched, to enlarge them in terms of economic analysis supplied by Engels, and then elevate them *à la hauteur des principes* in terms of a reinterpretation of Hegel's *Phenomenology of Mind*.'[10]

To these suggested connections we can add two more: Heine already described Hess as 'one of the most outstanding of our political writers,' and it was Hess who converted Engels to communism. In a letter to Auerbach on July 19, 1843, Hess reports that they were talking about the problems of the time, and Engels, 'ein Anno Eins Revolutioner, schied von mir als allereifrigsten Kommunist' (a Year One revolutionary, left me as a full-blown Communist).

Although inevitably I shall have to talk about influences, they are not my primary concern. I shall agree with Carlebach that reading Hess's *On the Essence of Money* will help us understand better what Marx is doing in his 'Economic and Philosophical Manuscripts' rather than what he is saying in his articles 'On the Jewish Question,' but not on the grounds of the type of historical data on which Carlebach based his arguments. Instead of influences I shall be looking for the choreography of the movements of ideas.

Historical influences do not just happen. They come about only in those configurations of conceptual forces where a new conceptual move either has to be made or is welcome. They have to arrive when someone is already grappling independently with a train of thought, and then they provide the missing link, creating either a confluence or a combustion under the right conditions.

I intend to trace one of the configurations in a kaleidoscope of complex patterns. I find presentations of other configurations of ideas in this field not only possible but sometimes even convincing. The very nature of our subject matter is such that we can entertain different possibilities without having to choose between them. Understanding here consists of seeing as many interesting possibilities and configurations as possible rather than in finding an orthodox line of development, parts of which, like tributaries, must all contribute to the final formulation of Marxism. Anyone who looks for such orthodoxy should, I think, take Althusser's way out and claim that there was a 'radical break' in Marx's development. Just as something radical happened on the river Jordan, so that the person who spoke after the Spirit descended on him was not merely the son of a carpenter whom his kinsmen knew and who was influenced by all the complex turmoil in Galilee and in the Judean desert, but someone who spoke with authority; so one might claim that at some time in Marx's life there was a similar radical break. I for my part do not think so but would like to present the essay here translated as just one of the many Dead Sea scrolls of Marxism.

In what follows I shall first give a brief outline of Hess's life and then analyse some theoretical themes that have a bearing on the significance of Hess's essay on money.

The first theme will be a brief consideration of Hess's first two works, *The Sacred History of Mankind* and *The European Triarchy* where, through two different triadic patterns, Hess sets the scene for the development of the ideas we shall be concerned with.

Then I shall try to decipher the recurring symbolism of 'head, heart and stomach,' which, I hope, will throw new light on the relationship of Marx's ideas to those of Hess, especially with regard to the problem of True Socialism and the role of the proletariat.

My final theme will concern *On the Essence of Money* most directly. I shall show that it is neither an economic nor a sociological treatise but a transformation of certain key ideas from Feuerbach's *The Essence of Christianity*. In tracing this we shall see what it is that Hess and Marx wanted to eliminate when they wanted to eliminate money and private property, and what result they expected. Since, as we saw, strong claims have been made for the influence of Hess's essay on Marx's articles 'On the Jewish Question,' I shall make some tentative comments on this problem, but my main preoccupation will be to decipher the structural transformation of both Hess's and Marx's conceptual systems insofar as the essay on money throws some light on these transformations.

II

Hess was born in Bonn's Judengasse in 1812. When he was five his parents moved to Cologne where his father established a sugar refinery. Apparently there was no Hebrew school in Cologne and young Moses was left behind in Bonn to be educated by his grandparents. Later Hess described his grandfather as 'a man very learned in the Scriptures who had the title and knowledge of a rabbi without making a profession of it'. He was only thirteen when his mother died and his father asked him to join him in Cologne. In fact his father would have liked him to join his firm, but there was a growing estrangement between the two. The young Hess with his keen and restless intellect threw himself into reading Spinoza, Rousseau and Fichte, and travelled to Holland and France where he was impressed by the various socialist and liberal ideas and movements. Although he attended Bonn University for a short time while Bauer was still teaching there, he was virtually a self-taught man. Even more than most of the Young Hegelians, whose circle he now joined, he distanced himself from the traditions of his upbringing. In the intellectual milieu that he now moved in outside his home, Judaism was regarded as it were symbolically, as a type, representing limitation, particularness and heteronomy. Christianity represented the middle stage in the development of consciousness, but even Christianity had to be overcome in the highest universality. Hess acted out in his own life that view of mankind's development which Bauer was to express later in its most succinct form, the view that while Christians had to make only one move to emancipation, the Jews were two steps behind. If one accepts the view that the history of mankind's journey to full emancipation is the history of religious consciousness from Judaism through Christianity, then no wonder Hess rejected what he came to regard as narrowness and particularness—and these characteristics for a socialist also meant egoism—to dedicate himself with the same love and concern that was his grandfather's to the universal liberation of mankind.

Even in his marriage he may have acted out his theories and ideals. Legend has it that his wife Sibylle Pesch was a prostitute, whom he married either in order to rescue her from her way of life, or perhaps as an idealistic act of atonement for the sins of the bourgeois world. Silberner disputes this legend, arguing that it partly originates from the disapproval of Hess's family towards his living with an uneducated Christian girl of humble origins.[11] Jenny Marx mentions 'Hess und seine Frau' as belonging to Marx's circle in Paris in 1844, but in fact Hess and Sibylle were not officially married until 1852, after the death of Hess's father.

My own contribution to this is the perhaps unscholarly remark that a biographer of Hess might well wish that the legend were true. Although the social crime which would have called for such an act of atonement was thought to have been committed by the bourgeois world that had forsaken true humanity, one cannot help thinking of the Book of Hosea: 'When the Lord first spoke through Hosea, the Lord said to Hosea: "Go, take yourself a wife of harlotry and have children of harlotry, for the land commits great harlotry by forsaking the Lord"... And the Lord said to me: "Go again, love a woman who is beloved of a paramour and is an adulteress; even as the Lord loves the people of Israel, though they turn to other gods and love cakes and raisins".' As we shall see, it was the love of cakes and raisins, 'the sense of having,' that Hess found so abominable.

'It was perhaps this childlike quality,' wrote Isaiah Berlin, referring to this legend, 'Hess's unworldliness and purity of character, rising at moments to genuine saintliness, that so deeply irritated the tough-minded "realists" among his fellow socialists, who looked on him as a benevolent ass. Yet even Marx, who utterly despised him, could discover no moral vice or fault to cast in his teeth.'[12]

Hess's first published work was *The Sacred History of Mankind, by a young disciple of Spinoza*, as he described himself in the title.[13]

Then in 1841 Hess published, also anonymously, his *The European Triarchy*. It was published by the avant-garde publisher Otto Wigand and it brought him into the Young Hegelian circle. While in the *Sacred History* it was said to be Spinoza who proclaimed the third age, now it is Hegel who stands at the threshold between the old age and the new. By its content Hegel's philosophy belongs to the new age but insofar as it is still a spiritual act of knowing it belongs to the previous age. Hess refers to Cieszkowski's *Prolegomena zur Historiosophie*, as equally acknowledging the perfection of theory and as giving the direction to the next step, to practical action in history, by bringing the perfected theory into this world. Thus Hess, along with Cieszkowski, gives the signature tune to one of the main preoccupations of the Young Hegelians, the problem of how to 'realise philosophy,' or, in terms of another symbolism, how to unite 'head' and 'heart'.

During the summer of the same year, in 1841, Hess was asked by George Jung, a Hegelian liberal, to co-operate with him in founding a paper in Cologne, which first appeared in January of 1842 as the *Rheinische Zeitung*. Hess was editing the paper until December when he went to Paris to become its Paris correspondent. This was of course the paper of which Marx became the editor. Hess first met Marx in the late summer of 1841, without converting him to communism, but about a year later he converted Engels to communism. From the articles of this time one can have a general idea of the grand reasonings he must have used to convert Engels. As to how he argued in person there is an interesting description of him in an intriguing document prepared for the Zurich authorities in 1843 under the title: *Die Kommunisten in der Schweiz, nach den bei Weitling vorgefundenen Papieren.* It was compiled by Dr J. Bluntschli, who was then a professor of law and a councillor at Zurich. In one of these papers 'a correspondent from Paris' in a letter dated 15th May 1843 reports to Weitling that Hess is a communist because he is the most consistent of the Young Hegelians, one of the purest type, and communism follows with the sharpest necessity from the Hegelian system. 'Hess is very effective,' he goes on to say,

> in converting the highly educated, but he talks in concepts and not directly, and so is unintelligible to those who are not highly educated. So far all German philosophers are the same. He realises this and says he will improve. He also has some baroque turns of phrase... But apart from these weaknesses Hess is very good.

Hess, through his reports from Paris, and mainly by his review of Lorenz von Stein's *Socialismus und Kommunismus des heutigen Frankreichs* for the *Rheinische Zeitung,* was largely responsible for the transmission of French socialist ideas into the German environment. In 1843 he contributed several articles for the *Einundzwanzig Bogen aus der Schweiz.* In the following year Marx wrote in his 'Economic and Philosophical Manuscripts':

> It goes without saying that besides the French and English socialists I have also used German socialist works. The only *original* German works of substance in this science, however,—other than Weitling's writings—are the essays by *Hess* published in *Einundzwanzig Bogen* and *Umrisse zu einer Kritik der Nationalökonomie* by Engels...

The title *Einundzwanzig Bogen aus der Schweiz* was specially designed to spite the censors, as a publication with twenty-one pages or more was considered to be scholarly work and exempt from censorship. Hess contributed to this collection the *Philosophie der Tat, Die eine und ganze Freiheit,* and *Socialismus und Kommunismus.* This latter is partly a continuation of his discussion of Stein and a further elaboration of his views already expressed in *Die Europäische Triarchie* on the partnership of German philosophy and French political practice. We shall see how important this recurring theme of the unity of German philosophy and French practice is among the Young Hegelians, but its present significance in the life of Hess is that here he is now in Paris during the preparation of the *Deutsch-Französische Jahrbücher*. He met Arnold Ruge, with whom Marx was to edit this paper, in August 1843. Even the title of the journal should be seen in the light of these ideas and not as an indication of some practical German and French co-operative effort. In fact there were no French contributions to the journal, but later in one of his essays Hess refers back to the *Jahrbücher* as only the first step in the all-important union of German Theory and French Praxis. It was to this journal that Hess first submitted *On the Essence of Money*, along with his 'Letters from Paris'. The essay was not published however, and was printed only a year and a half later in the *Rheinische Jahrbücher* in Darmstadt.

The fact that the *Deutsch-Französische Jahrbücher* went bankrupt after the first issue cannot explain why Marx did not publish Hess's essay on money, for we have a letter of Marx written from Paris to Fröbel, the publisher, dated November 21st, in which he writes: 'I have had to reject the articles so far sent to me by the local people (Hess, Weill, etc.) after many protracted discussions'. McLellan suggested that Marx 'copied heavily from Hess's essay presuming it would not be published' without implying that this was Marx's reason for not publishing it.[14] Carlebach speculates that Hess's dogmatic unequivocal call for the adoption of communism went too far for Marx, especially against his editorial policy.[15] I find this unlikely, especially as Marx, at least soon after reading it, adopted so many of its crucial ideas, including the idea that communism is the resolution of our alienation.

This is only the first of the complex and controversial problems about the relationship between Hess and Marx until their final break in 1848. Hess returned to Cologne and continued publishing articles and working in communist associations. The following year he joined Engels in Wuppertal and organised meetings in the Gasthof in Elberfeld. Engels wrote the most enthusiastic letters to Marx about their success, saying that everybody talks of nothing but communism, 'there is truly communism in Wuppertal, it is really a force'. Their only complaint was that there was not a single proletarian among them. In view of the fact that the essay on money begins with a long quotation from

'Queen Mab' it is interesting to note that one of the activities at these meetings was to have readings from Shelley. What complicates the relationship between Hess and Marx before 1848 is that it is during these years that Hess became the leading figure of the 'True Socialists' and it is also during these years that Marx turned against his former associates, which included the 'True Socialists'. He never explicitly criticised Hess however, not even in the sections devoted to the 'True Socialists' in *The German Ideology* and in the *Manifesto*. In fact Hess himself contributed to *The German Ideology* in the small section on George Kuhlmann.[16]

If we observe that Hess's style would have been an ideal target for Marx's sarcastic kind of criticism, the silence is even more puzzling. Let us consider only the examples which Hess took from nature to illustrate his contention that man consciously sacrifices his life for the life of the species if there is a conflict between the two, and that hence love is mightier than egoism. To prove this he says:

> The hen takes up a quite unequal fight if it has to defend its chickens from an attack. Cats will allow themselves to starve if they must, in order to satisfy their sexual desires, or in their sorrow when wicked men take away their kittens. Nature is always concerned with the preservation of the species, with the preservation of the life of the species, with the real life-activity.[17]

Now consider against this the sensible and refreshing reference to nature in St. Matthew's gospel: 'Consider the lilies of the field.' Marx's comment on this is also refreshing: 'Yes, consider the lilies of the field how they are eaten by goats, transplanted by man into his button-hole, how they are crushed beneath the immodest embraces of the dairymaid and the donkey driver!'[18] Imagine what Marx could have made out of the immodest embraces of stray cats in order to ridicule Hess's contention that love is mightier than egoism—a view that in fact Marx wanted to ridicule.[19]

György Bence, to whom I owe this lively illustration, follows Mönke in suggesting that Hess differs from the other 'True Socialists' in not neglecting the importance of revolutionary *praxis*, and that is why Marx spares him. This presupposes the idea that Marx's main concern at this time was to safeguard what later became some of the main tenets of Marxism. Rather, he had many other problems to contend with, and the moves he made to overcome these problems later became part of what we now know as Marxism.

I think that in this matter Hess's personality was just as important as his theoretical views. I do not just mean that his unworldly character made Marx reluctant to offend him, but that with Hess's disposition for admiration and enthusiasm, his readiness to change his mind and 'to improve,' he had the makings of a potential disciple of the sort Marx needed. As it turned out later, he did not after all become a shadow of Marx, a 'second fiddle', as Engels described himself to Hermann Becker after Marx's death.

We should also ask another question: why is it that Marx in *The German Ideology* criticises so many of his own recent views in general terms only, without ever referring directly to any of his own writings?

If someone changes his mind and yet would like to preserve the image that he has always been right, then he has to adopt one or another version of a historical theory of knowledge. He has to maintain that certain theories were at one time true and correct, and in fact were appropriate and historically necessary stages in the development of Truth, while at the same time denying that they are any longer true or appropriate. In order then to stay attuned to the development of the Truth a scheme must be created in which one can so place oneself that one's statements are guaranteed by one's very position within that scheme. This cannot be demonstrated in detail here, but this psycho-conceptual device of justifying one's own correctness while abandoning one's views must be kept in mind as at least partially explaining why Marx is criticising both his own and Hess's recent views without specifically criticising their own actual writings. 'Matters,' writes Marx in the *German Ideology*, 'which are quite vague and mystical even in Hess, although they were originally, in the *Einundzwanzig Bogen*, worthy of recognition, and have only become tiresome and reactionary as a result of their perpetual reappearance..., at a time when they were already out of date, became complete nonsense in Herr Grün's hands.'

On 28th July 1846 Hess wrote to Marx: 'Necessary as it was in the beginning to tie communistic efforts to the German ideology, so it is now just as necessary to base them on historical and economic assumptions, otherwise we will never be finished with the "Socialists" or with opponents of all colours.' He does not say that they were ever mistaken. He tried to show that 'True Socialism' was justified in the early forties but was no longer so under the changed historical circumstances.

Now the only event one can think of which changed the 'historical circumstances' is the publication of Stirner's *The Ego and His Own*, which had a shattering effect on the Young Hegelians. Stirner was no ordinary opponent. The threat did not come from his bulky and wild arguments, but from the logical force of his position within the Young Hegelian development of ideas.[20] We shall be able to appreciate the shattering effect of Stirner only after we have analysed in the last section of this discussion how far Hess's thesis depended on Feuerbach and how far Marx's ideas during his Paris period were a combination of the ideas of Feuerbach and Hess. Here I might mention a small point, referring explicitly to Hess. Ruge's ground for refusing Hess's request for further collaboration at this time was that Stirner had destroyed Hess's philosophical communism.

Hess and Engels were among the first to receive an early copy of Stirner's work, and Engels in turn sent it on to Marx. It was Hess who straight away got down to work writing his reply 'Die Letzten Philosophen,' while Marx and Engels, with some help from Hess, began work about a year later on their own reply, the unpublished *German Ideology*.[21]

However much Hess and Marx might have fought different wars, during these years they fought the same battle. In the event they had to evacuate their positions and move to new ground, and then they themselves attacked their own previous positions. This is why it was 'necessary' at the beginning 'to tie communistic efforts to the German ideology' but later 'just as necessary to base them on historical and economic assumptions'. Besides Engels, Hess was perhaps Marx's only ally in these manoeuvres, which explains why Marx in all his criticisms of their recent theories never criticised Hess himself, or acknowledged his own involvement with those theories.

For a while Hess himself moved towards expressing his theories in economic terms. In his article 'Die Folgen einer Revolution des Proletariats' published in 1847 in the *Deutsche-Brüsseler Zeitung* he argued that wages were governed by the same laws as the prices of other commodities; the value of labour, like that of other commodities, will be what it costs to produce it, hence wages will be kept at the subsistence level.

But these were not only times of revolutionary theory but also of political manoeuvrings in which Hess was too honest to be successful. He stood by Weitling and tried to defend Kriege. Weitling, writing to Kriege in America, was complaining about the cunning intrigues: 'I am to be polished off first, then the others and finally their friends, whilst in the end of course they will cut their own throats... Hess and I are quite alone on this side, but Hess is boycotted also'.

One episode from all this intrigue is worth mentioning. When in June 1847 members of the 'League of the Just' renamed it the 'Communist League' with branches among German workers in London, Brussels and Paris, they wanted to formulate their aims and ideals in a manifesto, or, as they put it at the time, in a 'confession of faith,' and they canvassed various branches for suggestions for such a confession. At the end of October Engels wrote to Marx from Paris:

> *Strictly between ourselves*, I've played an infernal trick on Mosi [Moses Hess]. He had actually put through a delightfully amended confession of faith. Last Friday at the district [a committee of the Communist League] I dealt with this, point by point, and was not half way through when the lads declared themselves *satisfaits*. *Completely unopposed*, I got them to entrust me with the task of drafting a new one which will be discussed next Friday by the district and sent to London *behind the backs of the communities*. Naturally not a soul must know about this, otherwise we shall be unseated and there'll be a deuce of a row.[22]

It is of this that Engels wrote again to Marx a month later: 'Give a little thought to the Confession of Faith. I think we would do best to abandon the catechetical form and call the thing: Communist *Manifesto*...'[23]

With Marx's criticism of the 'True Socialists' in the *Communist Manifesto* the final break came. We will look at one aspect of this criticism later on when we analyse the apparent disagreement between Hess and Marx with regard to the role of the proletariat in the final transformation of mankind. We should note, however, that it is in the section on the 'True Socialists' that Marx denounces the use of the term 'alienation'. Marx ends that section of the *Manifesto* by saying that 'with very few exceptions, all the so-called Socialist and Communist publications that now circulate in Germany belong to the domain of this foul and enervating literature'.

Defeats of revolutions have the most varied effects on those who were waiting for them, worked for them, or participated in them. There are many studies of what happened during and after the successful revolutions to those who worked for them; studies, too, of how they were betrayed or eliminated. But we also need comparative studies of the effects of unsuccessful revolutions on those who were looking forward to them. Even a small group such as the Young Hegelians might yield interesting results.

Engels added a footnote to the section on the 'True Socialists' in the 1890 edition of the *Communist Manifesto*: 'The revolutionary storm of 1848 swept away this whole shabby tendency and cured its protagonists of the desire to dabble further in Socialism...' In fact Hess's revolutionary as well as theoretical activities continued unabated. According to his wife he was even condemned to death *in absentia*, which may not be true, but no such pious legend originated about Marx or Engels. Hess was head of the Geneva section of the Bund der Kommunisten, but more importantly he co-operated with Lassalle in the formation of the Allgemeine Deutsche Arbeiterverein, the General Federation of German Workers, which is the foundation of all organised social democracy, not only in Germany but in the whole of Europe. In 1863 Lassalle asked him to represent his movement in the Rhineland. In his first speeches to Lassalle's organisation in Cologne and Dusseldorf he admitted the possibility of reform, and appealed again to such favourite True Socialist notions as the 'creative spirit of the people' to build a better world.

Marx in London was furious. He wrote: 'So Lassalle collects those who were excreted from our party twenty years ago for his dung factory with which world history shall be manured. So he has named Moses Hess his viceroy in the Rhine province. Oh youth, oh youth, what were you thinking when you let yourself be hanged on Herwegh and Moses Hess.'[24]

A more empirical attitude characterised Hess's work now. Like Marx, he abandoned the 'species-being,' though not because of Stirner's theoretical criticisms but for empirical historical reasons. From the abstract universality of mankind he returned to practical problems, and by turning to the particular he even returned to the community of his grandfather. As Nathan Rotenstreich has said, 'The return of Hess to Judaism was clearly the result of his rejection of myth and his adoption of a more genuinely historical attitude.'[25]

With his publication of *Rome and Jerusalem* in 1862 one can say that he became the father of Zionism, and so he was the founder of two important movements originating in the nineteenth century, social democracy and Zionism.[26]

The fact that Hess abandoned the 'iron laws of history' in favour of 'the creative spirit of the people' also pointed up the difference between the two prophets. One in London regarded the failures of 1848 as showing that the time was not yet ripe for the still inevitable destruction, and thus he studied yet more urgently the signs of the coming deluge. The other, Hess, saw in 1848 a sign that after all God loved the world and would not destroy Nineveh with all its wickedness and inadequate institutions; this, however, was no reason to be complacent.

III

Some theories, especially some theories of history, are like devices with which people can hoist themselves into favourable positions vis-à-vis other people, or can help themselves out of predicaments when they are conceptually cornered or feel themselves conceptually defeated. Theories can do this when they are not about an independently existing world of which we are spectators but when they are about a world in which we are participants as in a drama.[27] To be in a predicament from which such devices can provide a way out one must already be a participant in some drama on a world stage. The device rewrites the script.

One such theory of history is associated with the name of Joachim of Flora, a late twelfth century Calabrian monk. Joachim gave a temporal twist to the Christian doctrine of the Trinity. He believed in the unity of the three Persons of the Trinity but gave them each a special age, a special sphere of influence. It was not only respect for authority that made him continue to believe in the unity of the Trinity; it is an essential part of such a theory to show that it is the same principle which is developing and which is now coming to fruition.

The age of the Father was characterised by law and obedience. The age of the Son, beginning from the time of Christ, is devoted to the upbringing of mankind through education, through institutions and through the sacraments to the time when, as some modern theologians would say, 'man comes of age'. This may sound pious and edifying until we realise the revolutionary implications of the claim that the third age supersedes the second as the second superseded the first. Man come of age will do without institutions, without the sacraments and without the authority of those who educated him up to now. What must make such a theory infuriating to those who are representatives of the second age is that they are not rejected as non-believers. Their conceptual system is well equipped to cope with such a rejection. The heralds of the Third Age patronisingly insist on the importance and even validity of the Second Age 'for its time,' and by the help of the very logic of the Second Age they incorporate the representatives of the previous age within their own conceptual system.

One of the most important ingredients of such a theory of history was provided by the early Christians when they claimed to live in the age of Grace which superseded the age of Law, believing that their new covenant replaced the old. The claim lifted a whole people above another people by virtue of placing themselves in a new historical epoch. The simplest Christian was thereby on a higher level than the most learned Jew. Another permanent consequence of the claim was that it turned the continued existence of Judaism into a conceptual oddity.

But has the promise of the New Age been fulfilled? Is *this* what it looks like? To answer this uneasy feeling, which was already in existence among the first generation of Christians, Tertullian devised the triadic version of history, claiming that the present dispensation is only a transition to the age of the Spirit which is about to come. He reported eyewitnesses who saw above the old city of Jerusalem a new Jerusalem descending.

The pattern is so attractive that one does not necessarily need to be influenced by a previous formulation of it in order to employ it when the need arises. All the same Lessing probably had Joachim and his followers in mind when he adopted it to proclaim the arrival of the Enlightenment:

> Perhaps even some enthusiasts of the thirteenth and fourteenth centuries had caught a glimmer of this new eternal gospel, and only erred in that they predicted its arrival as so near to their own time.
>
> Perhaps their 'Three Ages of the World' were not so empty a speculation after all, and assuredly they had no bad intentions when they taught that the new covenant must become as antiquated as the old has become. There remained with them the same economy of the same God. Ever, to put my own expression into their mouth, ever the self same plan of the education of the human race.
>
> Only they were premature. They believed that they could make their contemporaries, who had scarcely outgrown their childhood,

without enlightenment, without preparation, at one stroke men worthy of their *third age.*

And it was just this which made them enthusiasts. The enthusiast often casts glances into the future, but for this future they cannot wait....[28]

In Lessing's view the revelation of the second age, what we normally call Christian revelation, spoke to men from the 'outside,' it spoke to the 'material man,' and, what might sound more of a paradox, it is polytheistic. The revelation of the third age, on the other hand, speaks from the 'inside,' it is the voice of reason, and (with this the paradox in the remark about polytheism disappears) it is universal.

Lessing did not say that he preferred reason to Christianity; he claimed that reason was the final revelation, its voice the real Eternal Gospel, its age the Age of the Holy Spirit for which Christianity was a preparation, valid 'for its time,' during the time when people could not yet hear the voice of reason and thus had to listen to the teaching of the Church. But now, as some present-day theologians would say, 'God has taught us to do without Him'.

Some might think that Lessing's way of expressing the claims of reason is still tainted with theological and metaphysical views characteristic of his age, whereas we in our scientific age would no longer put our case in his way. But to think this only shows the attractiveness of the scheme. For Comte, who also referred to Joachim, replaced the content of the three ages by claiming that the first age was the theological, the second the metaphysical, and that now we begin to live in the age of science.

We noted earlier that Hess's first publication was *The Sacred History of Mankind.* The Age of the Father lasted until Christ, but the Age of the Son now extends to the French Revolution, and the Age of the Holy Spirit is about to begin. He subdivided each age and made various patriarchs and representative figures preside over each subdivision. Such an elaborate scheme is very similar to Joachim's detailed subdivisions of each age. According to Joachim the new age was heralded in by St. Benedict, so his own time was already the gestation period of the Third Age. Anyone who would simply copy the story of the three ages might want to leave out such details as irrelevant, just as manuscript copiers were wont to leave out bits of the script that did not make sense to them, but such details do serve a purpose in the scheme:

they give an assurance that the third period is already under way. In Hess's *Sacred History* Spinoza replaces Benedict as the herald of the period of the Holy Spirit. 'With Spinoza began nothing less than the time which he [Christ] and his first disciples desired, hoped for and prophesied,' said Hess in his *Sacred History.* 'The time of the Holy Spirit began, the Kingdom of God, the New Jerusalem.'

Moreover, this gestation period is characterised both in Joachim and in Hess by an intensification of the conflict between the old and the new. Thus the empirical evidence which might be against the coming of the new age becomes evidence in *favour* of its coming: the worse things are, the more they are evidence for the coming of the better, spiritual age; not only has the decisive event already happened but it has brought about a powerful resistance on the part of the old dispensation, which is surely the proof of its death struggle. Some people who see themselves as actors in such a drama might even see it as their duty to conjure up and polarise the forces of evil as a service to the progress of mankind.

So Joachim interpreted the corruption of the secular clergy and of the Church as a sign and necessary prerequisite of the coming age of the Holy Spirit. In Hess we find the increasing concentration of capital, the tendency of the rich to become richer and the poor to become poorer, as the sign of the coming new age.

Hess gives support to his argument for the three ages by an analogy from nature:

> What is born in time develops in three periods. In the first period it takes root, forms a unity, and lives internally—that is the root of life. In the second period it grows, is divided and lives externally—that is the crown of life. In the third it waxes, is united again and ripens— that is the fruit of life.

Weiss, in a footnote to his study of Hess, comments that political theorists in the first half of the century tend to draw their analogies from plants, animals and men, while after 1850 it is more customary to find analogies from physics and chemistry, which shows the growing prestige of science and is 'one more indication of the transition from romanticism to realism'.[29] This may be true of writers who merely want to use illustration. Otherwise an analogy has a logical force of its own, and its use cannot be governed only by fashion or familiarity. Even in analogies drawn from nature there is an important difference between those drawn from plants and those that make use of the human body. As far as I know Plato did not draw any analogies from plant life. It would have implied growth and development. The organic theory of society Plato wanted to illustrate can use only the human body. Though the human body grows, growth in the analogy is not like that in a plant; the growth does not produce new shoots. On the other hand when Maimonides wanted an illustration to show that the maker has a special knowledge of his creation, he used the analogy of a clock to illustrate this, well before the industrial age.

Joachim is a master of illustrations, and apart from his triangles and his eagle the prominent illustration he uses is the tree. A tree with its root and trunk and branches, or even better, with its flowers, is the most compelling image by which to put across the Joachimite triadic view of history. Similarly, well into the industrial age, Kandinsky made use of the same image when he argued that he was not rejecting previous forms of art. Representational art might have been valid for its time, for a more material man who had to use perceptions from the outside. Kandinsky's spiritual or abstract art is only a necessary culmination of all previous developments; it is the art of the third, spiritual epoch. All this is accompanied by a characteristically relativist theory of knowledge.

'"Truth" in general and in art specifically is not an X, not an always imperfectly known but immovable quantity…,' writes Kandinsky in his *Reminiscences*. 'Art is like religion in many respects. Its development does not consist of new discoveries which strike out new truths and label them errors.' Its development consists of illuminations which show

new perspectives in a blinding light, new truths which are basically nothing more than the organic development, the organic growing of earlier wisdom which is not voided by the later, but as wisdom and truth continues to live and produce. The trunk of the tree does not become superfluous because of a new branch: it makes the branch possible. Would the New Testament have been possible without the Old? Would our epoch of the threshold of the 'third' revelation be conceivable without the second? It is a branching of the original tree trunk in which 'everything begins'. And the branching out, the further growth and ramifications which often seem confusing and despairing, are the necessary steps to the mighty crown: the steps which in the final analysis create the green tree.

One would not expect that the third age in art, as opposed to that in the social or moral world, should be born in apocalyptic travail, or that there should be a worst time before the best can arrive, but this is how Kandinsky announced the new age:

> Today is the great day of one of the revelations of this world. The interrelationships of these individual realms were illuminated as by a flash of lightning: they burst unexpected, frightening, and joyous out of darkness. Never were they so strongly tied together and never so sharply divided. This lightning is the child of the darkening of the spiritual heaven which hung over us, black, suffocating, and dead. Here begins the great epoch of the spiritual, the revelation of the spirit. Father — Son — Holy Spirit.[30]

This is no digression. If one had the space even more attention should be devoted to the analysis of various triadic patterns throughout history, in order to understand the Young Hegelians and in particular Feuerbach, Hess and Marx. One or another form of triadic pattern, or a combination of them, took such a hold on the Young Hegelians, that if I were another Young Hegelian myself I would like to say that the triadic pattern is their alienated essence which took on an independent existence and dominated them. For a proper study one should analyse in more detail the variety of patterns with their various logical forces.

Hess in the *Sacred History* superimposed on the model of organic development another model which has elements of Feuerbach and of Spinoza's theory of knowledge incorporated in it. In the first age, from Adam to Christ, mankind lived in natural unity and harmony, but during this time men could not separate the universal from its concrete manifestations, they could not discern the essential nature of things. Adam was also unaware of the conflict between fact and hope, real and ideal. It was 'perfection unearned'. It was also a time innocent of private property. During the second period the universal, the proper object of intellectual knowledge, was freed from its concrete manifestations—but at a terrible price. The price mankind had to pay for this was the fragmentation which resulted from the separation of the ideal and the real. In the third age the lost unity will be regained by knowing each object as a part of a total unity and by each human being becoming part of a harmonised whole. No wonder that the third age was said by Hess to be heralded in by Spinoza.

The power of the triadic model here is different from the Joachimite model. Here each of the first two stages has a 'positive' aspect and a 'negative' aspect. The first stage is harmony and unity, but on a primitive, undeveloped level. It is implied that there can be no further development in that stage without a drastic transformation. This is achieved by some sort of inner spirit or essential element of the original unity escaping and freeing itself. It can then perfect itself in its liberated form, which is the important 'positive' contribution of the second stage. Its 'negative aspect' is that this perfection happens outside those whose essence is so perfected.

I spoke of the 'power' of the model advisedly. There is no logical reason for all this to happen, and far less is there any logical reason for expecting that the alienated essence, now perfected, will return in the third stage. Yet until one stops to ask the simplest questions about the model one has a feeling that 'of course' this will happen.

Rousseau operates with such a triadic model. The 'positive aspect' of the first stage in his scheme is that we are free, while the 'negative aspect' is that we are not social. In the second stage we are social but not free. Although there is not alienation on a grand scale in the second stage, nevertheless one has the feeling of 'of course' when the third stage unites only the positive aspects of each of the previous stages and we become social beings and yet free, both at a higher stage.

Now turn the kaleidoscope slightly and we have a new configuration. Hess begins his next work, the *European Triarchy*, with a claim which, as we noted, is like a signature tune for much of the Young Hegelian endeavours:

> German philosophy has fulfilled its mission, it has led us to full truth. What we have to do now is to build bridges which will again lead us from heaven to earth. What remains in separation, be it truth itself, when it remains in its high distinctness, is untrue. Just as reality which is not penetrated by truth, so truth which is not realised, is imperfect.

As we know, Marx also, along with other Young Hegelians, wanted to 'realise philosophy'. We shall consider that move in the next section.

Let us notice that the description Hess just gave us is the description of the second age, Philosophy perfected, waiting to be reunited with the world. It is German philosophy which is perfected, and for the Young Hegelians that means Hegel's philosophy. In the *European Triarchy* Hegel's philosophy is now also one element in a further triad: it is Germany's contribution to a triad, other parts of which are French political life and English economic life.

But to want to realise philosophy is the most un-Hegelian thing to want to do. Not only does Hegel explicitly warn against such a project but his views on the cunning of reason should warn us that any conscious effort of ours would produce, so to speak, inadvertent results. More important is the fact that Hegel's philosophy is not about a subject knowing itself merely as a thinking subject, but about a subject knowing itself as it develops in nature and history. If Hegel's Spirit has not in fact developed *in the world*, in nature and history—if it has perfected itself only as a thinking subject thinking about its own thinking—then there is just no Hegelian philosophy to realise.

There were others, philosophers, who continued developing and arguing in detail about Hegel's philosophy. Had the Young Hegelians done this they would be called neo-Hegelians, not Young Hegelians. The Young Hegelians' relationship to Hegel was of a different nature: they regarded what they believed to be Hegel's achievement as itself an event, a decisive event, not only in human but in cosmic history. Their disagreement about Hegel's philosophy was not the continuation of Hegel's philosophical thinking, but a disagreement about the nature of this event and a disagreement about their own various schemes, within which Hegel's philosophy as an event plays but one role.

Some theologians and Scripture scholars argue that the early Christians transformed the role of Jesus in a similar way and they describe the process by the phrase 'the proclaimer became the proclaimed'. I suggested earlier that such claims that a decisive event has happened can create crises when people look around and see that the world does not after all look as though such an event took place. I believe the Young Hegelians lived in such a conceptual crisis for a few years in the 1840s. One solution to such a crisis, as we saw, is to characterise the present as a transitional age, thus saving the existence of the Kingdom by expecting it to come as a third age.

As we noted, in the opening paragraph of the *European Triarchy* Hess gives us a characterisation of the second age. But there is also an additional assurance: perfection has arrived, but only in theory. The world does not look as if perfection has arrived because the task of the present age is precisely *to realise* philosophy. Some Young Hegelians argued that criticism will turn all institutions into rational institutions. Others argued that this is the age of *praxis*. Still others argued that 'it is not enough that thought should seek to realise itself, reality must strive towards thought'. The empirical conditions in Germany are far from being a refutation of the approach of the Kingdom; it is precisely because Germany is most backward that it will be the agency of the coming realisation of the already perfected philosophy. This is made to look plausible by superimposing the notion of perfected theory onto our triadic model, turning the perfected theory into the perfected alienated essence against which stands the world emptied of its own essence. Hence the sphere which is most empty and degraded is the candidate for the crucial role of receiving the perfected essence. '*The emancipation of Germany*,' says Marx, 'is the *emancipation of man*. Philosophy is the *head* of this emancipation and the *proletariat* is its heart.'

Before we turn to the triad of 'head,' 'heart' and 'stomach' in the next section, let us complete the picture that was formed in Hess's *European Triarchy* by turning the kaleidoscope. As the title of this work suggests, the need is for a unity of the three leading nations of Europe, each with its specific contribution: Germany with her philosophy, France with her political praxis, and England with her economic development.

We are familiar with the claim made by Marx that Germany's revolutionary past is theoretical, it is the Reformation, and 'as the revolution then began in the brain of the *monk*, so now it begins in the brain of the *philosopher*'. It is this claim which is argued by Hess in *The European Triarchy*. He compares the French Revolution to the German Reformation to demonstrate that Germany too has had a revolution. The comparison still bedevils orthodox Marxist historiographers who try to accommodate such claims about Luther in their scientific history.

The role of France is in the world of praxis. 'The speculative German lives in the ideal, while the action-loving Frenchman works in the real,' said Hess. Along with Cieszkowski, Hess introduced the notion of *praxis* into this discourse. This did not make it, however, less of a discourse. It turned it into a theory claiming itself to be not a theory, it turned it into a theory claiming itself to be *praxis*.

We need a new Section to investigate how the proletariat replaced France as the symbol of *praxis*.

IV

That the coming of socialism is tied to the special role of the proletariat is supposed to be one of the crucial areas of difference between Marx and the True Socialists. For the True Socialists socialism was a moral demand which should appeal to anyone who could respond to such demands. As we noted, Hess appealed to the 'creative spirit of the people' and not to socio-economic trends and necessities. To be sure, the coming of socialism was tied to historical factors, but only to those historical factors which indicated to so many of the Young Hegelians that 'the hour is nigh,' and which gave them urgency and assurance that they lived in the fullness of time. Otherwise, however, socialism should have a timeless and classless appeal.

Marx's critique of the True Socialists in the *Manifesto* brings out this difference well, or, as one might prefer to say, it in part creates and constitutes the difference. There he criticises the True Socialists for allegedly borrowing their demands for socialism from France, for being the 'silly echo' of French social criticism, but forgetting the different economic and political conditions of France and Germany. According to Marx's argument, France had already had a bourgeois revolution, therefore the next, socialist, revolution was proper for French conditions. In Germany, however, the bourgeoisie was still the growing revolutionary force destined to destroy the feudal conditions, especially the absolute monarchy. According to Marx, the True Socialists transferred to Germany the socialist criticism of the bourgeoisie before the conditions were ripe for such a criticism, and thereby in effect they joined forces with the absolutist feudal government: while the government resisted the bourgeoisie from above, the True Socialists attacked from below. They should leave the bourgeoisie alone, on this assumption, or even join forces with it while it carried on its historic mission of destroying feudal conditions and establishing its liberal institutions, and attack it only afterwards. Marx accused the True Socialists, in his characteristic style, of 'representing not true requirements, but the requirements of truth; not the interests of the proletariat, but the interests of human nature, of man in general, who belongs to no class, has no reality, who exists only in the misty realm of philosophical fantasy'.

I want to argue nevertheless that Marx, at the time of writing the *Introduction* to his *Toward the Critique of Hegel's Philosophy of Right*, when he first introduced the notion of the proletariat, entertained a distinctly True Socialist view of the role of the proletariat, a view which, because of later developments, is obscured in retrospect. For my argument we have to understand the symbolism of head, heart and stomach in the Young Hegelian iconography and also the symbolic significance for them of France, England and Germany.

We saw in the previous section that Hess in his *European Triarchy* advocated a dialectical union of the three leading nations of the time, Germany with her philosophy, France with her political life, and England with her economic and industrial developments, each contributing their historically allotted elements to the coming final synthesis. Heine had already drawn a parallel between German philosophy and French political life in 1835, the details of which Hess criticised, but the theme was a recurring one. Feuerbach wrote in his *Provisional Theses for the Reformation of Philosophy*:

> The true philosopher who is identified with life and man must be of Franco-German lineage. Do not be scared by this mixture, you chaste Germans. The *Acta Philosophorum* had expressed this idea already in 1716: 'If we weigh the Germans and the French against each other and judge that the latter have more nimbleness in their temperament and the former more weightiness, then we can say justly that the *temperamentum Gallico-Germanicum* is best suited for philosophy, or we can say that a child which had a French father and a German mother would (*ceteris paribus*) be endowed with a good *ingenium philosophicum*'. Quite right [commented Feuerbach on this], only we must make the mother French and the father German. The *heart*—the feminine principle, the *sense* for the finite, the seat of materialism—is a French disposition; the *head*—the masculine principle, the seat of idealism, is German. The heart revolutionises, the head reforms; the head brings things into being, the heart sets them in motion.[31]

Let us again read Marx in his *Introduction* to *Toward the Critique of Hegel's Philosophy of Right*:

But a *radical* revolution in Germany seems to encounter a major difficulty.

Revolutions need a *passive* element, a *material* basis... It is not enough that thought should seek to realise itself; reality must strive towards thought.

[G]ermany, which likes to get to the bottom of things, can only make a revolution which upsets the *whole order* of things. The *emancipation of Germany* will be an *emancipation of man. Philosophy* is the *head* of this emancipation and the *proletariat* is its *heart.*

There are two important points to note in this passage. One is that here the proletariat seems to be replacing France (I shall argue that it replaces France *only in Germany,* while in France, because France *still* represents the heart, there is *no need for the proletariat*). The other point is that the proletariat represents the heart, and I shall argue that, according to Marx at that time, only Germany needed such a heart.

For the significance of the proletariat representing the heart we have to return to Hess for a minute. We saw that in his long essay, *On the Socialist Movement in Germany,* Hess refers back to the *Deutsch-Französische Jahrbücher* as being only the first step in the all-important union of German theory and French praxis. More important, however, is the critical comment Hess goes on to make in the same essay on Lorenz von Stein, who in his work on the French social movement first diagnosed the difference between the poor and the proletariat, and who connected the emergence of socialism with the rise of the proletariat as a class. Hess's critical comment is this:

It is an error—and this error is due to the egoistic narrowness which cannot rise to a truly human outlook—yes, it is an error diligently spread by the reaction, and by Stein above all, that socialism develops only among the proletariat, and among the proletariat only as a question of fulfilling the needs of the stomach. The French have given no excuse for this error. The French socialism comes not from the necessity of thought, not from the need of the head, not from the need of the stomach, but from the need of the heart; it comes from the sympathy for the suffering of mankind.[32]

At first sight this might indicate a difference between Hess and Marx. As we have seen, Marx had just introduced the proletariat as an agency of revolution and here is Hess denying that the proletariat is the agency to bring about socialism. Much of the strength of the claim that Marx at this stage of his development already differed from the True Socialists rests on this apparent difference between them. As we saw, the argument runs that Marx, however vaguely, already recognised the important role of the proletariat, while Hess still believed in the generosity of the spirit, in the political idealism of the people, and relied on these to inspire political action. This is what enabled Marx to criticise the True Socialists in the *Manifesto* for not recognising the relative development of the bourgeoisie and the proletariat in France and Germany.

There is, however, no difference in substance between Hess and Marx at this stage of their development. Hess rejected the idea that the proletariat was the agency of socialist revolution only insofar as it was represented by Stein—or as Hess understood it to be represented by Stein—as acting out of selfish material interest. If we take our clue from Hess's claim that socialism is not 'a question of fulfilling the needs of the stomach,' nor does it come 'from the need of the head' but it comes 'from the need of the heart,' we find agreement between him and Marx. Marx is not talking about Stein's version of the proletariat; Marx introduces the proletariat as something that Germany needs, and needs as the heart of that emancipation of which philosophy is the head. As far as France is concerned, according to Marx, *there is no need for the proletariat.* 'In France,' says Marx, 'every class of the nation is *politically idealistic* and experiences itself first of all not as a particular class but as representing the general needs of society'. This observation about France, just as much as Marx's observations about the proletariat, is so removed from any empirical, historical or sociological study that it can make sense only as part of the iconography we are deciphering.

I said earlier that Marx substituted the proletariat for France as the heart. We can see now how this happened. In a way France is still the heart, as Germany is the head. This is why France *is* politically idealistic and there is there a generosity of spirit. Marx agreed with Hess that this appeal to the heart would do the work for France—provided that the French would learn more German philosophy as well. But Marx was sceptical about the generosity of the German spirit. He thought, so to speak, that if only the proletariat would become hungry enough their stomachs would turn into hearts. It is because, as Marx complains, in Germany there is lacking a 'generosity of spirit' that Germany needs a proletariat as a heart. Hess would not criticise this notion of a proletariat as he criticised that put forward by Stein. In Germany, says Marx,

> There is equally lacking in every class that breadth of soul which identifies itself, if only momentarily, with the soul of the people— that genius for inspiring material force toward political power, that revolutionary boldness which flings at its adversary the defiant words, *I am nothing and I should be everything...* In France it is enough to be something for one to want to be everything... In France every class of the nation is *politically idealistic* and experiences itself first of all not as a particular class but as representing the general needs of society...
>
> Where then is the positive *possibility* of German emancipation?
>
> *Answer.* In the formation of a class with *radical chains,* a class in civil society that is not of civil society, a class that is the dissolution of all classes, a sphere of society having a universal character because of its universal suffering and claiming no particular right because no *particular wrong* but *unqualified wrong* is perpetrated on it....[33]

The proletariat is then introduced as the suffering Redeemer: 'a sphere, in short, that is the *complete loss* of humanity and can only redeem itself through the *total redemption of humanity.* This dissolution of society as a particular class is the proletariat.'

I want to look, very briefly, at the well known economic interpretation of history in Marx's Introduction to *A Contribution to a Critique of Political Economy,* and argue that there is no place and no role for the proletariat in that scheme. The theory is a miniature model of a Hegelian dialectical development. Men, the Subject, in their productive activities create certain objectively existing conditions, the purpose of which is to help those activities. When new means of production come into being these, after a while, can no longer be accommodated within the objectively-existing conditions, and so these conditions become fetters of production. What was a rational arrangement turns into a self-contradictory irrational state of affairs. But why is it *irrational* to have steam engines under feudal modes of production? After all, they could be used for pumping up the ornamental fountains in the gardens of Versailles, or be used as playthings in village squares. In order to create a self-contradictory state of affairs that needs to be resolved in a higher, more rational synthesis, two further conditions are needed. One is that the new instruments should be regarded as *means of production* and not regarded under some other formal aspect such as 'amusements' or 'the devil's work'. If the invention of the steam engine is regarded as the devil's work devised by an alchemist, rather than a means of production invented by an engineer, then it will not come into conflict with the existing relationships of production. The other requirement is that the standard of rationality must be identified with the fullest possible use of productive forces. Only if we regard the fullest possible use of productive forces as the standard of rationality can we say that arrangements that do not help this are irrational and must give way, whether they are the land rights of feudal lords or primitive tribes, or such parts of our 'superstructure' as our enjoyment of the beauties of our lakes and countryside. It is never suggested that the alleged contradiction might be resolved by curtailing the means of production.

My point, however, is not that this model is the expression of the bourgeois entrepreneurial mentality universalised, as ideology, into a philosophy of history. My point is that the proletariat does not fit into this model. The peasants were the oppressed class of feudal society, but capitalism did not come about by peasants overthrowing the feudal lords in order to establish capitalism after a brief period of the dictatorship of the peasantry. Why would one even think of such an absurd idea if in this historical progression the proletariat as the new oppressed class had not been cast into this role of establishing the next stage of history? If there was a class struggle, it was not between the peasants and the feudal lords: a new class grew up with the new means of production, which wanted to create more liberal institutions for its economic practices, and also eventually brought forth people like Hess, Marx and John Stuart Mill who wanted to make these institutions even more liberal and human according to their image of what is human. But this new class, the bourgeoisie, was not the oppressed class of feudalism. If we want to follow *this* pattern of development, then we should expect within the capitalist world a new class to develop with new means of production, which leaves behind the bourgeoisie and the proletariat as the bourgeoisie left behind the feudal lords and peasants.

In order to claim that one has found a scientific law of history, one should be able to produce at least two examples to support that scientific hypothesis. And we have two hypotheses here. On one hypothesis it is the oppressed classes which by their struggle bring about the new stage of history, in which case we are committed to the claim that the peasants brought about capitalism by overthrowing the feudal lords. On the other hypothesis it is the new means of production and the people associated with those productive forces that bring about the new stage of history, in which case the proletariat is as irrelevant as the peasants were in the previous process.

As a matter of fact there is no place for the proletariat in this theory, nor did Marx intend one. Nor is there any possibility for the other scenario of a new class emerging with a new means of production that cannot be accommodated within the existing relations of production. For a revolutionary situation to occur, according to this scientific theory of revolution, the ossified relationships of production should be unable to accommodate the new instruments of production. But this is what Marx has to say about the bourgeoisie in the *Manifesto*:

> The bourgeoisie cannot exist without constantly revolutionising the instruments of production, and thereby the relations of production, and with them the whole relations of society. Conservation of the old modes of production in unaltered forms, was, on the contrary, the first condition of existence for all earlier industrial classes. Constant revolutionising of production, uninterrupted disturbance of all social conditions, everlasting uncertainty and agitation, distinguish the bourgeois epoch from all earlier ones. All fixed, fast-frozen relations, with their train of ancient and venerable prejudices and opinions, are swept away; all new-formed ones become antiquated before they can ossify. All that is solid melts into the air, all that is holy is profaned, and man is at last compelled to face with sober senses his real conditions of life and his relations with his kind.

This is a tremendous insight to have had in 1848. I also think that Marx's other insight in the *Manifesto*, that the True Socialists are actually helping the absolute monarchy by attacking the bourgeoisie whose natural task it is to break the shackles of absolutist governments, is a very important insight.

Marxism is composed of many strata and to understand Marxism one needs the skills of a geologist and an archaeologist. My claim is that the notion of the proletariat belongs to the layer where Marx was concerned with the iconography of head, heart and stomach and not to the layer of his economic investigations, even if various forces later pushed that earlier layer into a new stratum.[34] There are of course other elements in that layer. Marx's search for 'the capability of a universal class to be really universal'[35] is part of his criticism of Hegel, and I am not disputing the view that Marx's proletariat is also a substitute for Hegel's bureaucracy.

As far as empirical life is concerned, the example in front of Marx and Hess was the developing bourgeoisie. In fact Marx's disagreement with the True Socialists in *The Communist Manifesto* was not over the role of the proletariat, but, without their realising it, over the role of the bourgeoisie, and I think Marx might have been right in defending their role in working for those liberal institutions that he there so eloquently described.

V

Hess, like Marx, talks almost interchangeably about private property and money, and they both wanted to abolish private property and money. I do not wish to take issue with them for confusing the two, for we can separate them even conceptually only in our empirical socio-economic life, and neither Marx nor Hess was concerned with that. When we discover what it was that they wanted to abolish we shall find that in that respect the two are indistinguishable.

Hess in *On the Essence of Money* writes:

For our Philistines, our Christian shopkeepers and Jewish Christians, the individual is the end, while the life of the species is the means to life. They have created for themselves a world apart. In theory the classical form of this inverted world is the Christian heaven... Practically, therefore, in our commercial world, as it is in theory in the Christian heaven, the individual is the end, the species only the means of life. Here likewise the life of the species is not at work in the individual and by means of him; here, just as in heaven, it is placed outside individuals and reduced to a means for them; here, in fact, it is money. What God is for its theoretical life, money is for the practical life of this inverted world: the alienated potentiality, the bartered life-activity of men.[36]

A couple of months after Marx read this essay, he was writing some notes on James Mill in which he approved of Mill characterising money as the medium of exchange, and then went on to say:

> This *mediator* is ... the lost, estranged *essence* of private property, private property which has become *alienated*, external to itself, just as it is the *alienated* species-activity of man, the *externalised mediation* between man's production and man's production. All the qualities which arise in the course of this activity are, therefore, transferred to this mediator. Hence man becomes the poorer as man, i.e., separated from this mediator, the *richer* this mediator becomes. Christ *represents* originally (1) men before God; (2) God for men; (3) men to man.
>
> Similarly, *money* represents originally, in accordance with the idea of money: (1) private property for private property; (2) society for private property; (3) private property for society.
>
> But Christ is *alienated* God and alienated *man*. God has value only insofar as he represents Christ, and man has value only insofar as he represents Christ. It is the same with money.[37]

A few months earlier, in the second of his articles 'On the Jewish Question,' Marx had already written that 'Money is the general, self-sufficient *value* of everything. Hence it has robbed the whole world, the human world as well as nature, of its proper worth. Money is the alienated essence of man's labour and life.'[38]

As I said earlier, my primary aim is not to trace influences. Even if we could document precisely who read and wrote what at what time and could also document what was said when in the various Gasthauses, beer halls or coffee houses, the interesting question would still remain: Who would be influenced, by reading Hess, to write what Marx wrote? The point I want to make is that we have to recreate a frame of mind where Hess's remarks (or Marx's for that matter) would not just be swept aside as strange speculations but would be taken so seriously that a man would risk the wrath of governments or be prepared to suffer exile for them, and where a wrong step in an argument would be regarded as a wrong step for mankind.

What I want to investigate is what it was they wanted to abolish when they wanted to abolish money and private property, and why they thought it should be done, or indeed would happen anyway in the progress of world history. The abolition of private property has been advocated many times and for several reasons ever since men yearned for a better world. But never was it argued, I think, for more grandiose reasons or with the expectation of more profound results.

Before we come to Hess and Marx I want to consider briefly two types of reasons for wanting to abolish private property, reasons which have been systematically confused with each other, and both of which are very often mistakenly thought to be Marx's reasons. Arguments that mistake them for Marx's reasons usually switch back and forth between the two types of reasons. So, for clarity's sake, before turning to Hess and Marx, we should look at them first.

We should distinguish between what I want to call the moral reason from what I want to call the economic reason for abolishing private property.[39] The economic and moral considerations are the opposites of each other in every way. The economic considerations are about the means of production, while the moral considerations are about private consumer goods that we want to buy or to have. Whether the arguments are right or wrong, the economic considerations are concerned with the better functioning of our economy, with more efficient production. These arguments do not say that we shall be better persons, but that we shall be able to produce more, or that our economic life will run more smoothly if the means of production are not privately owned. Rather, on the contrary, it is claimed sometimes by the proponents of these arguments that—at least temporarily—economic developments should take precedence over favouring liberal institutions which would help the development of freer autonomous persons. According to Durkheim these considerations have their origin in the modern state and the industrial mode of production, and these arguments want to connect the two; it should be the concern of the state to develop the economy, and it should be economic considerations that influence state policy.

The moral considerations are not tied to any historical conditions. They go back to Plato and come up over and over again throughout our history, as for instance in Campanella or Thomas More or in any one of a host of thinkers whose concern was to liberate us from the pernicious influence of money and the greed that is supposed to accompany it. When St. Francis threw away all his money and expressed his loathing of it in demonic terms he did not go on to organise co-operative economic associations for the poor in order to improve their standard of living, nor did he dig sewage systems for them. He thought that to be poor, to be without possessions, was a good thing. When Plato recommended the abolition of private property for the rulers of his city, he did not do so because this was the best way to overtake the olive oil production of a more advanced city by the end of the second five-year plan. He did so because the vocation of the rulers was virtue and wisdom, and this could be developed only if the sense of having, along with other inclinations toward the particular, was radically eliminated from their lives. He did not connect, but separated, economic affairs from state affairs. The 'appetitive' class, the stomach of the city, had to have private property as an incentive to fulfil its vocation which was production, but those who were supposed to have wisdom and virtue could have these qualities only if their 'sense of having' was eliminated by making it impossible for them to have anything.

We must also note, surprising as it may seem, that the moral consideration is *not* concerned with the just distribution of goods. The desire to redistribute property at all, in equal or unequal rations, still originates from the 'sense of having,' as against the moral consideration which aims at creating a better type of man by freeing him completely from the possession of any property at all and thus from the sense of having. Marx describes the redistribution of goods as crude communism in his 'Third Manuscript':

> [T]he domination of *material* property bulks so large that it wants to destroy *everything* which cannot be possessed by everyone as *private property*... Immediate, physical *possession* is for it the sole aim of life and existence. The condition of the *labourer* is not overcome but extended to all men. The relationship of private property remains the relationship of the community to the world of things... This communism—in that it negates man's *personality* everywhere—is only the logical expression of the private property which is this negation. Universal *envy* establishing itself as a power is only the disguised form in which *greed* re-establishes and satisfies itself in *another* way... Crude communism is only the fulfilment of this envy and levelling on the basis of a *preconceived* minimum.[40]

Marx's own version of communism is a '*positive* overcoming of *private property* as *human self-alienation*, and thus as the actual *appropriation of the human essence* through and for man.' It is this 'positive' overcoming of private property which is so essential for Hess and Marx. This leads us to a third type of reason for abolishing private property and money. Abolishing private property here means abolishing human self-alienation. The reason for abolishing private property is none other than *the regaining of our human essence*. But now since the Feuerbachian alienated essence, God, is replaced by the Hessian alienated essence, money, and at the same time the relationship of alienated men to each other and to the world of things is described as the relationship of private property, private property and money are spoken of interchangeably.

The abolition of private property and of money will bring a new type of man onto the stage of world history. We are not talking here of moral effort or of any practical steps on the part of moral agents to achieve a better human life. The new type of man will arrive as the culmination of cosmic history. The end result of this history will be not only an organically organised mankind, but mankind existing on a qualitatively higher plane because of the transformation of human sense-perception. To understand how a transformation of perception can result in an ontological transformation of both the perceiver and the perceived we shall have to turn to Feuerbach. Such a combination of epistemology and ontology is an indispensable part of Feuerbach's argument for the divinity of our species. It seems however that Marx in his Paris Manuscripts did not apply it to his purpose directly from Feuerbach. It was Hess, in his articles in the *Twenty-One Pages*,[41] who saw how this theory of knowledge can be applied to show the dehumanising effects of private property. Marx in his third 'Manuscript' refers to Hess to indicate what he means:

> [P]rivate property has made us so stupid and one-sided that an object is *ours* only when we have it... Hence *all* the physical and spiritual senses have been replaced by the simple alienation of them *all*, the sense of *having*. Human nature had to be reduced to this absolute poverty so that it could give birth to its inner wealth. (On the category of *having*, see *Hess* in *Twenty-One Pages*.)
>
> The overcoming of private property means therefore the complete *emancipation* of all human senses and aptitudes....

> For not only the five senses but also the so-called spiritual and moral senses (will, love, etc.), in a word, *human* sense and the humanity of the senses come into being only through the existence of *their* object, through nature *humanised.* The *development* of the five senses is a labour of the whole previous history of the world.[42]

Let us sum up briefly what seems to be the theory we shall have to make sense of. Both Hess and Marx claim that parallel to a story of alienation in terms of religious consciousness there is an alienation in terms of private property and money. Our essence is productive life-activity and this essence is alienated into private property and money, so the abolition of private property and money will result in our regaining our human essence. But the effect of alienation is also described in terms of our *perception*, both empirical and the 'so-called spiritual (or mental) and moral (or practical) senses'. The abolition of private property/money will result in a state of affairs which is also described in terms of a transformation of our human senses, along with the transformation of the objects of our senses, and all this has some world-historical significance.

One way of making sense of all this is not to take it seriously but to water it down to something within our everyday experience and translate it into an aesthete's critique of cultural philistinism. But just as it is bad sociology or anthropology to express a tribal mythology in our own familiar cultural terms so it would be shallow to read the Young Hegelians through our own preoccupations. Rather, I shall try to make sense of these claims by placing them within the context of some of Feuerbach's arguments. In particular we should investigate (a) Feuerbach's arguments for the divinity of our species, and (b) the triadic pattern of original unity, separation and return.

Feuerbach suffers from being 'well known' and from having been 'placed' in relation to Hegel and Marx by a popularly accepted line of development. I say this by way of warning because there is often a 'reader's resistance' to an exposition of a theory when the theory is both puzzling and strange *and* unfamiliar, or even runs counter to a popularly accepted view.

Feuerbach did not argue against the existence of God but only about His location: he relocated Divinity in the human species. And he did not argue for our divinity by turning Hegel the right way up, by making us the subject and God the predicate. In fact we shall see him claiming explicitly that *individual* human beings *are 'predicates,'* 'each new man is a new predicate, a new phasis of humanity'.[43]

Feuerbach's argument for our divinity hinges on a theory of knowledge which is at the same time an ontology. I have coined the term 'episto-ontology' to refer to this theory which is at the same time both materialist and idealist. 'The essence of a being,' says Feuerbach in his *Principles of the Philosophy of the Future*, 'is recognised only through its object; the object to which a being is necessarily related is nothing but its own revealed being.'

As we can see, this is not only a theory of knowledge. In the same sentence in which he claims that the essence of a being is recognised only through its object, he goes on to say that 'the object to which a being is necessarily related is *nothing but its own revealed being*'. So we not only recognise what an object is by observing what it, in its turn, takes as its object. The nature of the object is determined by what it takes as its object. This applies right through the scale of being, from inanimate things like stones, through plants to other living organisms like caterpillars to human beings.

It is as if he applied our notion of intentional objects to the inanimate world as well, in the sense that *their* objects are, as it were, intentional objects. At the same time *our* relationships to our intentional objects are to be interpreted in the sense in which the relationships of material objects to each other are to be interpreted. It is in this sense that the theory is inseparably both materialist and idealist at the same time.

When Feuerbach says that 'the object to which a being is necessarily related is nothing but its own revealed being,' the term 'necessarily' is ambiguous. If one were to put a piece of paper in front of the clarinet in an orchestra playing Mozart, Feuerbach would mean by 'necessary relationship' both the vibration of the paper in response to the waves coming out of the clarinet and the enjoyment of the audience in response to the music played. This is how I recognise that one object is paper and the other object is a special type of human being, or a human being at a special level of development, i.e. a music lover. Moreover, the *objects* of these objects are different: it is waves to the one and music to the other, and the next step in this theory is that their respective objects are nothing but *their own nature.*

In *The Essence of Christianity*, after stating that 'the object to which a subject essentially, necessarily, relates is nothing else than this subject's own, but objective nature,' the first example he goes on to give is this:

Thus the Sun is the common object of the planets, but it is an object to Mercury, to Venus, to Saturn, to Uranus, under other conditions than to the Earth. Each planet has its own sun. The sun which lights and warms Uranus has no physical (only an astronomical/scientific) existence for the Earth; and not only does the Sun appear different, but it really is *another* sun on Uranus than on the Earth. The relation of the Sun to the Earth is therefore at the same time a relation of the Earth to itself, or to its own nature... Hence, each planet has in its sun the mirror of its own nature.[44]

Feuerbach, to be consistent, should have said that if a planet has only astronomic/scientific existence for an object, then that object is not another planet but a scientist, and this is what makes him a scientist. For a scientist there exists neither Sun nor music but only waves; and waves, light or sound waves, exist only for a scientist.

We can already see that on the basis of a theory like this, if we were inclined to claim divinity for ourselves what we would need to establish is that *our* object is the Infinite. But before I come to outline how Feuerbach does this, or attempts to do this, I would like to dwell briefly on an example Feuerbach gives, the example of musical sounds. I do this partly for its own sake, as it further illustrates Feuerbach's theory, and partly because, through what I call the archaeology of examples, this example links his theory to Marx's views in the manuscripts he wrote in Paris.

If thou hast no sensibility [says Feuerbach], no feeling of music, thou perceivest in the finest music nothing more than in the wind that whistles by the ear, or than in the brook which rushes past thy feet ... The splendours of the crystal charm the sense, but the intellect is interested only in the laws of crystallisation.

[T]he animal is sensible only to the light beam which immediately affects life; while man perceives the ray, to him physically indifferent, of the remote star. Man alone has purely intellectual, disinterested joys and passions; the eye of man alone keeps theoretical festivals.[45]

Now turn to some of the familiar passages from Marx's third Manuscript:

> It is obvious that the *human* eye appreciates differently from the crude, inhuman eye, the human *ear* differently from the crude ear etc... [T]he most beautiful music has *no* meaning for the unmusical ear—is no object for it, because my object can only be the confirmation of one of my essential capacities and can therefore only be so for me insofar as my essential capacity exists explicitly as a subjective capacity, because the meaning of an object for me goes only so far as *my* senses go (only makes sense for a corresponding sense)...
>
> *Sense* subordinated to crude, practical need has only a *narrow* meaning. For the starving man food does not exist in its human form, but only in its abstract character as food. It could be available in its crudest form and one could not say wherein the starving man's eating differs from that of *animals.* The care-laden, needy man has no mind for the most beautiful play. The dealer in minerals sees only their market value but not their beauty and special nature; he has no mineralogical sensitivity.[46]

This is how the 'forming of the five senses is a labour of the entire history of the world down to the present'. There is no music if there are no musical ears, and only if I perceive what is there *as music* am I the type of being that I am. If, as a being, I responded to 'it' not by enjoying it, but, say, by growing, then I would perhaps be a plant. It is interesting to note how Feuerbach himself connects the division of labour to this theory. In the *Principles of the Philosophy of the Future* he says:

> [T]he object of herbivorous animals is the plant; however, by means of this object they essentially differentiate themselves from the other animals, the carnivorous ones. Thus, the object of the eye is neither tone nor smell, but light. In the object of the eye however its essence is revealed to us... We therefore also name in life things and beings only according to their objects; the eye is the 'light-organ'. He who cultivates the soil is a farmer; he who makes hunting the object of his activity is a hunter; he who catches fish is a fisherman; and so on.[47]

Hess and Marx operated with this episto-ontology. 'Private property has made us so stupid and one-sided that an object is only ours when we have it,' and so 'the sense of having' replaced all other senses. This perception, the perception of all objects as commodities, reduced us and the world to a lower, in fact to the lowest level of existence, not only figuratively but literally, ontologically; and, in a reciprocal relationship, the world is also correspondingly 'dehumanised'.

This is an ontology and not just an aesthete's complaint about our vulgarity. The aesthete's prejudice does come through, however, in that neither Hess nor Marx argues why it is more *human* to see the beauty of minerals than to make steam engines out of iron, and why it is against nature, akin to a medieval natural-law sense of 'against nature,' to do the latter rather than the former. When Marx says that 'a dealer in minerals has no mineralogical sense' he does not explain why we all ought to be lapidarists rather than only some of us.

But we still have to return to Feuerbach to see how he argues for our divinity and for the alienation of our divinity. As I remarked, in order to show that we are infinite he has to show that our object is infinite. And indeed this is what Feuerbach is doing in the first chapter of *The Essence of Christianity*. There are however at least four or five different senses of 'infinity' in these pages and Feuerbach moves from one to the other almost imperceptibly. There is a sense in which everything is infinite. Then there is the sense in which only we, as against the brutes, are infinite in that we have consciousness. This kind of infinity itself has two varieties: one is that we are infinite because we are conscious of the infinite, the other that we are infinite because everything and anything can be the object of our thought. In the last two crucial senses the imperfect individual is contrasted with the species which is infinite and then with mankind as a collective. I say this not so much to show some inconsistency but because the last two senses will be crucial for illuminating Hess's remarks on the Christian heaven and on egoism and because they are also the proper targets for Stirner's criticism.

In a sense for Feuerbach everything is infinite, for the limit of any creature's perception is the limit of its world, and in this sense even a caterpillar is infinite. 'A being's understanding is its sphere of vision. As far as thou seest, so far extends thy nature; and conversely. The eye of the brute reaches no farther than its needs, and its nature no farther than its needs. And so far as thy nature reaches, so far reaches thy unlimited self-consciousness, so far art thou God.'[48] But the genuine sense of infinity comes with consciousness. By definition, 'consciousness, in the strict proper sense, is identical with consciousness of the infinite'. 'The consciousness of the infinite is nothing else than the consciousness of the infinity of the consciousness; or, in the consciousness of the infinite, the conscious subject has for his object the infinity of his own nature.'[49]

In a very important little footnote on this page Feuerbach adds:

> The obtuse Materialist says: 'Man is distinguished from the brute *only* by consciousness—he is an animal with consciousness superadded'; not reflecting, that in a being which awakens to consciousness, there takes place a qualitative change, a differentiation of the entire nature.

It is in this sense that Feuerbach wants to say that it is religion that distinguishes man from the brute; not in the sense in which we talk about a religious person or a religious institution but in the vacuous sense in which even an atheist is, insofar as he is a conscious being, a religious being. It is in this context that we should read Marx's claim in *The German Ideology* that it is not religion that distinguishes us from the brutes but the fact that we produce, while in the 'Manuscripts' he still follows Feuerbach: 'The animal is immediately one with its life-activity... Conscious life-activity distinguishes man immediately from animal life-activity. It is just because of this that he is a species-being.'

The sense in which even the brute is infinite leads Feuerbach to the crucial claim that it is the species and not the individual which is infinite. The brute is not aware of any limitation but man is, though allegedly this rests on an error, partly on an intellectual and partly on a moral error:

> Every limitation of the reason, or in general of the nature of man, rests on a delusion, an error. It is true that the human being, as an individual, can and must—herein consists his distinction from the brute—feel and recognise himself to be limited; but he can become conscious of his limits, his finiteness, only because the perfection, the infinitude of his species, is perceived by him, whether as an object of feeling, of conscience, or of the thinking consciousness. If he makes his own limitations the limitations of the species, this arises from the mistake that he identifies himself immediately with the species—a mistake which is intimately connected with the individual's love of ease, sloth, vanity, and egoism. For a limitation which I know to be

merely mine humiliates, shames, and perturbs me. Hence to free myself from this feeling of shame, from this feeling of dissatisfaction, I convert the limits of my individuality into the limits of human nature in general.[50]

This imprecise sense of the infinitude of our species is replaced or specified a few pages later by the notion of our species as a collectivity of which the members complement each other in such a way that the whole conglomeration adds up to an infinity.

Each new man is a new predicate, a new phasis of humanity. As many as are the men, so many are the powers, the properties of humanity. It is true that there are the same elements in every individual, but under such various conditions and modifications that they appear new and peculiar. The mystery of the inexhaustible fullness of the divine predicates is therefore nothing else than the mystery of human nature considered as an infinitely varied, infinitely modifiable, but, consequently, phenomenal being.... One man is a distinguished musician, a distinguished author, a distinguished physician; but he cannot compose music, write books, and perform cures in the same moment of time. Time, and not the Hegelian dialectic, is the medium of uniting opposites, contradictories, in one and the same subject.[51]

The striking relationship of Feuerbach to Hess's message in *On the Essence of Money* comes out when we see how in the section on 'Christianity and Heathenism' Christianity is made into the villain of the piece. According to Feuerbach 'The ancients sacrificed the individual to the species; the Christians sacrificed the species to the individual.... [But] the Christians are distinguished from the heathens in this, that they immediately identify the individual with the species...'[52] To do this, for Feuerbach, is also a sign of egoism.

This leads us back to the passage I quoted from Hess's essay on money at the beginning of this section. He begins Part V of his essay, from which I quoted the passage, by saying: 'The individual elevated to an end and the species debased to a means: that is an absolute reversal of human and natural life.' Feuerbach's idiosyncratic notion of Christianity is Hess's model for his 'inverted' world. 'In theory the classical form of this inverted world is the Christian heaven.' What Hess did was not only to replace the Feuerbachian alienated essence, God, with money, but to argue for some sort of relationship between the two which is an embryonic version of economic base and theoretical superstructure. It is somewhat confused, but not more confused than Marx's similar double-decker view of economic and religious life in his second article 'On the Jewish Question'.

'Christianity is the theory, the logic of egoism. The classical basis of egoistic practice, on the other hand,' says Hess, 'is the modern Christian commercial world'. He also describes the practitioners of this modern Christian commercial world as 'Christian shopkeepers and Jewish Christians' for whom 'the individual is the end, while the life of the species is the means to life'. Not always, but often, the economic base takes primacy in our emancipation. 'We may emancipate ourselves theoretically from the inverted world-consciousness as much as we please, but so long as we have not escaped it in practice, we are obliged, as the proverb has it, to hunt with the pack.'

Although at the end of his second article 'On the Jewish Question' Marx also comes down on the side of the empirical base as the prime agency of change, he does so not for any sound or unsound sociological reasons but as a further move in the choreography of symbolic characters. He does it, as we shall see, to short-circuit the triadic progression of Judaism, Christianity and full emancipation. In the bulk of the article, however, the causal connections between the two levels run both ways, and we shall discover only a thin line of reason why this should be so.

'The Christian egoism of eternal bliss in its practical fulfilment necessarily becomes the material egoism of the Jew,' says Marx; 'heavenly need is converted into earthly need...' In the very next sentence, however, he reverses the direction: 'We do not explain the Jew's tenacity from his religion, but rather from the human basis of his religion, from practical need, from egoism.'[53] Hess, by replacing Feuerbach's egoistic Christian heaven with the world of egoistic Christian shopkeepers and 'Jewish Christians,' while keeping the Christian heaven as a sort of theoretical counterpart, with reciprocal relationships between the two, generated the theory of economic base and superstructure.

In order to see whether there are any important connections between Hess's views and Marx's two articles 'On the Jewish Question' we have to turn to the other topic we set out to investigate: the triadic pattern of original unity, separation and return. So far we have only investigated Feuerbach's argument for our divinity, and we saw that he operated with several notions of 'infinity' in arguing for the infinity of our species. Some of Feuerbach's arguments rested on what I called his 'episto-ontology'. Hess and Marx made substantial use of this theory in their characterisation of our alienated state. To conceive and to practise our relationship to each other and to the world as the relationship of private property is akin to perceiving the world and each other through the 'sense of having,' and this has drastic ontological consequences both for us and for the world we perceive.

Feuerbach then slides into another sense of the infinity of our species. This is not an infinity for which he argues by claiming that our object is infinite and we are what our object is. This other sense of the infinity of our species is the sense in which mankind as a whole makes up an infinitely perfect organic being where individual imperfections and limitations are compensated for by corresponding virtues in others. Christianity is then, oddly, taken to task for regarding *each individual* as somehow perfect and identical with the species, as against the proper view which is that each individual is a partial predicate of the perfect whole. This is then taken over by Hess as 'the inverted world' of the Christian heaven, as the theory, the logic of egoism. This egoistic heaven is realised in the individualist bourgeois world and in the political and human rights of individuals: '... the egoism of heaven was also achieved on earth... Practical egoism was sanctioned by declaring men to be single individuals, ... by proclaiming human rights, the rights of independent men, ... and so making out isolated persons to be the free, true and natural men.'[54] These are the rights that Marx criticised in his comments on the American constitution.

But Feuerbach is better known for the claim that God is our alienated, projected essence. We have seen however that as individuals we *have* to project the best of our nature onto our species. It would be 'egoistic' and 'Christian' to do otherwise. It was precisely because we tended to project our failings onto our species through claims like 'to err is only human,' that we obscured from ourselves the truth that on the contrary, the essential human nature, our species, is perfect. What Feuerbach considers to be wrong with the Christian theological view of God is that it is an *overprojection.* He does not express it in these words, but his point is that divinity is projected further than it should be. It is as if in casting our essence onto mankind it leapt off as in a game of ducks and drakes and ended up in heaven.

However, this looks like *overprojection* only if we take real individual human beings as our starting point. It did not look like overprojection to Feuerbach, Hess and Marx, but only as a simple projection or alienation of our essence; for to them the organic unity of mankind was the natural order of things. This natural unity which existed during a heathen or a primitive stage of human development was torn asunder by Christianity, and now we are waiting for the reunion which will result in unity on a higher level. We have seen this model already in Hess's *Sacred History of Mankind.*

As Hess presents it, in the first stage the human essence is united to us but in an undeveloped manner and scattered among our communities. The positive aspect of this stage is that we are united with our essence, though in an undeveloped form. Our essence however cannot develop or perfect itself in this stage. In the next stage our essence is liberated from its scattered embodiments and in its liberated form attains its perfection. It does this, however, outside ourselves, turning us into scattered individuals, into lifeless, alienated beings. In the third stage there are two possibilities. One is the communist, the other the anarchist model. Or, to give them philosophical nicknames, one could be called the Spinozistic model, in which each individual is taken up into one perfect being as an indivisible part of a whole, the other the Leibnizian model, where each individual is a complete monad mirroring all aspects of the universe. In both models the perfected essence is, as it were, re-contained, and this is the culmination of the whole development.

Hess's influence is not evident in the first of Marx's articles 'On the Jewish Question'. Marx in that article speaks of our human essence as being *political life*, rather than the Hessian *mutual exchange* between productive human beings. It is only in his notes on James Mill, which he wrote a few months after reading Hess's essay on money, that Marx himself spoke of the Hessian mutual exchange, rather than political life, while setting out his triadic model. Still later, in *The German Ideology*, Marx spoke of *productive forces* rather than political life or mutual exchange as being the true human essence.

In his first essay 'On the Jewish Question', Marx explicitly draws the analogy with the original content of the model which was the model of alienation in terms of religious consciousness. The first stage in this case is not located in prehistoric time but in feudal times:

> The old civil society had a *directly political* character, that is, the elements of civil life such as property, the family, the mode and manner of work, for example, were raised into elements of political life in the form of landlordism, estates and corporations... Thus the vital functions and conditions of civil society always remained political, but political in the feudal sense....

Then, in the next stage:

> The political revolution ... *abolished* the *political character of civil society.* It shattered civil society into its constituent elements—on the one hand *individuals* and on the other the *material* and *spiritual elements* constituting the vital content and civil situation of these individuals. It released the political spirit, which had been broken, fragmented and lost, as it were, in the various cul-de-sacs of feudal society. It gathered up this scattered spirit, liberated it from its entanglement with civil life, and turned it into the sphere of community, the *general* concern of the people ideally independent of these *particular* elements of civil life.[55]

We see here a vivid description of how the political element, which in the feudal society was scattered and fragmented but in a primitive way united to individuals and communities, was liberated and became universal, leaving behind the individuals now merely fragmented without the political element.

> Political emancipation is a reduction of man to a member of civil society, to an *egoistic independent* individual on the one hand and to a *citizen*, a moral person on the other.

Then, in the third stage:

> Only when the actual, individual man has taken back into himself the abstract citizen and in his everyday life, his individual work, and his individual relationships has become a *species-being*, only when he has recognised and organised his powers as *social* powers so that social force is no longer separated from him as political power, only then is human emancipation complete.[56]

Marx draws a clear parallel with the Feuerbachian model. In the second stage, the stage of political emancipation, when the political spirit is liberated, the political state does achieve its perfection and universality, but this perfected universality now stands over against us, as God stood over against us in our religious alienation. Some of the phrases in which Marx describes this do echo Hess, but, as I said, the content is not yet Hessian.

> Where the political state has achieved its full development, man leads a double life, a heavenly and an earthly life, not only in thought or consciousness but in *actuality*. In the *political community* he regards himself as a *communal being*; but in *civil society* he is active as a *private individual*, treats other men as means, reduces himself to a means, and becomes the plaything of alien powers. The political state is as spiritual in relation to civil society as heaven is in relation to earth. It stands in the same opposition to civil society and goes beyond it in the same way as religion goes beyond the limitations of the profane world, that is, by recognising, re-establishing, and necessarily allowing itself to be dominated by it.[57]

It is worth stopping to see what this triadic development which Marx presents to us means in practical terms. It is tempting to assume that since political emancipation was a good thing, however partial it was in its achievements, the next emancipation, social emancipation, will be an even better thing, completing what political emancipation left undone. The story however has a happy ending only in terms of our triadic sacred history. In real terms the picture looks quite different.

Before political emancipation the possession of various political rights depended on man's status, whether as peasant or lord, Jew or Christian, Catholic or Dissenter. In simple terms, political emancipation made all these and other differences irrelevant for the possession of political rights. It indeed separated, if one wants to put it that way, the political element from one's social life. The possession of political rights now does not depend on a man's being a Christian or a Jew, on being the lord of the manor or a pioneer settler in New England. The struggle for this ideal was and is long and it is a different struggle from the one which tries to eliminate or ameliorate our social disadvantages and problems. When the Jews in Germany, like Catholics and Dissenters in England, tried to gain political emancipation they did not regard their respective religions as disadvantages—like poverty—that they wanted to be rid of. They wanted political rights because they wanted to practise their religions unhindered by political restrictions. Marx's point about political emancipation was just the opposite of this: the fact that you are a Jew, a Christian, a Muslim or a believer in the Australian Aboriginal Dreamtime is taken by him to show that you are still a limited, partial being. Social emancipation is not a further improvement on political emancipation but is its reverse. It aims to eliminate that for the practice of which political emancipation was demanded. This applies not only to religion but to anything in which one has an interest and for the sake of which one would wish to form what Rousseau described as a 'partial association' such as a trade union or a students' or a writers' association. The claim that only those who possess the universal and true consciousness can express the will of society is already present here in the 'early,' supposedly 'humanist,' Marx. It is significant that Marx quotes Rousseau towards the end of this article:

> Whoever dares to undertake the founding of a nation must feel himself capable of *changing*, so to speak, *human nature* and *transforming* each individual who is in himself a complete but isolated whole, into a *part* of something greater than himself from which he somehow derives his life and existence, substituting a *limited* and *moral existence* for physical and independent existence. *Man* must be deprived of *his own powers* and given alien powers which he cannot use without the aid of others.[58]

The triadic sacred history is not empirical history, and the remedies it prescribes are not remedies of this world. We are asked to envisage a kind of substance which continues to be the same throughout its development; it attains perfection while separated from us, and the remedy for the imperfections of mankind is for us to be reunited with this perfected substance which is really our essence. This can be transcribed into Rousseau's language by saying that in our fragmented state we are like Rousseau's individuals following our particular wills, while when we are in the possession of our universal essence we express the General Will.

Hess envisages this essence almost literally as the organic life-giving and sustaining substance. 'Life is the exchange of productive life-activities… What is true of the bodies of small units is also true of large ... social ones.'[59] The social world is envisaged by Hess as a large organic body where mutual exchange is like the nervous system and the circulation of the blood in the body. When this essence is alienated and turns into money Hess describes it as if our blood had been solidified into money. 'Money is the congealed bloody sweat of the wretched who bring to the market their inalienable property, their most intrinsic powers, their life-activity itself, so as to exchange it for its *caput mortuum*, a so-called capital, and to dine like cannibals off their own fat... Because money, which we live off and for whose acquisition we work, is our flesh and blood, which, in its alienated form we must struggle for, grab and consume.'[60]

Here the organic analogy is no longer a tree. The dead branches of the tree could not be used as an image for the purpose Hess has in mind here. One might describe members of a movement one wants to be rid of as 'dead branches' to indicate that they should be left behind for good, and to reassure oneself that they are not living opponents who diminish the life of one's own movement. Now Hess wants to introduce an *evaluative* distinction in terms of what is 'natural' into a world the whole of which is supposed to be 'nature'. He achieves this by distinguishing between a living, organic body and dead matter. 'This general trash, money, is not an organic, living body. Yes, it is *supposed* to represent the social body, the organic species-life and our social relationships, but it *cannot* do this because by its very nature it is inorganic and without articulation or inner differentiation; it is nothing else but dead matter, a sum or number.' Part XII of *On the Essence of Money* is an especial elaboration of this theme. Here he also makes use of the Lockean notion of property as the extension of one's body, through the shades of meaning in the German words 'Eigenthum,' property, and 'eigenthümlich,' that which is proper. 'Money can never be *property* [Eigenthum] ... it must appear *im*proper to man [dem Menschen nicht Eigenthümlisches betrachten werden] ... The man of honour, the genuine man, is so wholly identified with his property, with his real social possessions, that he is fused into and absorbed in it as his soul is with his body.'[61] Part XII of Hess's *On the Essence of Money* reads more like the attitude of the gentry or of the aristocracy to the rising commercial world than the voice of someone from the next stage of historical development after capitalism.

The cruder expressions of organic analogies could not have been to Marx's taste, though there are echoes of such analogies in his early writings, and so there should be, because part of the evaluative force of Marx's writings does rest on what is presented as *natural*, living, organic and proper. Marx did, however, take over the real content of Hess's essay, which is that our essence is productive life-activity and exchange, and it is this which is alienated in money. So, within a few months in the development of Marx's thought, the role which he had assigned to political life was now assigned to productive life-activity, and in the second stage of the triadic development, in place of the Christian God, it is money rather than the perfected political state which dominates us. In his 'Comments on James Mill' Marx wrote:

> [T]he *mediating activity* or movement, the *human*, social act by which man's products mutually complement one another, is *estranged* from man and becomes the attribute of money, a *material thing* outside man ... It is clear that this *mediator* now becomes a *real God*, for the mediator is the *real power* over what it mediates to me.

We noted earlier, quoting from this same passage, that money is 'the alienated species-activity of man'.[62] Perhaps the neatest way Marx puts the case is in his Paris Manuscripts:

> The more the worker exerts himself, the more powerful becomes the alien objective world which he fashions against himself, the poorer he and his inner world become, the less there is that belongs to him. It is the same in religion. The more man attributes to God, the less he retains in himself.[63]

About two years later Marx assigned yet another content to our essential natures. It might look as though there is only a shift of emphasis from 'exchange of productive life-activities' to 'productive forces' but the shift indicates Marx's move away from his earlier philosophical positions and from his Young Hegelian friends. But although he moved to new ground in *The German Ideology*, the pattern of movement of productive forces still reflects the triadic pattern of sacred history. In this new version Marx discusses what he calls the 'natural division of labour': for one individual it could be, say, shoemaking, for another carpentry, and so on. The productive forces are themselves fragmented but united to individuals. Under the capitalist mode of production these productive forces are separated from the individuals and belong to them only insofar as they constitute property. Even in the case of the capitalists who alone are assumed to have property, this new relationship between individuals and productive forces no longer constitutes an organic unity; even capitalists are alienated because even their relationship to productive forces is now in the form of private property. This is then the second stage:

> Thus, on the one hand, we have a totality of productive forces, which have, as it were, taken on a material form and are for the individuals no longer the forces of the individuals but of private property ... On the other hand standing over against these productive forces, we have the majority of individuals from whom these forces have been wrested away, and who, robbed thus of all life-content, have become abstract individuals....[64]

In the third stage everything falls into place: 'the appropriation of a totality of instruments of production is, for this very reason, the development of a totality of capacities in the individuals themselves'. Furthermore, just as in the second stage the alienated essence has to be perfected before it can return, the productive forces have to be perfected in their alienated form in the capitalist mode of production, before their return in socialism.

Earlier in this section we had to consider various reasons for wanting to abolish private property and money, in order to distinguish them from the reasons Hess and Marx had for wanting to do so. Unless we understand these reasons we cannot fully appreciate that there are arguments for saying that nationalising the means of production results not only in practical changed social and economic arrangements but also in the arrival of an ontologically and morally new man on the stage of world history, though few would put it so eloquently as to say that it would result in 'the true resolution of the antagonism between men and nature and between man and man', and that 'it is the true resolution of the conflict between existence and essence, objectification and self-affirmation, freedom and necessity, individual and species. It is the riddle of history solved and knows itself as this solution.'[65]

Shortly I shall make a few critical comments about the whole logical scheme, especially about the logical blind-spot which allows us to assume that the power of a formal structure which received its original impetus from a specific content can be indefinitely transmitted to new and different contents which are successively put in place of that original content. First, however, I would like to make a few observations about the second of Marx's articles 'On the Jewish Question,' and again I limit my observations to further decipherment of the triadic model.

Carlebach's detailed arguments to show that Hess did not influence Marx's articles 'On the Jewish Question,' which rest mainly on the accurate dating of the compositions of the respective documents, could allow for an influence on the second of Marx's articles, for I can well imagine that Marx could have written such a short angry outburst in a matter of hours, and these hours could be fitted in somewhere between Marx's reading of Hess's essay on money and the publication of the *Jahrbücher.* What would be hard to comprehend, however, is how the reading of Hess could explain such an outburst.

I am fully aware that I am dealing with a very delicate problem here. At one extreme Marx's remarks could be interpreted as an uncharacteristic aberration on his part, and on the other they could explain most of his life's work. Luckily I have the excuse of restricting myself to the variations of the triadic pattern.[66] I shall concentrate on Bauer's claim that while the Jews have to take two steps to full human emancipation, the Christians need take only one. Bauer's actual argument is more subtle, but here we have a triadic progression, a progression that Hess himself lived out in his own life before he returned to Judaism.

Now if an orthodox Benedictine monk would read, say, Charles Reich's once-popular *The Greening of America* he would not be offended if he found that according to the arguments of that book he might belong to 'consciousness one' or 'consciousness two' and that he would have to take one (or two) steps to reach 'consciousness three'.[67] The reason why he would not be offended is that as long as he is an orthodox monk he would not think for a moment that this is the direction in which history is going and he would not think that he has to take any steps at all. My guess is that an orthodox Jew would similarly be unoffended by Bauer's argument and would not know what Bauer is talking about except as an odd theory; certainly he would not apply the invitation to himself to take two steps while he is outside the Young Hegelian conceptual framework. Bauer's suggestion could seem rather impertinent only to someone who is using the Young Hegelian road map to find his way in the world.

Whether Marx was offended or not, he certainly made a master-move to short-circuit Bauer's triadic development, even though his master-move created or reinforced a tragically misguided symbolism. In reply to Bauer, Marx asserts that Christianity did *not* overcome Judaism. Christianity is *not* the second stage. These are daring and revolutionary remarks in the context of the Young Hegelian conception of history—indeed in the whole Christian conception of history. But now comes the hitch. The Judaism which is still continuing is the world that Hess described as the world of 'our philistines, our Christian shopkeepers and Jewish Christians'. Hess uses startlingly gory language:

> Money is social blood, blood externalised, blood which has been shed. The Jews, whose world historical mission in the natural history of the world of social animals was to evolve the predator out of mankind, have at last fulfilled the work they were called to. The mystery of Judaism and Christianity is revealed in the modern Jewish-Christian world of shopkeepers.[68]

It is however on the structure of Marx's argument rather than merely on his language that we might detect some Hessian influence. After eliminating Bauer's three stages and indeed the Christian view (before Joachim added the third stage) that Christianity overcame Judaism, Marx recreates the second stage of the triad in the form in which we have met it in Hess. The reason why Christianity could not overcome Judaism was that Christianity was 'too *noble*, too spiritual, to eliminate the crudeness of practical need except by elevating it into the blue.' Judaism whose essence is practical need is still continuing in our civil society; civil society is its continuation. Thus we get the double-decker universe we considered earlier. 'Christianity is the sublime thought of Judaism, and Judaism is the common practical application of Christianity.' As it should be in the second stage, the ideal is perfected: this application of Christianity 'could only become universal after Christianity as a religion *par excellence* had *theoretically* completed the alienation of man from himself and from nature. Only then could Judaism attain universal dominion and convert externalised man and nature into *alienable* and saleable objects subservient to egoistic need, dependent on bargaining.'

The content of the triadic model in Marx's second essay 'On the Jewish Question' differs markedly from that in the first of his articles. Although Hess's influence is not as clear as it is in his notes on Mill,

Hess's gruesome imagery and his double-decker triadic pattern might
have given hints to Marx as to how to tackle Bauer whose views preoccupied him at the time. Not that Marx copied Hess. It was Feuerbach,
not Hess, who wrote that 'Judaism is worldly Christianity; Christianity, spiritual Judaism,' and that 'Christianity has spiritualised the egoism of Judaism into subjectivity'.[69] If Hess had an influence it was in
providing a pattern within the choreography of symbolism. To fully
appreciate that the second of Marx's essays just as much as the first is
constructed on a triadic pattern but with a different content we should
observe that the third stage, the resolution, is again expressed in terms
of overcoming the conflict 'between the individual sensuous existence
of man and his species-existence' by transcending it.

> When society succeeds in transcending the *empirical* essence of
> Judaism—bargaining and all its conditions—the Jew becomes *impos-*
> *sible* because his consciousness no longer has an object, the subjec-
> tive basis of Judaism—practical need—is humanised, and the conflict
> between the individual sensuous existence of man and his species-
> existence is transcended. The *social* emancipation of the Jew is the
> *emancipation of society from Judaism.*[70]

In this strange last sentence, 'Jew' stands for the actual Jew, and 'Judaism'
for the universalised egoism that has been realised in civil society and
idealised in Christianity. Marx talks here about the religious nature of
the Jew and about the consciousness which is a reflection of the conditions of civil society. This consciousness will disappear when that of
which it is a reflection is transformed. According to the logic of this
model, however, this reflection should be Christianity and not the Jewish
religion, which according to Marx was always practice, not theory,
and is now continuing in civil society. Indeed, as we know, he will talk
of Christianity and our whole intellectual life, and it is in its later version that we meet the familiar tag that 'religion will wither away' and
that all our intellectual life is but a reflection of our economic base.
Much has been written by some historians and sociologists taking this
view as their scientific theory of history. Marx never made this view
clear, and never gave arguments for it, but here we can see its origin.
    I described Marx's move in his article as a master-move, but it is
so only insofar as it was a transformation of Bauer's three stages into

the three stages of Hess's and his own sacred history. Otherwise I did not mean it as a word of praise. Sometimes it is argued in Marx's favour that he did not talk about the real actual Jews but about a type, but this is precisely what is wrong with what he does. But even by the standard of his own conceptual pattern and symbolism it is a confused piece of work.[71] My main critical comment, however, is not about the confused version of the conceptual framework we have been surveying but about its purest form.

The original use of the alienation model, or the use which gave it its power, was a certain creation story combined with a theodicy explaining the existence of evil and imperfection. Creation is the externalised objectified Deity, and the imperfection of creation is gradually eliminated by the gradual struggle of this alienated essence to become again what it is supposed to be, divine. This optimistic view of progress and history makes sense only if it is rationality which tries to realise itself by the gradual elimination of contradictions in progressive stages. Only in connection with what is rational can we talk of contradictions, and only that which wants to achieve rationality wants to do so by eliminating its contradictions. Here God's relation to nature and history is God's relation to Himself in an externalised manner. Now already the Feuerbachian version of this story should not make sense. The feeling that it does make sense needs to be analysed. If for the sake of argument we suppose that God made us, then reversing the argument we suppose that we, on the contrary, made God, it is clear that the suppositions of making, the makings in question, are very different. The claim that God created us is a claim about a real movement, about the coming into being of some objective entity, the world. The claim that we created God is not a claim to the effect that we brought into being a real existing entity; rather it is the denial of the existence of a supposed entity. By eliminating an 'alienated essence' we are not re-absorbing into ourselves a really-existing essence, but are eliminating an imaginary object; and we are left as we were before, only now without thinking about an imaginary object. The claim that 'God is really man' may be true or false but, if it makes sense at all and is not just a meaningless metaphor, it makes sense only if there is a Divine Being who either chose to become human in a special act of Incarnation, or happened to become human through alienating Himself. If, however, the existence of a supposed Divine Being is a mere stage in the development of our religious consciousness, then the claim 'God is really man' is a figurative and misleading way of denying His existence, and all the statement means is that 'man is really man'.

If imperfect beings project a perfect Being above themselves, then it is true that one has to do something practical to cure the imperfection. What certainly does not follow however is that the cure will result in perfect beings. It is a fallacy to suppose that a person who is cured of imperfection will be as perfect as the Being that he was imagining as a result of his illness. Someone with distorted vision who keeps seeing giants will not himself become a giant if we restore his proper eyesight. He will have his eyesight corrected, and stop seeing giants. The man might even become more wretched and full of *angst*, having lost his imaginary giants whom he also imagined to be his protectors. For better or for worse, however, one can see how Feuerbach's recommendation to us to rid ourselves of the idols that dominate us would have some effect, precisely because they are imagined idols. Here I am myself trying to get rid of a conceptual model that holds some of us captive. If however we replace our imagined idols with money, steel works, coal mines and factories, then however much it is true that we have to manage them better than we do, our triadic model cannot cope with them.

The curious logic of preserving the power of the story when the original content from which it derived its power no longer exists, is beautifully illustrated by a *Peanuts* cartoon. Lucy and Linus are looking at something which is lying on the ground. 'Well, look here!', says Lucy, 'A big yellow butterfly! It's unusual to see one this time of year unless, of course, he flew up from Brazil ... I'll bet that's it! They do that sometimes, you know ... They fly up from Brazil, and they ...' 'This is no butterfly ... This is a potato chip!' interrupts Linus. 'Well, I'll be! So it is! I wonder how a potato chip got all the way up here from Brazil?'[72]

Feuerbach once remarked that '"the Absolute Spirit" is the "deceased spirit" of theology which as a spectre haunts the Hegelian philosophy'. Indeed the 'deceased spirit' still haunts Hess's and Marx's systems, as the idea that big yellow butterflies come from Brazil still haunts Lucy when she is confronted with a potato chip.

Moses Hess:
On the Essence of Money

Commerce has set the mark of selfishness,
The signet of its all-enslaving power
Upon a shining ore, and called it gold:
Before whose image bow the vulgar great,
The vainly rich, the miserable proud,
The mob of peasants, nobles, priests, and kings,
And with blind feelings reverence the power
That grinds them to the dust of misery.
But in the temple of their hireling hearts
Gold is a living god ...
All things are sold: the very light of Heaven
Is venal; earth's unsparing gifts of love,
The smallest and most despicable things
That lurk in the abysses of the deep,
All objects of our life, even life itself,
And the poor pittance which the laws allow
Of liberty, the fellowship of man,
Those duties which his heart of human love
Should urge him to perform instinctively,
Are bought and sold as in a public mart
Of undisguising selfishness, that sets
On each its price, the stamp-mark of her reign.
Even love is sold; the solace of all woe
Is turned to deadliest agony, old age
Shivers in selfish beauty's loathing arms ...
But hoary-headed Selfishness has felt
Its death-blow, and is tottering to the grave:
A brighter morn awaits the human day,
When every transfer of earth's natural gifts

Shall be a commerce of good words and works;
When poverty and wealth, the thirst of fame,
The fear of infamy, disease and woe,
War with its million horrors, and fierce hell
Shall live but in the memory of Time,
Who, like a penitent libertine, shall start,
Look back, and shudder at his younger years.

(Shelley: *Queen Mab*)

I

Life is the exchange of productive life-activities. The *body* of every living thing, plant, animal or man, as the *medium* through which the productive life-activity of that thing is *exchanged*, is its indispensable means of existence, the *medium of its life*; consequently those parts of the body that are the centres of exchange are its noblest and most indispensable organs, as for instance the brain and the heart. What is true of the bodies of small units is also true of large, and equally true of inanimate celestial bodies, so-called, as of conscious, social ones. The atmosphere of the Earth is the indispensable medium for the exchange of earthly products, it is the earthly life-element; the sphere in which men exchange their social life-activities—i.e. intercourse in society— is the indispensable social life-element. Here men relate as conscious and consciously acting beings to the sphere of exchange of their social life, just as they relate unconsciously, as bodily units, to the sphere of exchange of their bodily life-activities, to the atmosphere of the Earth. If separated from the medium of their social life they can no more live than they are able to exist physically if separated from the medium of their physical life, that is, if the life-giving air is denied to them. They are related to the whole social body as the individual members and organs are related to the individual body. They perish if they are separated from each other. Their real life consists only in the mutual exchange of their productive life-activity, only in co-operation, only in their connection with the whole social body.

II

The reciprocal exchange of individual life-activity, intercourse, the mutual arousal of individual forces: such co-operation is the real essence of individuals, their real potentiality. They cannot realise their powers, cannot utilise, actualise, manifest or bring them to life at all—or if they have done this, will again find them dying—so far as they do not mutually exchange their life-activities in intercourse with fellows of the same community, or members of the same body. As the terrestrial atmosphere is the workshop of the Earth, so the intercourse of men is the human workshop wherein individual men are able to realise and manifest their life or powers. The more vigorous their intercourse the stronger also their productive power and so far as their intercourse is restricted their productive power is restricted likewise. Without their life-medium, without the exchange of their particular powers, individuals do not *live*. The intercourse of men does not originate from their essence; it *is* their real essence, and is indeed both their theoretical essence, their true life-consciousness, and also their practical real life-activity. Thinking and acting come into being only through intercourse, through the co-operation of individuals—and what we speak of mystically as 'spirit' is in fact this life-giving air, this workshop, this co-operation. Every free activity—and there is no other but free activity, because what a being does not do from himself, that is freely, is *no* act at all, or at least not his own but another's—every real life-activity, therefore, either practical or theoretical, is an act of the species, a co-operation among different individuals. Such co-operation first realises the productive power, and hence the real essence of each individual.

III

The essence of man, man's intercourse, develops like every other, in a historical process through many struggles and disturbances. Like everything authentic, the true nature, the co-operation of individuals constituting the human species has a history of its development or origin. The social world, the organising of men, has its own natural history, its genesis, its creation story, like every other world, and like every other organic body. The natural history of mankind however began when the Earth's natural history had come to completion, when the Earth, that is, had already brought into existence its last and highest organism, the human body, and with it the sum-total of its bodily organisms. The natural history of the Earth, which in the opinion of geologists probably lasted several million years, stopped and came to a close several thousands of years ago; the Earth is complete. On the other hand the natural history of mankind has not yet come to an end; we are still immersed in the struggle. Mankind is not yet completed but it is close to its completion. We already see in the distance the vaunted land of organised mankind; already we can reach it with our eyes, this promised land to which all man's previous history points, though we cannot yet set foot upon it. It is false to see in the completion of nature's history, in the end of man's creation-history, the end, the 'doomsday,' of mankind itself: an optical illusion which has ever imposed itself upon those who could think of no reality save the existing one—though that did not satisfy them and they therefore wished for another—and who therefore saw in the downfall of their evil world and the coming of a better, the end of this world and the beginning of the next. So likewise are they victims of the 'doomsday' illusion who expect no better afterworld, but also no better world than that now existing—who accept the Christian dogma of the imperfection of this world, but without the consolation of a hereafter—who dream of infinite progress, but suppose no other end or completion for it save death, or some lifeless phantom they call 'spirit'. The philosophers, likewise, are among those who can think of no other reality than the present evil one— are among the antediluvian creatures who see in the downfall of the old world their own destruction, and nothing but death in the completed organism of mankind—because a correct instinct tells them that they themselves form an integral part of the old, decaying, evil reality. If the monsters before the flood—which were spawned by the Earth, while still in its 'raw youth,' before it had ripened and reached maturity—if these monsters had possessed consciousness they would have argued and speculated precisely in the manner of our philosophers, theologians and priests. They too would not have believed in any higher creations, in any completed product of Earth, in any man; they too would have fancied they saw in the destruction of the primeval fauna the approaching destruction of the world. However, just as the completed pattern of Earth makes, not the end, but rather the beginning of its real life, so the completed pattern of mankind, its perfection that is, makes, not the end of man, but rather his true beginning.

IV

Human development, its genetic or natural history, the *story of the creation* of man, requires as a necessity its mutual *destruction*, proceeding from the contradiction of its *intercourse* in the context of its *isolation*. The developmental history of human nature or of mankind appears primarily as a self-destruction of this nature. Men were already sacrificing themselves to their heavenly and earthly gods long before there was a heavenly or earthly, religious or political *economy* to justify it. They destroyed each other because at first they subsisted only as isolated individuals, because they could not co-operate in harmony as members of one and the same organic whole, as members of mankind. If an organised exchange of products, organised activity, the co-operation of all, had already existed beforehand, then naturally there would have been no necessity for men to wrestle or work for their mental and material needs as isolated individuals, by their own efforts, with brute force and cunning deceit; they would not have needed to seek their mental and material goods outside of themselves; they could have developed themselves through themselves, that is, could have exercised their capacities in common. But this would have amounted to saying that human beings would have come into existence as developed human beings, and in this case they would not have had to go through their development history. In other words: if mankind had not begun with isolated individuals it would not have needed to fight out its egoistic struggles for the goods that were still alien and external to them. By now, at the end of this brutal struggle for our nature, once that nature—in theory anyway—has been formed, we can at least think of a human society *without* self-destruction and carry it into practice, a rational, organic human society, with manifold, harmoniously co-operative forms of production, with manifold, organised spheres of activity, which would correspond to the varying proclivities, the manifold activities of men, so that every mature individual can freely exercise his capacities and talents in society, as calling and inclination suggest. This we can do now; for human capacity, human nature (production and dissemination of the propensity to consume products, for the sake of further production) are now developed to excess. The forces of nature no longer confront man as alien and hostile; he knows and uses them for human purposes. Men themselves draw daily closer together. The bounds of space and time, of religion and nationality, the bounds of individuality, are falling asunder, to the horror of narrow minds and the joy of all men of good will! We have only to hail the dawn of freedom, to banish the guardians of night, and we can all clasp hands in rejoicing. Yes, now man has come of age; nothing prevents him from entering at last into his heritage, the fruit of so many millennia of slavish toil and primitive endeavour! His present misery is indeed the most striking proof of this; for it is not a consequence of want, but of superfluity, in productive capacity. England is pressing into the Earth's remotest corners to seek consumers; but already, or before long, the whole Earth will be too small a market for her products, which continue to multiply in geometrical progression, while her consumers increase only in arithmetical progression, so that Malthus' theory—whereby consumers grow in geometrical, and production in arithmetical progression—is really the very opposite of the truth. Yes, now indeed are men ripe for the full enjoyment of their freedom, or their life. This was not so in the beginning. The human productive powers had first to be developed, the human essence evolved. At first there were merely raw individuals, simple elements of mankind, who had either not yet come into mutual contact and drew their sustenance and bodily needs directly from the earth as plants do, or had made only such contact with each other as to join forces in the brutish warfare of animals. Hence the first form of product-exchange, of intercourse, could only be murder-for-gain, the first form of human activity the labour of the slave. On this basis of historic right, as yet uncontested, no organised exchange could take shape, and only a bartering of products was possible—which was what in fact occurred. The laws that rest on this historical basis have merely regulated murder-for-gain and slavery, have merely erected into a rule or principle what at first occurred by chance, without consciousness or will. Past history till now is no more than a history of the regulation, justification, execution and universalisation of murder-for-gain and slavery. We shall show in what follows how we have at last reached the point where we all, without exception and at every moment, traffic in our activities, our productive powers, our potentialities and our very selves; how the cannibalism, mutual murder and slavery with which human history started have been elevated into a principle—and how out of this general exploitation and universal vassalism the organic community can first be born.

V

The individual elevated to an end and the species debased to a means: that is an absolute reversal of human and natural life. Man consciously sacrifices his individual life for the life of the species if there is a conflict between the two. Even the as yet unthinking creatures, the animals who only feel, forget their instinct of self-preservation, their drive to self-maintenance, if it clashes with their drive to self-propagation, their nature as a species or productive instinct. Love, wherever it may appear, is mightier than egoism. The hen takes up a quite unequal fight if it has to defend its chickens from an attack. Cats will allow themselves to starve if they must, in order to satisfy their sexual desires, or in their sorrow when wicked men take away their kittens. Nature is always concerned with the preservation of the species, with the real life-activity. Individuals always die in the natural order of things and begin to do so, indeed, the moment they have ceased to be able to reproduce. For many members of the animal kingdom, the very day of their mating is the day of their death. In man, who can also do service to his species by means of thought, feeling and will, the gradual decline of his mental powers is the sure presage of his natural death. On this order of things is based the natural world-outlook which sees life itself in the species and regards the individual only as the means to life. In the state of egoism, however, the inverted world-outlook rules because it is itself the state of an inverted world. For our Philistines, our Christian shopkeepers and Jewish Christians, the individual is the end, while the life of the species is the means to life. They have created for themselves a world apart. In theory the classical form of this inverted world is the Christian heaven. In the real world the individual dies; in the Christian heaven he goes on living; in real life the species is active in the individual and by means of him; in heaven the essence of the species, God, lives outside individuals, and they are not the medium whereby God works, whereby the essence of the species lives, but on the contrary, it is individuals who live by means of God. Here the essence of the species is reduced to a means for the life of the individual; the Christian 'self' needs his God, needs Him for his own individual existence, for his holy immortal soul, for his spiritual salvation! 'If I did not hope to partake in immortality, I should care nothing for God, nor for all the creeds.' These few words, uttered by a man of great piety, contain the whole essence of Christianity. Christianity is the theory, the logic of egoism. The classic basis of egoistic practice, on the other hand, is the modern Christian commercial world—another heaven, another fiction, another imagined, suppositious benefit to the life of the individual, sprung from the morbid egoistic craziness of corrupt mankind. The individual, who does not wish to live through himself for the species, but through the species for himself alone, has also to create for himself in practice an inverted world. Practically, therefore, in our commercial world, as it is in theory in the Christian heaven, the individual is the end, the species only the means of life. Here likewise the life of the species is not at work in the individual and by means of him; here, just as in heaven, it is placed outside individuals and reduced to a means for them; here, in fact, it is money. What God is for its theoretical life, money is for the practical life of this inverted world: the alienated potentiality, the bartered life-activity of men. Money is human value numerically expressed—it is the seal of our slavery, the indelible brand of our servitude—men who can buy and sell themselves are in fact slaves. Money is the congealed bloody sweat of the wretched who bring to the market their inalienable property, their most intrinsic powers, their life-activity itself, so as to exchange it for its *caput mortuum*, a so-called capital, and to dine like cannibals off their own fat. And all of us are wretches such as these! We may emancipate ourselves theoretically from the inverted world-consciousness as much as we please, but so long as we have not escaped it in practice, we are obliged, as the proverb has it, to hunt with the pack. Yes, we are obliged continually to alienate our nature, our life, our own free life-activity in order to sustain our miserable existence. We continually purchase our individual existence by the loss of our freedom. And of course it is not just we proletarians but also we capitalists who make up these wretches who suck their own blood and feed upon themselves. We none of us are able to live our lives freely, to create our work for each other—all of us are able merely to eat up our lives, to prey simply upon each other, if we do not want to starve. Because money, which we live off and for whose acquisition we work, is our own flesh and blood, which, in its alienated form we must struggle for, grab and consume. All of us—and we should not hide it from ourselves—are cannibals, predators, vampires. And remain so as long as we are not all working for each other, but are each obliged to fend for ourselves.

VI

According to the principles of political economy, money is held to be the universal means of exchange, and hence the medium of life, the power of man, the real force of production, the real treasure of mankind. If this externalised treasure really corresponded to the internal one, every man would be worth just so much as the amount of cash or credit he possesses—and as a consistent theology values a man solely according to the measure of his orthodoxy, so a consistent economics ought to value him only according to the weight of his moneybags. In fact, however, neither economics nor theology cares anything about human beings. Political economy is the science of the earthly acquisition of goods, as theology is the science of their acquisition in heaven. But men are not commodities! For the strictly 'scientific' economists and theologians people have no value at all. But where these two sacred sciences are applied, in the practice of our modern world of commerce, man is indeed valued only according to his moneybag— just as in the practice of the Christian Middle Ages, which to some extent still flourishes, he was valued according to his profession of faith.

VII

Money is the product of men mutually alienated, of the externalised man. Money is not 'precious metal'—we have now more paper money, state- and bank-notes than metal coinage—money is what does duty for human productive power, the real life-activity of mankind. Capital, therefore, according to the economists' definition, is accumulated, stored up labour—and insofar as production comes about through the exchange of products, money is exchange value. What cannot be exchanged, cannot be sold, has no value. In that men can no longer be sold, they are now not worth a rap—though they certainly are so insofar as they sell or 'commodify' themselves. The economists maintain, indeed, that a man's value increases to the extent that he can no longer be sold and is therefore obliged to sell himself in order to live, and concludes from this that the 'free' man is 'worth' more than the slave. This is quite correct. Hunger is a stronger motive to work than the whip of the slave-owner, and avarice is a stronger incentive for the private owner to do his utmost than the gracious smile of the satisfied master. What the economists forget, however, is that the 'value' of 'freedom' must again decline, the more widespread it becomes. The more 'free' men flock into slave-labour, the more available, and thus the cheaper, they are or become. The bane of competition lowers the price of 'free' men—and the truth is that on the basis of egoistic private ownership there is no other way of increasing their 'value' again but by the re-establishment of slavery.

VIII

Ancient slavery is the natural form of the social order based on murder and robbery; it is also its most human form. It is natural and human to allow oneself to be sold only against one's will. It is, however, unnatural and inhuman to sell oneself freely. Only the modern commercial world, through Christianity, the epitome of the unnatural, has been able to attain to this supreme degree of baseness, unnaturalness and inhumanity. Man had first to learn to despise human life in order to cast it freely away from him. He had first to cease regarding real life and freedom as priceless values, in order that he might offer them for sale. Mankind had first to go through the school of serfdom so as to pay homage, in principle, to slavery. — Our modern traders are worthy descendants of the medieval serfs, as these latter, the Christian slaves, were worthy descendants of the pagan slaves. As medieval serfdom is ancient slavery raised to a higher power, so the modern Christian commercial world is a similarly enhanced form of medieval serfdom. The ancients had not yet turned the alienation of human life into Christian self-alienation, were not yet conscious of the decadence of human society, had not yet made a principle out of this fact. The ancients were naive; they accepted uncritically what lay in the nature of the world they moved in (and in which we still move today)—the alienation of man. As religion took over from the ancients the human sacrifices it demanded, so politics did the same, without trying to provide any 'scientific' justification for this barbarism, or to excuse it hypocritically to their still unawakened consciences. — When the latter awoke, Christianity came into existence. Christianity is the sophistical expression of depraved mankind's awakened bad conscience, the desire to be freed from its reproaches. But the Christian does not free himself from remorse by freeing the wretched of the earth from their misery; he persuades himself rather, that this human wretchedness is not crazy but right and proper, that real life is by right the external form of life, that the alienation of life is the normal condition of the world as such. — The Christian distinguishes between the 'inner' and the 'outer' man, that is, between the real and the unreal. The human soul, that is, the remainder left over when everything corporeal is taken away—and this remnant is invisible because it is actually nothing—the human soul is the sacred and inalienable life of man; the human body on the other hand is an unholy, bad, contemptible, outer and therefore alienable life. The unreal man cannot sell himself as a slave; but the real man is in any case a depraved being, so he not only can but ought to be wretched; the poor shall inherit the Kingdom of Heaven. — The immediate consequence of this teaching was to leave the reality of slavery as it was, and even to regard it as justified, save only that it was no longer men but mere bodies that were sold—a great step forward—but a step yet further into the morass. Once the principle of saleability had triumphed in this fashion, the road was open for universal serfdom, for the general, mutual and free self-bartering of present-day commerce.

IX

The essence of the modern commercial world, money, is the realised essence of Christianity. The mercenary state, the so-called 'free' state, is the promised Kingdom of God, the commercial world the promised kingdom of heaven—just as, conversely, God is but idealised capital, and heaven merely the commercial order in theoretical form. — Christianity discovered the principle of saleability. It did not yet worry, however, about the application of its principle. Since reality for it was evil and transitory, it could have no concern for reality at all, and so none for the realisation of its principle. It was therefore quite indifferent whether people really became alienated, that is, became serfs, bodily slaves. It left this 'outside' practice to the 'outside,' 'worldly' powers. And so long as these too were still in a state of theoretical alienation, were more or less in the grip of Christian belief, and so long as they had not yet arrived at practical Christianity, the real serfdom in spite of its theoretical justification remained something purely accidental. Christianity did not in reality change anything in classical slavery to begin with; the existing slavery remained—it was merely enriched with a principle. A new principle, however, is not yet a new existence, a distinction with which our newest Christians, the most recent philosophers, are very familiar. Can anyone, indeed, be surprised at such acumen? If only a theory is given—and Christianity, like philosophy, has merely provided a theory—then its relationship to the *praxis* of life becomes a matter of indifference; the theory is a 'truth' which is taught and learned, offered and accepted 'for its own sake,' not for the sake of its application. For this reason in the Middle Ages as in the ancient world, it was just as much a matter of accident whether a man actually became a slave or remained free in the 'real world'. The difference between medieval serfdom and ancient slavery lies only in the idea involved. In their reality on the other hand there was not a hair's breadth of difference between them. Neither was better or worse. Neither in the Middle Ages nor in antiquity could one lay claim to real freedom on the ground of one's nature—for in antiquity they did not recognise this nature and for this reason did not acknowledge it, while in the Middle Ages the nature of man was acknowledged only in 'spirit' and in 'truth,' in the divine hereafter, and for this other reason did not acknowledge it in real life;—but still there was no more intention in the Middle Ages than there was in antiquity to enslave man as such, that is, to turn every man into a real slave. Thus in both cases there was *some* freedom; in the Middle Ages as in antiquity, there were *in fact*, that is, *accidentally*, besides those 'certain' people who, as Aristotle thought, were 'born' to be slaves, also 'certain' others who were born free, 'well-born,' 'very well-born,' 'of noble birth'. Thus serfdom was still in reality the natural form of the order based on robbery and murder. Medieval serfdom in reality was not a self-alienation of men, nor could it have been so; for man cannot turn himself directly into a natural serf on his own account. Man's immediate life, his natural body, can be appropriated only by other men. Direct serfdom required other people who were not serfs. The medieval serf could not possess serfs, he had nothing—he did not possess even his own body as his property—so how could he possess other bodies? Had Christians cared about the legislation of this world, they must soon have seen that 'worldly' circumstances still contradicted their principle, that far too much 'naturalness' still held sway there. But they did not worry about this since Christians were *theoretical* egoists. But when in course of time people became enlightened and practical, and wanted to realise Christianity also in this world, when they sought to apply 'pure' Christianity and to realise its 'idea', they then came to see that the 'spiritual' freedom and equality proclaimed by Christianity was still not realised at all. In order to carry the clever distinction between body and soul into life as well, one had to go about it very much more cleverly than the purely theoretical egoists had done. One had to find a form of social life in which the alienation of men was effected just as universally as in the Christian heaven. Free disembodied spirits had also to appear in this world—a truly colossal absurdity, but one which the cleverness of our modern, Christian-educated legislators and political economists has brought into existence. Christianity is realised in the contemporary commercial world.

X

The modern legislators, who as enlightened and practical Christians could not rest content with legislating for the next world but wanted to realise the Christian world, their heaven, on earth, had to make the spirits of heaven appear in this world. Such a conjuring of ghosts was not witchcraft however; everything was already prepared for it and the modern legislators, though no sorcerers, were thus able to bring about this piece of magic conjuring act. All that was needed was to canonise and sanctify the already available private man of the medieval bourgeois society which had evolved from serfdom—to sanctify this abstract 'personality,' this dead remnant of the real man, who had stripped and divested himself of everything belonging to the life of his species, abstracted it and offered it in heaven, i.e. in theory, to God, and on earth, i.e. in practice, to money. Thus was the neuter, emasculated individual of the Christian heaven made real also in this world. In other words: it was only necessary for what had already happened to *theoretical* life from the point of view of religion and theology to happen to *practical* life from the point of view of politics and economics—it was necessary only to elevate into a principle not merely the theoretical but also the practical alienation of life; and the egoism of heaven was also achieved on earth. This in fact was done. Practical egoism was sanctioned by declaring men to be single individuals, by asserting abstract bare persons to be the true men, by proclaiming human rights, the rights of independent men, and hence alleging men's independence of each other, their separation and individualisation, to be the essence of life and freedom, and so making out isolated persons to be the free, true and natural men. These monads, naturally, could no longer enter into traffic with each other, which in our kind of trade, based as it is on robbery and murder, amounts to this: they are no longer to be brought to market to be bought and sold directly. This direct trading, this immediate dealing in men, this outright slavery and serfdom had to be abolished, for otherwise people would have still depended on each other;

but in place of immediate serfdom there had to be a mediate kind; in place of serfdom in fact there had to be serfdom in principle, which makes all men free and equal, i.e. isolated and done to death. — With the abolition of actual slavery, it was not murder and robbery that were abolished, but direct murder and robbery. That which now did away with ancient and medieval slavery was nothing else but the application of logical egoism. Only now could the principle of slavery—the externalisation of human nature by the isolation of individuals and the degradation of this nature into a means for their existence—be generally realised in life. The thoroughgoing egoism of the modern commercial world abolishes all direct relationships, all direct life, in theory as in practice, in this world as in the next, and permits this life only as a means to private existence. But where all human relationships, all human activity, is directly abolished and can still be exercised only as a means to egoistic existence; where from the most natural love, from the relationship of the sexes, to the exchange of ideas in the whole cultural world, nothing can be done without money; where there are no other practical men but those who are cashed and traded; where every heartbeat has first to be turned into money before it can come to life: there the heavenly souls wander on earth, there the dehumanised man exists also in this world, there the 'blessedness' of the next world has become the 'good fortune' of this, there theoretical egoism has become practical egoism, the mere fact of actual slavery has been elevated into a principle and is systematically put into effect.

XI

The distinction between private man and member of the community, between domestic and public life, has always existed in fact, for it is nothing else but the distinction between person and property. The abstract 'personality,' separated from all the means of his existence, this bodiless and lifeless ghost, has been seeking his lost body from the beginning of history, and has sought it at times in the *heavenly* otherworld, in God, the purveyor of ever-distant, never-attainable blessedness, and at times in the *earthly* otherworld, in money, the purveyor of ever-distant, otherworldly, never-attainable happiness. This separation of person and property, which has existed in fact ever since religion and politics have existed, needed only to be recognised in principle and to be sanctioned, and it was thereby asserted that money alone was the essence of the community or the state, while man was merely its paid servant, and indeed a mere ragged purse-bearer. In the modern state, therefore, not man but the moneybag is the lawgiver, and just as the private man replaces the holy 'personality,' so the functionary replaces the holy 'property'. Just as in old times the legislators received their authority from God, so they now receive it from property, from money. The sanctity of abstract 'property' divorced from persons and people presupposes no less the sanctity of the abstract, naked, empty 'personality,' divorced from its property, as this latter presupposes the former. The abstract, alienated, external and alienable 'property' can only appear in its holy purity, separated from everything human, if 'personality' likewise appears in its holy purity, separated, that is, from all genuine property. So a sharp boundary-line was drawn round every individual, within which the holy personality was to be located. These holy personalities are the blessed spirits of heaven walking on earth; they are the bodies of these shadows—their boundary-line is their outer skin. The objective atmosphere of men, however, which in heaven is God, the superhuman good, is on earth the extra-human, non-human, tangible good, the object, the property, the product divorced from the producer, its creator, the abstract essence of relationships: *money*. This is how the 'person' came to be declared holy, not indeed because it is a human essence—on the contrary its essence is completely separated from it; in egoism the universally human is left out of account—but because it is an 'I'. — On the other hand 'property' came to be declared holy, again not because it is human—for it is indeed only an object and not even a superhuman one, like God in heaven, but something extrahuman—it is holy, rather, because it is the means of egoistic existence, because the 'I' uses it (in practice the egoism of the next world becomes tangible). But egoism, which seeks to preserve only the naked person, removed from or independent of its natural and human environment, separated from its physical and social atmosphere, and endeavours to maintain that person in a lifeless, inorganic, inactive, stony existence—egoism which cannot feel beyond its outer skin and cannot see beyond its nose—this narrow-minded essence is in fact destructive of the real life of the individual himself. It simply did not occur to the wise Christian lawgivers that one cannot separate man from the atmosphere in which he breathes without miserably suffocating him in his isolation; that his natural or physical life includes not only what lies within the boundaries of his body which they had drawn, but the whole of nature; that his spiritual or social life-activity includes not only the products, thoughts and feelings that remain within him, but all the products of social life. It did not occur to them that the man cut off from his environment is an emasculated, flayed being with no more life in him than raw meat with the hide off, or a breathing creature deprived of air. They took all life-giving social atmosphere away from man, and left it to him instead to create a vapour around himself, and if possible to preserve himself with money, the materialised Christian spirit of God. And this spiritualised holy corpse they declared to be the free man, the untouchable, holy, infinite personality! — What do these holy corpses do in order to preserve themselves? They try to take away from each other this spirit, their discarded essence, without which they would rot; they rob each other in order not to be without property—they murder each other to live, that is, in order to exist in misery. Thus human freedom and equality were taken to be established by systematically realising the freedom of beasts of prey, based on the equality of death. This freedom was called man's natural freedom! What enlightened lawgivers! They spoke to poor men somewhat as follows: 'You are free by nature, and your natural freedom, your naked personality, are to remain your untouchable, inalienable property. But as to that which pertains to your social life (and of course everything belongs to this; you cannot even sustain your natural life if you do not acquire the food produced by society), you must wrest it individually from each other. You must use your natural freedom to obtain the means for life. And you obtain these by alienating your natural freedom—but by alienating it voluntarily. Nobody is *forced* to alienate his natural freedom, to sell, hire, or commodify himself, if he prefers to starve. But take care not to disturb others who understand better how to cash and convert their natural freedom; do not disturb these worthy folk in their acquisition! If you want to acquire, you have to surrender voluntarily your natural freedom and offer it for sale, as the other worthy people do. In return, however, when you have acquired something, you can buy and use the natural freedom of other people.'

The trade in human beings, the trade in human freedom and human life, has become too universal nowadays for it to be noticeable at first sight. Indeed one cannot see the wood for the trees. It is by no means only the propertyless who barter away their freedom for the means of their existence; the more a person has 'acquired' already, the more he wants to go on 'acquiring' until in the end he would like to drain the whole world for his private purpose. Yes, we get so used to trading with our own and other people's freedom that finally we are hardened to it and are left with no idea or memory of free activity and real life. If slavery is more visible among the propertyless, among the propertied it is all the more a state of mind. But for this generation of born slaves, even visible slavery is invisible! Our working men and women, our day-labourers, servants and maids who are happy to have found a master, these are free workers, according to our modern notions, and the master who keeps many hands busy and feeds many mouths is 'respectable' (usually also extremely enlightened), and is a 'useful member of civil society'... But what about those blacks in 'free' North America who work for a master exactly as our 'free' workers do, for slave-owners, who exactly resemble our worthy, enlightened, useful members of civil society, in keeping many hands busy and many mouths fed? — Oh, how un-Christian! But at any rate there is a difference between the 'infamous' human trade on the coast of Africa and the respectable human trade at our doorsteps! There is even an essential difference between the modern slavery of the Christian North America and the ancient slavery of pagan Greece. The Greeks kept slaves so that they could devote themselves to public life, live in freedom, and cultivate the arts and sciences in a free manner; the ancients still had no machines which might have made the slaves, the human machines, superfluous, but had they possessed the new discoveries, then, as Aristotle clearly stated, they would have had no slaves to labour for their greed. The moderns on the other hand, the Christians, buy human beings only because it is cheaper to work with bought rather than with hired men, but yet they declare infamous this trade in human beings, as soon as it threatens to become less profitable or even dangerous to the trader's existence. And now what of the human trade at our doorsteps! What an essential difference! With us slavery is no longer one-sided but mutual: not only do I make you, but you make me, a slave, not by directly robbing each other of our freedom, for this cannot be done, but by mutually taking away the means to our freedom and our life. Thus we can no longer be sold against our will; we have to sell ourselves voluntarily! We cannot even *sell* ourselves any more; no, we must simply hire and make a commodity of ourselves— as I said, we must simply give up our freedom in a wholly voluntary fashion. Yes, our modern lawgivers have distinguished well between selling and putting on the market. Such cleverness is frightful! But alas! The cleverness of our modern lawgivers is only the slave mentality. — As I said, to the modern commercial world even visible slavery is invisible.

XII

The world of commerce has solved the problem of realising Christianity. This is the task of taking away absolutely all and every kind of ability from men, not only in fantasied theory, but in genuine real life and practice, and conferring all this on an imaginary chimerical Being; it is the task under pretence of turning the earth into a palpable heaven, of converting it into an equally palpable hell—of depriving men of all the life-giving human air of social life and putting them into the air-pump of egoism, and then representing the death-struggle of these miserable beings as the normal life-activity of men. — Compared with our social relationships, not only antiquity but even the Middle Ages were still human. Medieval society, with all the accursed appendage of its barbaric laws and institutions, did not disfigure men through and through as modern society does. In the Middle Ages, beside the serfs who were nothing and had nothing, there were also people who had a social position, and social character, people who were something. The estates and guilds, merely egoistic associations as they were, had a social character, and a social spirit, however limited; the individual could enter into his circle of social activity and be absorbed into the community, in however limited a way. — It is quite different now, when the formula has been found for *universal* serfdom. The social life of man is now completely devoid of any noble motives. There is no social property or living possession; no man who may really have or be something. This general trash, in which people fancy themselves to possess something, is a phantom we pursue in vain! — What does genuine social property consist of? It consists in the means of living and functioning in society. Property is the body of social man and as such is his first requirement for living in society, just as the natural body, our natural property, is the first requirement of living at all. But what is *our* social property? — This general trash, money, is not an organic, living body. Yes, it is *supposed* to represent the social body, the organic species-life and our social relationships, but it *cannot* do this because by its very nature it is inorganic and without articulation or inner differentiation; it is nothing else but dead matter, a sum or number. How can the value of a living being, the value of man and his highest life and activity, how can the value of social life be expressed in sums and numbers? We were able to arrive at this absurdity only by robbing the real life of a man's soul, dividing and dismembering it and placing one half in the other world and the other half in this. Let us imagine on the one hand a world of spirits without bodies, a chimaera, and on the other a bodily world without spirit, without life, a dead world of matter, and thus another chimaera—and now let us suppose these bodiless spirits rushing after this soulless matter in order to grab hold of smaller or larger bits of it and make off with them: we then have a faithful picture of the chimerical world in which we live. However much we seize and acquire of this dead, soulless and inorganic matter, this general trash that we pursue as ghosts hunt for their lost bodies, we still do not gain from it any genuine living property or social possession, nor anything which would determine and make possible our life and function in society, our social activity; we gain only the materialised Christian God, the ghost or spirit in which we can preserve and maintain our earthly corpses in a dead stony existence. Money can never in any way be *property* [*Eigenthum*]; on the contrary, to anyone whose nature is not yet corrupted it must appear so alien, so *im*proper to man [*dem Menschen nicht Eigenthümliches betrachten werden*], that precisely what is characteristic of all genuine and real property, the internal fusion of owner and owned, appears here as the most repulsive and contemptible vice. The man of honour, the genuine man, is so wholly identified with his property, with his real social possessions, that he is fused into and absorbed in it as his soul is with his body; he fills his post so completely that it is quite impossible to think of him as separated from his sphere of activity—a phenomenon that is now the exception since the content of all social endeavour nowadays is money. For what makes a man man is not the Christian and philosophical aloofness from ordinary life, but the mutual devotion of living and working for each other. The fusion of possessor and possession is thus what characterises genuine property, the social no less than the natural, as such. Everything that I have really appropriated, which is thus my living property, is intimately fused with me; must be, and therefore ought to be. — But what is he who has become fused with our *so-called* property? Who so far identifies himself with his money that he cannot be separated from it? A miserable creature! — And yet we have to regard this general trash as the first requirement of our lives, as our indispensable property, because without it we cannot preserve ourselves. Hence you must strive eternally to appropriate something which cannot be appropriated, which eternally remains remote and inaccessible to you. In your money you can own only a soulless body that you can never animate, that can never become your property. You must count yourself lucky to have a body that does not belong to you; lucky to be able to exchange your *own* flesh and blood, your life-activity for this trash, and thus to be able to sell yourself—a thing that in the Middle Ages and in antiquity was at least still considered a misfortune,—whereas now you must count yourself lucky to be a modern serf. For you are constantly exposed to the danger of lapsing into that original state of the blessed spirits which our legislators conjured down from the Christian heaven and have declared to be the normal state of 'natural' men; you are constantly exposed to the danger of becoming a pure, free, naked person.

XIII

The commercial world is the practical world of appearances and lies. Under the appearance of absolute independence, absolute necessity; under the appearance of the most lively communications, the deadly isolation of each man from all his fellows; under the appearance of an untouchable property assured to all individuals, an actual deprivation of all their powers; under the appearance of the most universal freedom, the most universal servitude. No wonder that in this realised world of lies fraud is the norm and honesty an offence; that baseness achieves all the honours and the lot of the honourable is misery and shame; that hypocrisy rejoices in triumph while truthfulness is held indecent; that the half-hearted half-hold a majority while firmness is firmly in the minority; and finally, that the freest vision is the most destructive while the crassest servility is the most conservative element.

XIV

A man torn off from his life-giving roots and from his life-element, like a rotten fruit fallen from the tree of life, and thus a dying, isolated individual, can only artificially be preserved from decay. A living being does not conserve himself but is active and creates himself anew at every moment. But in order really to live, that is, to be able to bestir or create oneself, the different individual members of the self-same greater organic body must be inseparably connected with each other as well as with their communal life-element or life-material; they and their bodies and their life-atmosphere must not be separated from each other. This separation, isolation and disintegration of individuals is the characteristic feature of the animal world and egoism, and the reason why mankind have hitherto had this animal characteristic is that they were still developing; for the animal world itself is nothing else but mankind caught in the process of development. Mankind, in fact, has a two-fold history of development: one, men's first history, represents the development of their still unconscious or bodily existence, and this we find in the *natural* animal world; the other, their second history, which follows from and after the first, and whereby they first exist in a completed, developed and perfect form, consists in the development of their conscious, spiritual or social existence, and this we encounter in the social animal world. We find ourselves now on the peak, at the culminating point of the world of social animals; and hence we are now social predators, complete, conscious egoists, who sanction in free competition the war of all against all, who uphold in the so-called rights of man the rights of the isolated individual, the private person, the 'absolute personality,' who condone in the freedom of trade the mutual exploitation of each other, the lust for money, which is nothing else but the blood-lust of the social beasts of prey. We are no longer herbivores like our guileless ancestors who, though also social animals, were not yet social predators, in that most of them, like good-tempered domestic animals, only required to be fed: we are bloodsuckers who mutually flay and devour each other. As the animal enjoys in blood his own life merely, though in a bestial, brutal fashion, so man enjoys in money his own life in a brutal, bestial, cannibal manner. Money is social blood, but blood externalised, blood which has been shed. The Jews, whose world historical mission in the natural history of the world of social animals was to evolve the predator out of mankind, have at last fulfilled the work they were called to. The mystery of Judaism and Christianity is revealed in the modern Jewish-Christian world of shopkeepers. The mystery of Christ's blood, like that of the veneration of blood in ancient Judaism, appears here at last quite openly as the mystery of the predator. In ancient Judaism the blood cult was only a prototype; in medieval Christianity it became theoretically, ideally, logically realised: one really consumed the externalised, poured-out blood of mankind, but only in imagination the blood of the God-man. In the modern Jewish-Christian world of shopkeepers this besetting urge of the world of social animals has at last appeared, no longer symbolically or mystically, but in wholly prosaic form. In the religion of the social predators there was still poetry. Even if not the poetry of Olympus, it was still the poetry of Walpurgisnacht. The world of social animals became ordinary and prosaic only when nature again reasserted its rights and the isolated man, this poor slave of antiquity and serf of the Middle Ages, was no longer content with heavenly food; he began to strive, not for spiritual but for material treasures, and wished to juggle his alienated life, his shed blood, no longer into his invisible belly but into his visible pocket. Then the sacred conjuring trick became profane, the heavenly fraud an earthly one, the poetic contest of gods and devils a prosaic animal struggle, the mystical God-eating [*Theophagie*] an open devouring of man [*Anthropophagie*]. God's church, the heavenly tomb, where the priest, the hyena of the social animals, conducted an imaginary funeral feast, has now been transformed into the money state, a worldly battlefield where predators with equal rights guzzle each other's blood. In the money state, the state of free competition, all privileges and differences of rank are at an end; here, as we said, there prevails an unpoetic freedom of the predator, based on the equality of death. Against money, kings have no more title to command because they are the lions among human animals, than does the black-garbed priest still have the right among them to regale himself upon the odour of death because he is their hyena. On the contrary, they have their rights, like other human animals, only by virtue of their common right of nature, their common quality as predators, blood-suckers, Jews and wolves of money.

XV

Money is the means of exchange which has turned to a dead letter and kills life, just as letters are the means of communication which have turned to dead money and kill the spirit. The invention of both money and the alphabet is attributed to the Phoenicians, the same nation which also invented the Jewish God. A literary wit supposed, therefore, that he was making a very telling point against the elimination of money when in one of his writings, under the title of 'The Movement of Production,' he compared the spiritual capital that we possess in writings (especially his own) to the material capital that we possess in money, and then went on to say: 'The elimination of money would thus have the same significance as the elimination of writing: it would be a command to world history to return into its womb.' But, to begin with, Herr Schulz has overlooked the difference between the material capital that we possess in money and the spiritual capital that we can appropriate through writing. This difference is nothing less than the difference between genuine and false property. Without doubt I can appropriate spiritual treasures through writing. But it would not occur to anyone to label the treasures that we appropriate through words and writing as the individual's private property that he could in turn bequeath to private heirs. Of course I can inherit or acquire a library, a so-called treasury of literature; I can even obtain so-called revelations through holy writ; but the more this acquisition approximates to the acquisition of money, the more external and accidental it is, the more it is subject to loss and gain, the more valueless, the more spiritless, my 'spiritual' treasure becomes. Or does Herr Schulz think that I have already garnered the spirit with the letters and the books? Language is the living, animate means of communication but it is not the letters that count. Spiritual money has value only so far as it is organically interfused with man. Language can be organically fused with men because it is an organic, structured whole. But, as was already shown earlier, money cannot fuse organically with men, and therefore resembles writing, not in the sense of living language, but in the sense of dead letters. It is said—and it is indeed very significant—that letters, like money, were invented by those who invented *Moloch.* Language, however, was not invented in this place or that. If an invention is no longer needed or useable, and has even become harmful, then people no longer use it though without therefore needing to return to the 'womb'. That letters and coins were 'useful' inventions, and even 'necessary' discoveries is not in dispute. The question is simply whether they will therefore also be 'useful' and 'necessary' in the future. It is perfectly true that in the isolated condition and mutual alienation of men that has existed until now, an external symbol had to be invented to represent the exchange of spiritual and material products. During this period of alienation such an abstraction from genuine, spiritual and living relationships strengthened men's capacity and productive power; for in this abstract means of relationship they had in fact a

mediating essence of their own alienation; because they were themselves not human, that is, not united, they had to seek the uniting fac-
tor outside themselves, that is, in a non-human, superhuman being.
Without this non-human means of relationship they would simply not
have come into relationship at all. But as soon as men unite, and a
direct relation can occur between them, the non-human, external, dead
means of relation must necessarily be abolished. This dead and dead-
ening means of relation cannot and will not be abolished by an act of
choice; its abolition no more occurs by 'command' than its creation
did. Just as, during the inner fragmentation of mankind, the need for
an external means of unity brought spiritual and material idols into
being, so the need for direct inner unification of men will bring these
idols to nought again. The love, which took refuge in heaven when
earth was not yet able to comprehend it, will again have its dwelling
where it was born and nourished, in the human breast. We shall no
longer seek our life vainly outside and above ourselves. No foreign
being, no third intermediary will again force itself between us to unite
us externally and in appearance, to 'mediate,' while internally and in
reality it separates and divides us. Together with commercial speculation, philosophical and theological speculation will come to an end;
together with politics, religion will also disappear. Driven by the inner
necessity of our nature and the outer need of circumstances we shall
once and for all finish with all the nonsense and hypocritical rubbish
of our philosophers, learned men, priests and politicians which har-
monises so beautifully with the inhumanity and baseness of our bourgeois society; and we shall do it by uniting ourselves into a community
and by ejecting as alien bodies all these external means of relation, all
these thorns in our flesh.

XVI

The organic community we envisage could come into being only
through the highest development of all our powers, by means of the
painful spur of necessity and of evil passions. The organic community, the ripe fruit of human development, could not come into being
so long as we were not yet completely developed, and we could not
develop ourselves if we did not come into contact with each other.
During the development of contact, however, we have continued to
struggle with each other as isolated individuals. We have fought with

each other over our spiritual and material means of contact because as isolated individuals we needed these means of contact in order to live. We needed them because we were not yet united; but the unification or co-operation of our powers is our life. We have therefore had to look for our very life outside ourselves and to attain it by mutual fighting. Through this fight, however, we have attained something quite different from what we were trying and hoping to attain. We had thought to attain an outside good, and we have merely developed *ourselves* thereby. But this madness was beneficial and useful to us only so long as it really helped to develop our powers and capacities. After they are developed we would only mutually ruin each other if we did not turn to communism. The struggle no longer develops our powers any further, if only because they are now developed. But we can also see daily that on the one hand we merely squander our powers fruitlessly and that on the other they simply cannot develop any further because of the superabundance of our powers of production. If the bourgeois liberals still regale us with the necessity of progress through the competitive struggle, it is only because they are thoughtless twaddlers, because they perpetrate anachronisms, or because egoism has made them blind and incapable of grasping truths apparent to anyone who merely opens his eyes. If we do not unite with each other in love, then at the stage of development that we have arrived at we can only go on mutually exploiting and devouring each other. Not centuries, as the unthinking liberals assume, not even decades will pass before the hundredfold increase in productive powers will have pushed into the deepest misery the great majority of those who must live by the work of their hands, because their hands will have become valueless; while those few who busy themselves with the accumulation of capital will revel in abundance and ruin themselves in vile pursuit of pleasure, if they have not first hearkened to the voice of love and reason or succumbed to force.

XVII

The history of the development of society is completed; soon the last hour will strike for the world of social animals. The clock of the money machine has run down and our political exponents of progress and reaction are trying in vain to keep it on the move.

Endnotes

1. Julius Kovesi

1. Their experiences with the Australian immigration authorities were amusingly described in an article Julius wrote for the Australian *Observer* (20th August 1960) entitled 'Why Migrants Say No'.
2. It was the subject of an editorial in *Philosophy*, April 1976. See also Jill Paton Walsh's novel, *Lapsing* (London: Black Swan Press, 1995), 217.
3. Founded in wartime Oxford as an open forum for religious argument. See Roger Lancelyn Green and Walter Hooper, *C.S. Lewis: A Biography*, (London: Collins, 1974), 214–218.
4. See *The Economist*, July 15th, 1989.
5. *Mind*, No. 310, April, 1969.
6. 'Tom Wolfe,' *Quadrant*, October 1985.
7. Teilhard de Chardin, *Le Christique*, as quoted in Robert Speight, *Teilhard de Chardin* (London: Collins, 1967), 330. See pages 80–81 in this volume.
8. On this see the end of 'Nature and Convention,' pages 124–125 of this volume.

2. The Moral Philosophy Papers: Introduction

1. Taken from 'The Fallacy of One Good, One Bad, Or a Real Case of the Naturalistic Fallacy' (unpublished paper).
2. From 'Moral Judgments and Moral Decisions' (unpublished paper).

4. Against the Ritual of 'Is' and 'Ought'

1. *Philosophical Review* 73 (1964) reprinted in Philippa Foot, ed., *Theories of Ethics* (Oxford: Oxford University Press, 1967), 101–114.
2. R.M. Hare, 'The Promising Game,' *Revue Internationale de Philosophie*, 70 (1964), reprinted in Foot, *Theories of Ethics*, 115–127.
3. *The Language of Morals* (Oxford: Clarendon Press, 1952), 83–84.
4. 'The Promising Game,' reprinted in Foot, *Theories of Ethics*, 127.
5. *Aristotelian Society Supplementary Volume* XXXV (1961).
6. *Ibid.*, 74.

7. P.T. Geach, 'Good and Evil,' reprinted in Foot, *Theories of Ethics*, 82.
8. *Aristotelian Society Supplementary Volume* XXXV (1961), 77.
9. *Ibid.*, 69.
10. *The Language of Morals*, 168–9.
11. Montefiore, 'Goodness and Choice,' 74.
12. 'Geach: Good and Evil,' in Foot, *Theories of Ethics*, 79.
13. I am grateful to Dr John Colman for letting me read parts of the manuscript of his forthcoming book on the moral philosophy of Locke [*John Locke's Moral Philosophy* (Edinburgh: Edinburgh University Press, 1983)] and for drawing my attention to the similarity of Locke's views to what I am groping for. (I think one can gain some similar insights from Vico.)

5. Descriptions and Reasons

1. Thomas D. Perry, *Moral Reasoning and Truth* (Oxford: Clarendon Press, 1976), 132–134.
2. *Essay*, III, Ch. V, 5.
3. *Ibid.*, III, Ch.V, 14.
4. *Ibid.*, III, Ch.V, 7.
5. *Ibid.*, III, Ch.V, 6.
6. *Ibid.*, III, Ch. XI, 16.
7. *English Works* (London: Bohn, 1839–45), Vol. 7, 184.
8. Maimonides, *The Guide of the Perplexed* (Chicago: University of Chicago Press, 1963), Part III, Ch. 21, 484.
9. 'Against the Ritual of "Is" and "Ought",' *Midwest Studies in Philosophy*, Vol. III, 1978, 10–16, pages 25–42 in this volume, and 'Valuing and Evaluating,' in *Jowett Papers*, ed. by B.Y. Khanbhai, Blackwell 1970, pages 13–23 in this volume.
10. D.D. Raphael, *British Moralists* (Oxford: Clarendon Press, 1991), Vol. I, 245.
11. *Essay*, IV, Ch. IV, 8.
12. I worked on versions of this paper while I was Visiting Fellow at the Research School of the Social Sciences at the Australian National University. I would like to thank the University for its hospitality and especially Stanley Benn for his persistent helpful criticism.

6. *Principia Ethica* Re-examined: The Ethics of a Proto-Logical Atomism

1. Hume himself has equally been appropriated by contemporary British moral philosophy. But however inaccurately the tag 'Hume on "is" and "ought"' is used, it does identify the tradition that uses this tag.

2. *Principia Ethica* (Cambridge: Cambridge University Press, 1903), xi. For ease of reference I shall put further page references to *Principia Ethica* and to 'The Nature of Judgment' (*Mind*, 1899) into the text, abbreviating the references to *PE* and *NJ* respectively.
3. *International Journal of Ethics* (1903), 117.
4. I would like to mention here how much I learnt from discussion of these problems with Mrs Shasta Dawson.
5. See my 'Against the Ritual of "Is" and "Ought",' *Midwest Studies in Philosophy*, III (1978), 6, and pages 25–42 in this volume.

7. The Theological Papers: Introduction

1. See 'Marxist Ecclesiology and Biblical Criticism,' pages 82–83 in this volume.

8. Marxist Ecclesiology and Biblical Criticism

1. The drama which is *in principle* universal can have a rather provincial universality in reality, and large sections of the world can be ignored in the drama. Thus the universal gentile world comprised the Greco-Roman world, and if St. Paul had reached Spain he could have considered that the Gospel had indeed been preached 'universally'. Again, the world-spirit's development was expected to culminate in the limited area of early nineteenth-century Germany, France, and England. When the world outside the drama cannot be ignored, or forces its importance to be recognised, it creates a crisis in the self-understanding of the actors in the drama and can create an ecclesiological crisis. In this respect the place of Hinduism or Buddhism in the history of Providence presents problems for Christianity comparable to the role of the 'Third World' in the Marxist drama.
2. Eric Voegelin, *The New Science of Politics* (Chicago: Chicago University Press, 1952), 29.
3. Teilhard de Chardin, *Le Christique* as quoted in Robert Speight, *Teilhard de Chardin* (London: Collins, 1967), 330.
4. Marx, *The Poverty of Philosophy* (Moscow, n.d.), 120.
5. *Toward the Critique of Hegel's Philosophy of Law*: Introduction, in Loyd D. Easton and Kurt H. Guddat, *Writings of the Young Marx* (New York: Doubleday, 1967), 263.
6. Jaroslav Pelikan, *The Finality of Jesus Christ in an Age of Universal History. A Dilemma of the Third Century* (London, 1965; Richmond, Va., 1966).

7. *New Blackfriars* (May 1969). The article was printed in the same month in *Marxism Today* as part of an ongoing Christian–Marxist dialogue.
8. *Marxism and Beyond* (London: Paladin, 1968), 38.
9. *History and Class Consciousness* (London: Merlin Press, 1968), 1.
10. *Ibid.*, 16–20.
11. *Ibid.*, xxv.
12. D. Strauss, *Streitschriften* (Tübingen, 1841), III, 95.
13. I owe this point to a conversation with Professor Patrick Henry of Swarthmore College.
14. *Die Europäische Triarchie*, in *Moses Hess, Philosophische und Sozialistische Schriften*, ed. Auguste Cornu and Wolfgang Mönke (Berlin: Akademie-Verlag, 1961), 77.
15. *Toward the Critique of Hegel's Philosophy of Law*: Introduction.
16. Sartre, *Critique de la Raison Dialectique* (Paris: Gallimard, 1960), 23.

9. Some Philosophical Aspects of Demythologising

1. Editor's note: This article was written in 1979 but never published. Later, Kovesi planned to revise the introductory section and in particular the first two pages. The editor considers that the article deserves to be published in its original form, but that Kovesi would want the reader to know that he had come to be dissatisfied with the opening passages and intended to rewrite them.
2. Rudolf Bultmann, *Kerygma and Myth*, ed. Hans-Werner Bartsch (London: SPCK, 1957), 34.
3. *Ibid.*, 35.
4. *Ibid.*, 38–39.
5. J.C. Fenton, *The Gospel of Saint Matthew* (Harmondsworth: Pelican, 1963), 18–19.
6. *Ibid.*, 19.
7. *Ibid.*, 20–21.
8. *Ibid.*, 21.
9. *Peanuts Treasury*, Charles M. Schulz (New York: Holt, Rinehart and Winston, 1968).

10. The Historical Papers: Introduction

1. The account here is paraphrased from his unpublished paper 'Did Plato Turn Himself Upside Down?'

11. Nature and Convention

1. *De Corona,* 5.
2. Cf. his *Sense and Sensibilia* (Oxford: Clarendon Press, 1962), 70–73.
3. I cannot remember off-hand whether Arthur Lovejoy recorded over forty or over seventy different usages of 'nature' in his article '"Nature" as an Aesthetic Norm'.
4. *The Writings of the Young Marx,* ed. and tr. Loyd D. Easton and Kurt H. Guddat (New York: Doubleday Anchor, 1967), 141.
5. Diels, *Fragm.* 125.
6. *Treatise,* Book III, Pt. 1, Sec. 1.
7. *Commentary,* June, 1980.

12. Moses Hess, Marx and Money

1. Several years ago, after I translated Moses Hess's essay *On the Essence of Money,* I asked Professor Peter Heath of the University of Virginia whether he would be kind enough to read it. The result of this request was such a drastic transformation of my text that had my original version still not weighed on his elegant style I would have liked to call this a joint translation.

   While Peter Heath so improved on my English translation of a German text, my wife did her best to improve the English of my English discussion of Hess's thought. Though she wished I would turn to saner subjects, she helped with more than style.

   Professor Eugene Kamenka wrote copious helpful comments on an earlier version of this essay. Though he did not see this present completely rewritten text I would like to express my gratitude for his earlier comments as well as for his constant help whenever one turned to him.

   Anyone who writes on Moses Hess cannot help but be indebted to Professor Silberner's authoritative work on the life of Hess. I also relied on Professor John Weiss' work, and of course on Professor Isaiah Berlin's lively essay. Finally I would like to thank Robert Castiglione, who helped me to clarify so much while we were disentangling the complexities of Feuerbach.
2. 'Über die Sozialistische Bewegung in Deutschland,' *Neue Anekdota,* Darmstadt, 1845, in *Moses Hess, Philosophische und Sozialistische Schriften,* ed. W. Mönke (Vaduz: Topos Verlag, 1980), 2nd ed., 293–94.

3. Marx is quoting here from F.H. Semming, 'Communism, Socialism, Humanism,' in *Rheinische Jahrbücher*, 1845, Vol. 1. He quotes it in *The German Ideology* (New York: International Publishers, 1972), 95–96.

4. David McLellan, *Marx Before Marxism* (London: Macmillan, 1970), 141.

5. David McLellan, *The Young Hegelians and Karl Marx* (London: Macmillan, 1969), 158.

6. *Ibid.*, 158. The reference to Silberner is to Edmund Silberner, 'Die Tatigkeit von Moses Hess,' *Annali*, Milan, 1963, 431.

7. Edmund Silberner, *Moses Hess: Geschichte seines Lebens* (Leiden: Brill, 1966). Silberner discusses the problem on pages 184 ff. For the reference see page 192.

8. Robert C. Tucker, *Philosophy and Myth in Karl Marx* (Cambridge: Cambridge University Press, 1961), 112.

9. Julius Carlebach, 'The Problem of Moses Hess's Influence on the Young Marx,' *Year Book of the Leo Baeck Institute*, Vol. 18, 1973, 27–39. The article also forms part of Chapter VI of Julius Carlebach, *Karl Marx and the Radical Critique of Judaism* (London: Routledge and Kegan Paul, 1978).

10. Nicholas Lobkowicz, *Theory and Practice: History of a Concept from Aristotle to Marx* (Notre Dame: University of Notre Dame Press, 1967), 292.

11. For Silberner's arguments see E. Silberner, *op. cit.*, 166–169. Jacob Leveen in his brief pamphlet on Hess writes that 'Hess took for his wife a Christian woman, whom he had nobly rescued from a life of prostitution'. A nice little point is that in the British Library copy of this pamphlet someone has crossed out the word 'prostitution' and written 'degrading poverty' on the margin as a replacement. Hess was in no position to rescue anyone from degrading poverty, but the legend of the noble act must go on. (Leveen's pamphlet *Moses Hess* was published in London in 1926.)

12. Isaiah Berlin, *The Life and Opinions of Moses Hess*, 1957 Lucien Wolf Memorial Lectures (Cambridge: Heffer and Sons, 1959), 10–11, reprinted in his *Against the Current. Essays in the History of Ideas* (London: Hogarth Press, 1979).

13. Moses Hess, *Die Heilige Geschichte der Menscheit* (Stuttgart, 1837; reprinted Hildesheim, Gerstenberg, 1980).

14. David McLellan, *The Young Hegelians and Karl Marx*, 155.

15. Julius Carlebach, 'The Problem of Moses Hess's Influence on the Young Marx,' 30.

16. Hess's co-operation in *The German Ideology* is discussed by W. Mönke, 'Über die Mitarbeit von M. Hess in der "D.I.",' *Wissentschaftliche Annalen*, Vol. 6, 1957.

17. See Hess's essay, page 189 in this volume.

18. *The German Ideology*, 102.

19. I owe this point to György Bence's article on Hess, 'Moses Hess a Filozo-fiatörténelemben,' in *Magyar Filozofiai Szemle*, Budapest, 1967, Vol. XI, No. 2, 262.

20. To be fair, one must quote Ruge's remark in one of his letters that Stirner was responsible for 'the first readable book in philosophy that Germany has produced.' On Stirner's crucial role in the development and dis-integration of the Young Hegelian movement see especially Lawrence S. Stepelevich, 'Max Stirner and Ludwig Feuerbach,' *Journal of the History of Ideas*, Vol. 39, 1978, 451–463; Nicholas Lobkowicz, *Theory and Practice*; and Karl Lowith, *From Hegel to Nietzsche: the Revolution in Nineteenth Century Thought* (London: Constable, 1965). I took Bauer's remark from Stepelevich's article, page 457.

21. There exists now a translation of Hess's article 'The Recent Philosophers' in Lawrence S. Stepelevich's anthology *The Young Hegelians: An Anthology* (Cambridge: Cambridge University Press, 1983).

22. Engels to Marx, 25–26 October, 1847, *Karl Marx, Friedrich Engels: Collected Works* (London: Lawrence and Wishart, 1975–1994), 47 Vols, Vol. 38 (1982), 138–139.

23. Engels to Marx, 23–24 November, 1847, *Marx, Engels: Collected Works*, Vol. 38, 149.

24. Marx to Engels, 15 August 1863, *Karl Marx, Friedrich Engels: Werke* (Berlin: Dietz Verlag, 1961–1991), 43 Bände, Band 30 (1964), 369.

25. Nathan Rotenstreich, 'For and Against Emancipation—The Bruno Bauer Controversy,' *Year Book of the Leo Baeck Institute*, London, 1959.

26. That the two were not unrelated in Hess's mind is well argued by Shlomo Avineri, 'Political and Social Aspects of Israeli and Arab Nationalism' in Eugene Kamenka, ed., *Nationalism* (Canberra: Australian National University, 1973).

27. See Julius Kovesi, 'Marxist Ecclesiology and Biblical Criticism,' *Journal of the History of Ideas*, January–March 1976, Vol. 37, No. 1, 93–110, and pages 75–93 in this volume.

28. Gotthold Ephraim Lessing, 'The Education of the Human Race,' in *Lessing's Theological Writings*, tr. and ed. Henry Chadwick (London: Adam and Charles Black, 1956), 97.

29. John Weiss, *Moses Hess, Utopian Socialist* (Detroit: Wayne State University Press, 1960), 69.

30. Kandinsky, 'Reminiscences' in *Modern Artists on Art*, ed. by Robert L.

Herbert (Englewood Cliffs, New Jersey: Prentice-Hall, 1965), 38–40.

31. Ludwig Feuerbach, 'Provisional Theses for the Reformation of Philosophy,' which first appeared in Arnold Ruge's *Anekdota*, 1843. Now translated by Daniel O. Dahlstrom in Stepelevich, *The Young Hegelians*, *op. cit.*

32. Auguste Cornu and Wolfgang Mönke, eds., *Moses Hess, Philosophische und Sozialistische Schriften* (Berlin: Akademie-Verlag, 1961), 303.

33. *The Writings of the Young Marx*, ed. and tr. Loyd D. Easton and Kurt H. Guddat (New York: Doubleday Anchor, 1967), 261. Hereafter: Easton and Guddat.

34. It is interesting to see Engels' reference to 'the egoism of the heart' in a letter to Marx on the 19th November 1844. After referring to Hess's views on Feuerbach and Stirner, Engels goes on to say: Hess 'also hates any and every kind of egoism, and preaches the love of humanity, etc., which again boils down to Christian self-sacrifice. If, however, the flesh-and-blood individual is the true basis, the true point of departure for our "man," it follows that egoism—not of course Stirner's intellectual egoism *alone*, but also the *egoism of the heart*—is the point of departure for our love of humanity, which otherwise is left hanging in the air. Since Hess will soon be with you, you will be able to discuss this with him yourself.' *Karl Marx, Friedrich Engels: Collected Works*, Vol. 38, 12–13.

35. Karl Marx, *Critique of Hegel's 'Philosophy of Right,'* ed. Joseph O'Malley (Cambridge: Cambridge University Press, 1970), 50.

36. See Hess's essay, pages 189–190 in this volume.

37. Karl Marx, 'Comments on James Mill…,' *Karl Marx, Friedrich Engels: Collected Works*, Vol. 3, 212.

38. Easton and Guddat, 246.

39. I have based my distinction on a similar one made by Durkheim in his *Socialism and Saint Simon.*

40. Easton and Guddat, 301–302.

41. George Herwegh, *Einundzwanzig Bogen aus der Schweiz* (Vaduz: Topos Verlag, 1977).

42. Easton and Guddat, 307–309.

43. Feuerbach, *The Essence of Christianity*, tr. George Eliot (New York: Harper Torchbook, 1957), 23.

44. *Ibid.*, 4–5.

45. *Ibid.*, pages 9 and 5.

46. Easton and Guddat, 308–310.

47. Feuerbach, *Principles of the Philosophy of the Future*, tr. M.H. Vogel (New York: Bobbs-Merrill, 1966), 9.

48. Feuerbach, *The Essence of Christianity*, 8; see also 17.
49. *Ibid.*, 2–3.
50. *Ibid.*, 7.
51. *Ibid.*, 23. Echoing the familiar tag 'The king is dead, long live the king,' Marx writes in his third Manuscript: '*Death* seems to be a harsh victory of the species over the particular individual, and to contradict the species' unity, but the particular individual is only a *particular generic being* and as such mortal' (Easton and Guddat, 307).
52. *The Essence of Christianity*, 152 and 154; see also 158–159.
53. Easton and Guddat, 248.
54. See Hess's essay, page 195 in this volume.
55. Easton and Guddat, 238–239.
56. *Ibid.*, 241.
57. *Ibid.*, 225.
58. Rousseau, *Social Contract*, Book II, quoted by Marx in Easton and Guddat, 241. The italics are Marx's.
59. See Hess's essay, page 184 in this volume.
60. See Hess's essay, page 190 in this volume.
61. See Hess's essay, page 201 in this volume.
62. Karl Marx, 'Comments on James Mill...,' *Marx-Engels: Collected Works*, Vol. 3, 212.
63. Easton and Guddat, 289–290.
64. Marx and Engels, *German Ideology*, 65–66.
65. Easton and Guddat, 304.
66. For a proper study of the problem, see Carlebach, *Karl Marx and the Radical Critique of Judaism* and Rotenstreich, 'For and Against Emancipation, The Bruno Bauer Controversy'.
67. Charles A. Reich, *The Greening of America: How the Youth Revolution is Trying to Make America Livable* (New York: Random House, 1970).
68. See Hess's essay, page 203 in this volume.
69. Feuerbach, *The Essence of Christianity*, 120–121.
70. Easton and Guddat, 248.
71. To my amazement István Mészáros gives the impression that Marx, and he himself following Marx, is talking about actual history in his views about Judaism. See Mészáros, *Marx's Theory of Alienation* (London: Merlin Press, 1970).
72. *Peanuts Treasury* by Charles M. Schulz (New York: Holt, Rinehart and Winston, 1968).

Index